DO I MAKE MYSELF CLEAR?

"Have you heard of Harold Evans? Sir Harold Evans? Of course you have. He is one of the greatest and most garlanded editors alive...There is no better way of cultivating your inner editor than following Evans as he plies his craft...As a master editor and distinguished author, Evans is well qualified to instruct us on how to write well. But can he delight us in the process? After reading this book, I can affirm the answer is yes."

—Jim Holt, *New York Times Book Review*

"Clarity and wit have something in common, and it's Harry Evans. He clears a path through the thorny underbrush that stands between us and meaning, and he does it with cutting humor and graceful charm. He certainly does make himself clear, and us, too."

—Alan Alda

"Mr. Evans's skills are on display on nearly every page of *Do I Make Myself Clear?*...Evans introduces a crisp curriculum of do's and don'ts for the aspiring clear writer...He also urges writers to cut fat, check their math, be specific, organize their material for clarity, accentuate the positive, and never be boring."

—Edward Kosner, *Wall Street Journal*

"A writing manual so smart and incisive that it could surely benefit anyone—journalist, student, business executive, legislator—who has ever tried to craft an English sentence and fallen short."

—Malcolm Jones, *Daily Beast*

"*Do I Make Myself Clear?* goes well beyond the typical style guide's proscriptions against the passive voice, cliché, and so on...Evans rewrites health-insurance policies, governmental reports on terrorism, and even Jane Austen, in order to demonstrate the virtues of concision and clarity."   — *The New Yorker*

"A timely reminder that precision of language is the writer's greatest weapon. Harry Evans's methodical research and wry eye provide an entertaining lesson in intent, measured and exacting. At a time when public debate is shrill and filled by the overly assertive, Evans gives us a treat of a book that, through the use of practical examples, allows us to bathe in a language of clarity. *Do I Make Myself Clear?* shows that writing remains the gift of the ultimate explorer. Make more time for the journey."
— David Walmsley, editor in chief, *Globe and Mail*

"*Do I Make Myself Clear?* is a case for the value of clear writing, and a thorough guide for making writing clearer."
— Maddie Crum, *Huffington Post*

"In the tradition of George Orwell, who said that political language is designed to make lies sound truthful, Harry Evans reminds us how important it is to write clearly. Then he shows how. Those of us who have been edited by Harry marvel at his dexterity in unclogging dense prose, and in this book he reveals his secrets."
— Walter Isaacson, author of *Steve Jobs* and *Leonardo da Vinci*

"*Do I Make Myself Clear?* is full of enthusiasm for words and the struggling idea that they actually matter. And it is full of sound advice for anyone who wants to make themselves clearer, whether they write novels, articles, or memos to the regional sales director. It even applies to unwritten words."
— Matthew Engel, *Financial Times*

"The great French writer Émile Zola said that his prose style was 'forged on the terrible anvil of daily deadlines,' but the anvil of journalism is no use without the hammer of a great editor. Few if any wordsmiths hit harder than Sir Harold Evans. From the foggy corridors of Fleet Street to the lofty heights of Manhattan publishing, he has dedicated his life to hammering sloppy verbiage into plain English. Witty, wonderfully well written, but above all wise, *Do I Make Myself Clear?* should be required reading for all who scribble, type, or otherwise 'word process.'"

—Niall Ferguson

"Harry Evans is one of the great—indeed legendary—editors of our time. Over the course of his career, he has edited newspapers, books, and magazines, which surely qualifies as a publishing trifecta. All his talents—and irresistible charm—are on display in *Do I Make Myself Clear?* It's much more than a guide to English usage—it's a companion: informative, delightful and indispensable. Do not hit INT or SEND without it!"

—Christopher Buckley, author of *Thank You for Smoking*

"A sparklingly well-written book."   —Fareed Zakaria

"Harold (Harry) Evans is a writer and thinker of deep and celebrated accomplishment and marked independence, and his new book on how our government hides behind a word it's never even heard of—prolixity—is acutely on target."

—Peggy Noonan, author of *The Time of Our Lives*

"Read this book before you write another word. As original as it is entertaining, Harold Evans's guided tour of every nuance of our language amounts to a masterly reappraisal of English usage for our times by a consummate editor turned writer."

—Anthony Holden, editor of *Poems That Make Grown Men Cry*

ALSO BY HAROLD EVANS

My Paper Chase: True Stories of Vanished Times

They Made America: From the Steam Engine to the Search Engine; Two Centuries of Innovators
(with Gail Buckland and David Lefer)

War Stories: Reporting in the Time of Conflict from the Crimea to Iraq

The BBC Reports: On America, Its Allies and Enemies, and the Counterattack on Terrorism
(BBC Corporation and Harold Evans)

The Index Lecture: View from Ground Zero
(lecture prepared for the Hay-on-Wye Festival)

The American Century
(with Kevin Baker and Gail Buckland)

Good Times, Bad Times

Eyewitness

Suffer the Children: The Story of Thalidomide (with the *Sunday Times* Insight Team)

We Learned to Ski (with Brian Jackman and Mark Ottaway)

The Freedom of the Press: The Half Free Press
(with Katharine Graham and Lord Windlesham)

Editing and Design (five volumes: *Essential English, Newspaper Design, Text Typography, Newspaper Headlines,* and *Pictures on a Page*, with Edwin Taylor)

The Active Newsroom (with the International Press Institute)

DO I MAKE MYSELF CLEAR?

A PRACTICAL GUIDE TO
WRITING WELL IN THE
MODERN AGE

HAROLD EVANS

BACK BAY BOOKS
LITTLE, BROWN AND COMPANY
NEW YORK   BOSTON   LONDON

Back Bay Books / Little, Brown and Company
Hachette Book Group
1290 Avenue of the Americas, New York, NY 10104
littlebrown.com

Originally published in hardcover by Little, Brown and Company, May 2017
First Back Bay Books paperback edition, September 2018

Back Bay Books is an imprint of Little, Brown and Company, a division of Hachette Book Group, Inc. The Back Bay Books name and logo are trademarks of Hachette Book Group, Inc.

The publisher is not responsible for websites (or their content) that are not owned by the publisher.

The Hachette Speakers Bureau provides a wide range of authors for speaking events. To find out more, go to hachettespeakersbureau.com or call (866) 376-6591.

Credits appear at the end of the book.

ISBN 978-0-316-27717-4 (hc) / 978-0-316-50919-0 (pb)
Library of Congress Control Number 2016953762

10 9 8 7 6 5 4 3 2 1

LSC-H

Printed in the United States of America

To the memory of the brilliant Robert Silver,

our family's lost friend

CONTENTS

CONTENTS

Fog everywhere. Fog up the river, where it flows among green aits and meadows; fog down the river, where it rolls defiled among the tiers of shipping and the waterside pollutions of a great (and dirty) city. Fog on the Essex marshes, fog on the Kentish heights. Fog creeping into the cabooses of collier-brigs; fog lying out on the yards, and hovering in the rigging of great ships; fog drooping on the gunwales of barges and small boats. Fog in the eyes and throats of ancient Greenwich pensioners, wheezing by the firesides of their wards; fog in the stem and bowl of the afternoon pipe of the wrathful skipper, down in his close cabin; fog cruelly pinching the toes and fingers of his shivering little 'prentice boy on deck. Chance people on the bridges peeping over the parapets into a nether sky of fog, with fog all round them, as if they were up in a balloon, and hanging in the misty clouds.

—Charles Dickens, *Bleak House*

DO I MAKE MYSELF CLEAR?

INTRODUCTION

The year 2016 was the seventieth anniversary of George Orwell's classic polemic *Politics and the English Language* (1946) indicting bad English for corrupting thought and slovenly thought for corrupting language.

The creator of Newspeak, as he called the fictional language of his nightmarish dystopia, Oceania, did as much as any man to rescue us, but eternal vigilance is the price of intelligent literacy. For all its benefits, the digital era Orwell never glimpsed has had unfortunate effects.

As I write today, messages on Facebook and WhatsApp mourned the death of "martyr Rahul Upadhyay"[1] in the Indian state of Uttar Pradesh. It was news to Rahul; he was very much alive, but one man died in riots incited by the bogus report of his death. It's old news that words can kill,

---

[1] Suhasini Raj and Kai Schultz, "After Religious Clash in India, Rumors Create a False 'Martyr,'" *New York Times,* February 6, 2018.

but today we're vulnerable to a fusillade of digital bullets, reckless words unmonitored, unchecked, unverified, but with their credibility enhanced by traveling at the speed of light to the screen of your cell phone. The *New York Times* tracked months of "riots and lynchings...linked to misinformation and hate speech" following "Facebook's rapid expansion in the developing world whose markets represent the company's financial future."[2]

This book on clear writing is as concerned with how words confuse and mislead, with or without malice aforethought, as it is in literary expression: in the millions of raw and deceptive social media postings, in misunderstood mortgages, in the labyrinthine language of Social Security, in commands too vague for life-and-death military situations, in insurance policies that don't cover what the buyers were led to believe they covered, in instructions that don't instruct, in warranties that prove worthless. The 2008 implosion of the housing bubble revealed that millions had signed agreements they hadn't understood or had given up reading for fear of being impaled on a lien. But as the book and movie *The Big Short* make clear, the malefactors of the Great Recession hadn't understood what they were doing either.

Fog everywhere. Fog in the English Channel (and La Manche) obscuring the irreversible connection of the British Isles with Europe. Fog online, on seductive screens, and in print. Fog in the Wall Street executive suites. Fog in the reg-

---

[2] https://www.nytimes.com/2018/04/21/world/asia/facebook-sri-lanka -riots.html

"I like it — it's wonderfully editable."

ulating agencies that couldn't see the signals flashing danger in shadow banking. Fog in the evasions in Flint, Michigan, while its citizens drank poisoned water. Fog in the ivory towers where the arbiters of academia all over the world are conned into publishing volumes of computer-generated garbage. Fog machines in Madison Avenue offices where marketers invent dictionaries of fluff so that a swimming cap is sold as a "hair management system."[3] Fog in pressure groups that camouflage their real purpose with euphemism, fog in how "clean air" and "clear water" became dirty words, fog from vested interests aping the language of science to muddy the truth about climate change. Fog in the U.S. Supreme Court,

---

[3] http://www.speedousa.com, April 14, 2014.

where five judges in *Citizens United v. Federal Elections Commission* (2010) sanctified secret bribery as freedom of speech. But never come there fog too thick, never come there mud and mire too deep, never come there bureaucratic and marketing waffle so gross as to withstand the clean invigorating wind of a sound English sentence.

I

Tools of the Trade

1

A Noble Thing

Winston Churchill had problems talking to a table. His teachers at Harrow told him that the Latin word for *table* was *mensa* but if he wanted to invoke the thought of a table—address a table in the vocative case—he could not just blurt out the word. He must do as the Romans did and write or say, "O *mensa*." To Churchill's straightforward English way of thinking about such matters, it seemed "absolute rigmarole" to muck about with a good solid noun. He was further dismayed to learn it was not even permissible to talk *about* a table without changing its identity to *mensae*. Give these Romans an inch, and they'd take a passus.

In his captivating memoir *My Early Life*, Churchill admits a delinquency in the declensions of Latin grammar which had given "so much solace and profit" to the cleverest

Englishmen. He decided he would stake his destiny, instead, on the force of simple, natural prose rooted in the lexicon of Anglo-Saxon. "Thus," he writes, "I got into my bones the essential structure of the ordinary British sentence — which is a noble thing."

The world well knows how he marshaled the sentences. On February 9, 1941, he addressed a radio appeal for war matériel to President Roosevelt and the American people. He asked America to believe in Britain's ability to stand alone against Hitler's war machine, even then poised to invade. He cited British victories against the Italian armies in the North African desert war. He closed with three sentences. The first was an emotional pledge: "We shall not fail or falter; we shall not weaken or tire. Neither sudden shock of battle, nor the long-drawn trials of vigilance and exertion will wear us down." But then he ended his broadcast with ten taut words: "Give us the tools and we will finish the job!"

The sentence, a verb in the active voice, had the decisive urgency of a battlefield command, a shocking transition from literary elegance. No tears. No plaintive whining. No soft soap. Not a wasted syllable. Just, for God's sake, man, give us the tools and we will finish the job!

So many of Churchill's words are imperishable. He might have written "words are the only things that last forever; they are more durable than the eternal hills." For a time, like many, I thought he had, but they were written by the English essayist William Hazlitt (1778–1830). We know the observation to be true of those combinations of words we can none of us forget: Lincoln's resolve for "government of the people, by the people, for the people"; Martin Luther King Jr.'s "I have a dream," invoking the cadences of the Bible, "...from every mountainside, let freedom ring!"; John Kennedy's call to "my fellow Americans, ask not what your country can do for you, ask what you can do for your country"; and for many, the enduring inspiration of Shakespeare's *Henry V* battle speech at Agincourt, that from this day "to the ending of the world...we in it shall be remembered—we few, we happy few, we band of brothers." The words of Pope Francis in 2013 will surely pass into history—that an obsession with narrow political issues risks even the moral edifice of the church falling "like a house of cards, losing the freshness and fragrance of the Gospel."

Such pulsations of language memorably marry thought and expression. We cannot remember all the good writing we come across, but we know it when we see it. One of the cool sentences in E. B. White's essay on the "trembling city" of New York comes with me every day I walk to my office in Times Square. "No one should come to New York to live unless he is willing to be lucky."

We know the right words are oxygen, that dead English pollutes our minds every day. Those combinations of words don't last forever, but ugly words and phrases linger in the vocabulary. They are picked up and passed on like a virus by the unwary and by the pretentious who like to give the "appearance of solidity to pure wind." Orwell, of course:

> Political language—and with variations this is true of all political parties, from Conservative to anarchist—is

designed to make lies sound truthful and murder respectable, and to give an appearance of solidity to pure wind.

The critic Clive James defines the subtlety of composition that has given enduring life to that one sentence toward the end of Orwell's essay *Politics and the English Language:*

> The subject stated up front, the sudden acceleration from the scope-widening parenthesis into the piercing argument that follows, the way the obvious opposition between "lies" and "truthful" leads into the shockingly abrupt coupling of "murder" and "respectable," the elegant, reverse-written coda clinched with a dirt-common epithet, the whole easy-seeming poise and compact drive of it, a world view compressed to the size of a motto from a fortune cookie, demanding to be read out and sayable in a single breath—it's the Orwell style.

There is no compulsion to be concise on either the Internet or the profusion of television and radio channels; and in writing of every kind, Twitter apart, we see more words, more speed, less clarity, and less honesty, too, since with "demand media" you never know whether a review of *Swan Lake* will conceal a hard sell about toenail fungus. A new enterprise in print, on TV, or on the web is now a "platform" for "content" where if you can develop "core competency," there will be "measurable deliverables." My own observable "behavior-driven process" used to be to throw a shoe at the television whenever I heard *weather* expunged in favor of *existing weather conditions.* As for marketing-speak, I don't have enough shoes or energy for all the branding baloney; it induces the comatose condition Ben Bradlee defined as "MEGO."[1]

In 2012, Chris Hughes, a co-founder of Facebook, bought control of the *New Republic* magazine, renowned as a citadel of literacy. Two years later his new management decided it would no longer print the magazine; it would henceforth publish only online. Straightforward enough, you'd think. The magazine was losing money. It was better to be read than dead. It had lost none of its authority in the hard times for all print publications. It need lose none when the words were backlit on a screen.

What it did lose, on the announcement of a series of changes, was most of the gifted editors and writers. This is not the place to explore all the reasons for the resignations, much regretted by their readers, but one can empathize with the reluctance of writers to associate with the fakery of marketing-speak which regarded the magazine's history as a "competitive advantage" to be "leveraged." The new managers expected the digitized staff to "create magical experiences" through "cross-functional collaboration," and "align themselves from a metabolism perspective" to the needs of "a vertically integrated digital media company." It didn't, as they say, travel well. "Vertical integration?" asked *Slate*'s Seth Stevenson in a spirit of inquiry. "Are they going to, like, mine their own pixels?" Cynthia Ozick, the novelist and

---

[1] "My eyes glaze over."

critic, fretted that the magazine might be turned into a clickbait factory. She knocked out a rough lament inspired by Byron's "The Destruction of Sennacherib":

> The Siliconian came down like the wolf on the fold,
> And his cohorts were gleaming in wireless gold,
> Crying Media Company Vertically Integrated!
> As all before them they willfully extirpated:
> The Back of the Book and the Front and the Middle,
> Until all that was left was digital piddle,
> And Thought and Word lay dead and cold.

Lo and behold, in a nanosecond, Mr. Hughes, who initiated the debacle, announced in January 2016 he would "pursue conversations" with those interested in "taking on the mantle," i.e., buying the magazine. He was as good as his word. What the trade prefers to call a "liquidation event," i.e., a sale, took place a month later. Everybody was happy when, as Mr. Hughes put it, the philanthropist Winthrop McCormack donned the mantle. He assigned the literary figures Hamilton Fish and John Gould to sentry duty to keep out non sequiturs and marketing burble.

In his thoughtful book on rhetoric, *Enough Said,* Mark Thompson, the CEO of the *New York Times,* suggests that anger with conventional political leadership in the United States and Britain can be traced to a change in public language that has produced a mutual breakdown of trust, "leaving ordinary citizens suspicious, bitter and increasingly unwilling to believe anybody."

My contention in *Do I Make Myself Clear?* is that the

oppressive opaqueness of the way much of English is written these days is one cause for disaffection. Waffle dressed up as a high-level digital concept gets regurgitated by business leaders who promise to dedicate themselves to "improving the efficacy of measurable learning outcomes" (a *Financial Times* management statement). Another company urged staff to "deploy social listening tools to come up with consumer engagement strategy to inspire consumer conversations and advocacy."

Had Donald Trump talked like that he would not have won the election. His simple, repetitive assertions were brilliantly effective with his audiences, hypnotized by his insistent certainty:

> We have to stop illegal immigration. We have to do it. [Cheers and applause] We have to do it. Have to do it. [Audience: USA! USA! USA!] And when I hear some of the people that I am running against, including the Democrats. We have to build a wall, folks. We have to build a wall. And a wall works. All you have to do is go to Israel and say is your wall working? Walls work.

It's straightforward work to lay brick on brick to make a wall. It is harder to explain to people caught in the ice and snow of winter storms that the planet is in danger from global warming and that this has something to do with the cars they drive and the coal and oil they burn. Candidate Trump did not attempt to explain the difference between weather and longer escalations in temperatures. His reluctance to attempt that got him into enough of a language swivvet, but what he did say served him well because it connected with his audience. It may have offended the cognitive elite, but it did not deter his rally crowds. It was more or less what they felt; indeed, they may have resented the intrusion of physics into polite conversation. So these were his words:

> And actually, we've had times where the weather wasn't working out, so they changed it to extreme weather, and they have all different names, you know, so that it fits the bill. But the problem we have, and if you look at our energy costs, and all of the things that we're doing to solve a problem that I don't think in any major fashion exists. I mean, Obama thinks it's the number one problem of the world today. And I think it's very low on the list. So I am not a believer, and I will, unless somebody can prove something to me, I believe there's weather. I believe there's change, and I believe it goes up and it goes down, and it goes up again. And it changes depending on years and centuries, but I am not a believer, and we have much bigger problems.[2]

He identified with Republican sentiment—their anxieties, their bewilderment. In national polls, Democrats are as consistent worrying about the effects of climate change from human causes as Republicans are dismissive. More than half

---

[2] See, for instance, "What Is the Meaning of the Medium Is the Message?," by Mark Federman, chief strategist, McLuhan program in culture and technology, http://individual.utoronto.ca/markfederman/article_mediumisthemessage.htm

of Democratic voters trust the scientific consensus; 15 percent of Republicans say the scientists are motivated by political bias and advancing their careers.

Mischief has flowed from Marshall McLuhan's overused, enigmatic paradox "The medium is the message." He did not mean the message was irrelevant, but that we should be more aware of how changes in the medium affect our social interactions. Wasn't he just right? The digital era might have offered a vision of a universe of honest exchanges in search of mutual understanding. It didn't happen. Twitter's guillotine falling at 280 characters put a premium on conciseness, and a tweet fits neatly on the screen of a cell phone.

It breaks news, offers instant relief for the opinionated, makes sure Harry gets to the same meeting place as Sally. It became a megaphone for Donald Trump as a candidate, and then as twitterer in chief. He made an art form of creating stereotypes and pinning scurrilous adjectives to characters in his psychodrama—Lyin' Ted, Crooked Hillary, Psycho Joe, Goofy Elizabeth, Little Rocket Man, etc. You can despise or relish such tweets, but they had millions of loyal followers, even though Twitter Audit and other monitors have identified umpteen fake tweets generated automatically by code, not people.

Only in the wake of the 2016 U.S. presidential election did we become aware of the more sinister malefactions created by the digerati. Facebook's founder, Mark Zuckerberg, laughed off as "crazy" the fears that his site had been infiltrated by fake accounts. The joke was on the millions of Americans who were hoodwinked into believing they were reading the opinions of their fellow Americans when they weren't. They were suckers for a stealthy agitprop campaign by Russian secret services so massive that fully half the voting population was exposed to divisive messages—mainly, it seems, hostile to the Democratic candidate Hillary Clinton and to the benefit of Donald Trump. In 2018 we learned that Facebook had been sneaky about another covert political operation, this one funded in 2016 by the American billionaire Robert Mercer, in a scheme devised by Steve Bannon. In an attempt to underpin the Trump campaign, they engaged a company luxuriating in the faux academic name Cambridge Analytica to "harvest" private information from more than 50 million Facebook accounts. The aim was to identify themes for psychographic messaging that might influence voting attitudes and not incidentally further enrich Zuckerberg and his top staff.[3] Twitter, too, was corrupted. The agitators bought 36 million robot accounts ("bots") that tweeted 14 million times and reached half the 200 million eligible voters.

I would argue that the maelstrom of mendacity makes it all the more imperative that truth be clearly expressed. The great nineteenth-century editor C. P. Scott might have written his famous command just for today—that the unclouded truth must not suffer wrong. But if we care for truth, C.P.'s demand is more onerous since the digerati have secured legal immunity for transmitting falsehoods, as the

---

[3] Matthew Rosenberg, Nicholas Confessore, and Carole Cadwalladr, "Firm That Assisted Trump Exploited the Data of Millions," *New York Times*, March 17, 2018.

gun-making industry has secured immunity for marketing assault weapons.

Liars and their lies can be exposed, but can good writing be learned? I give the "best answer" cigar to Mark Forsyth, author of *The Elements of Eloquence,* whose title I will adorn with the alliterative adjective *entertaining.* He proves how Shakespeare learned to write. Yessir; Shakespeare had a lousy start then refined and mastered every trick in the rhetorical trade. If this attitude seems without reverence for God-given genius, beware: Mr. Forsyth advocates a hit, a palpable hit, on the noses of dissenters until they promise not to talk nonsense anymore.

Still, it may be impossible for any of us to avoid slovenly English. There is so much of it about. Words filtered through algorithms are not washed clean of impurities. Rust eats once-fresh metaphors. I've been reading about *crumbling* infrastructure for twenty years. Hasn't it crumbled away yet? Could it not make out with another adjective for a decade or two, deepen our depression by linking with the catalog of deadly *d* words, *disintegrating, dilapidated, decaying,* or just rot and collapse? Better, is it beyond the wit of the writers to get out from under the Latin *infra* and remind us that the abstraction covers a multitude of sins—corroded water pipes, leaking dams, archaic airports, decrepit overhead power cables?

Passages of obscurity, ugliness, and verbosity pop up as in the game Whac-A-Mole in news reports, business letters, academic journals, contracts, websites, school essays, job descriptions and the applications they attract; in magazines, publicity releases, Facebook posts, broadcasting, and even supposedly well-edited books. Bureaucrats have no monopoly on the opaque. Writers generally set out with good intentions, but something happens along the way. We don't really know what we want to say until we try to write it, and in the gap between the thought and its expression we realize the bold idea has to be qualified or elaborated. We write more sentences. Then more. We are soon in the territory defined by the French mathematician Blaise Pascal (1623–1662) but associated with others, too: I would have written something shorter, but I didn't have time. Soon enough we find ourselves trapped in a bad neighborhood. We whistle up reinforcements, more words. Thoughts collide midsentence. Abstractions suffocate narrative. Nouns dressed up as verbs sap vigor. Clichés avoid detection. Stale images creep in. Modifiers get detached from the words they are supposed to modify: "Walking into Trafalgar Square, Admiral Nelson's column is surrounded by pigeons reaching 169 feet into a pure blue sky."[4]

It's good to feel bad about something you've just written. It tells you there's a fat chance nobody else will feel good about it, so you'd better work out what's wrong and fix it. Kurt Vonnegut's seventh rule of writing[5] applies: "Pity the readers. Readers have to identify thousands of little marks on paper, and make sense of them immediately. They have to read, an art so difficult that most people don't really master it even after having studied it all through grade school and

---

[4] Limbering up to hunt danglers, you can exercise answering a Bristol university quiz: http://www.bristol.ac.uk/arts/exercises/grammar/grammar_tutorial/page_30.htm

[5] Maria Popova, https://www.brainpickings.org/2013/01/14/how-to-write-with-style-kurt-vonnegut

high school—twelve long years." Sonia Orwell and Ian Angus spelled out the obligation for the imperfect artist to meet the imperfect readers more than halfway. It means "rewriting, and rewriting, all of it or in bits and pieces, getting rid of redundant words, making complex sentences simpler, clarifying what you really wanted to say."[6]

A fair question—I am glad you asked—is what do I bring to the picnic? The short answer is that I have spent my life editing thousands of writers, from the urgent files of reporters on the front lines to the complex thought processes of Henry Kissinger in his memoirs and history of China. Forty years ago I wrote a manual for journalists that was adopted by the industry's Society of Editors[7] and another adopted by the Asian press.[8] I discovered early on how skilled are some people in politics and business in using words not for communicating ideas but concealing them. At the *Sunday Times* when we were investigating the cover-up of the great espionage scandal of the Soviet agent Kim Philby, who became head of British intelligence, we were educated in nuance by a former Foreign Office adviser who was a specialist in Anglican liturgy. "Oh, dear," he said, "why does no one read our statements with the care with which we drafted them?" Prime Minister Edward Heath had said in 1973 that the British government was "now aware" that Philby had "worked for the Soviet authorities

---

[6] George Orwell, *Politics and the English Language*, ed. Sonia Orwell and Ian Angus (New York: Harcourt Brace, 1968).

[7] *Newsman's English* (London: William Heinemann, 1972); new edition, *Essential English for Journalists, Editors and Writers*, introduced by Neil Fowler and Crawford Gillan (London: Pimlico, 2000).

[8] *The Active Newsroom* (Zurich: International Press Institute, 1969).

before 1946." In other words, they had known for some unspecified time that he was a Russian agent after 1946 and had then just discovered that Philby had been working for the Soviet Union before that—that is, all along. This made all the more pressing the question of what he was doing in British intelligence from 1940 onward. The finished articles read like John le Carré (who was incidentally of some assistance), but this book is all about nonfiction. I want to pass on what I've learned from trying to get a headlock on the world's most sinuous or deceptive writing; learned, too, from travels with a dictionary in the cascade of good books about writing well (see the bibliography).

If you are more into explaining your inner self to the waiting world than in conveying information, stop here and brood on to greatness. My approach is to start from the muddy field where the casualties lie, see what editing can do to make them whole, and generalize from there. I may note why nonfiction passages lose narrative tension, but I don't aspire to teach great writers; they can look after themselves. Nor do I wish to take the chalk from the grammarians' itchy fingers. When we get lost in unraveling how menaced we are by a software licensing agreement setting out what is forbidden by our "concurrent use," it's the Silicon Valley syntax, stupid. We should respect grammatical rules that make for clarity, but never be scared to reject rules that seem not to. In self-defense, I can call spirits from the vasty deep. A little more than a century ago, William Brewster insisted that the mere avoidance of grammatical barbarisms will not result in clear writing:

One might escape illiteracy but not necessarily confusion. To know what a sentence is saying is important, more important than anything else about it. That is rarely interfered with, directly, by the presence of barbarisms, and not grievously, for the most part, by improprieties and solecisms, as they actually occur in writing; these things cause sorrow chiefly to the erudite or the parvenu of style, whom they offend rather than confuse; the populace cares very little about them.

Fifty years later, Robert Graves and Alan Hodge took up the right end of the stick that the only relevant standard by which to judge any straightforward piece of prose is the ease with which it conveys its full intended sense, rather than its correctness by the laws of formal English grammar inherited from Alexandrian Greek. And around the same time, Orwell was rebuking the rebukers. Defending the English language, he wrote, "has nothing to do with correct grammar and syntax, which are of no importance so long as one makes one's meaning clear, or with the avoidance of Americanisms, or with having what is called 'a good prose style.'"

You can lose your mind trying to obey prescriptivists—the "linguistically brainwashed," in David Crystal's exuberant demolition. He advises: "Don't be conned, don't feel threatened or inferior when confronted by a menacing grammarian" [*that* but not *which* can introduce a noun clause (or argument clause or content clause), and *which* but not *that* can be used as a determiner with a plural noun (so *which books*, but not *that books*]. Go to a quiet room with Crystal's

The Fight for English or read Thurber's adventures with a which clause which rescued Ernest Hemingway from a which clause about which nobody had alerted him, which was a damn shame.[9]

Do I Make Myself Clear? is for everyman. I've read and respected the admonitions in scores of books on usage and debated their utility. What I got into *my* bones, early on, was the conviction that a concise sentence was more likely to be clear. At sixteen, as a junior reporter on a weekly newspaper, I longed to speed up the translation of the proceedings of councils, inquests, and courts I'd taken down verbatim in Pitman's phonetic shorthand.

At Durham University, writing essays on politics, economics, and ethics, I became infected with literary pretensions, squeezed out of me when I was hired by an electric evening newspaper, the *Manchester Evening News*. We edited words written on a typewriter, sent the marked folios to the Linotype operators to convert into column-width slugs, lines of hot lead, antimony, and tin. We prayed that the number of metal lines would fit into the space the page planner had allotted for their assembly in an iron frame (a chase). Every report we edited had to fit a prescribed space. ("We don't have rubber type.") No meandering in cyberspace. Omit a salient fact in editing to length, send the printer an excess of type, and you were looking for a job. The turnover of staff was scary.

I graduated from those disciplines to marshaling argu-

---

[9] "Which," by James Thurber, was first published in *The New Yorker* in 1929 and reprinted in Thurber's *The Owl in the Attic and Other Perplexities* (New York: Harper, 1931).

ments, as best I could, for the newspaper's formal editorials, as testing an exercise in making oneself understood in a short space as my spare-time efforts to pass on my understanding of Keynes to coal miners for workers' education classes. Both demanded as much clarity as I could manage.

Every day on the editorial page I had sixty minutes to write the *Evening News* pronouncement on whatever the editor, Big Tom Henry, decided was the issue of the moment. Housing! Suez Canal! The Test Ban Treaty! The National Health Service! I'd spend half the hour writing an arresting first paragraph. Too often for my self-respect, it didn't appear. It had been lopped off by Big Tom. I got the message: Get to the point. No throat clearing.

His next big thought was that I might now be qualified to clear up debris left by British imperialism. Governments of various countries in Southeast Asia had asked the International Press Institute for help in improving newspapers and broadcasting. Big Tom nominated me, so in a jiffy I was translated from Manchester's dark Satanic mills to the lovely Delhi garden of India's prime minister, Pandit Nehru (Cambridge and the Inner Temple 1907–1910). He gently explained how the florid Victorian mode of writing bequeathed by the Raj was standing between him as prime minister and his people's understanding of what he was trying to do.

I spent months on the temporary teaching assignment with editors in the subcontinent and the Philippines and Japan and South Korea. Paul Miller, the head of the Associated Press and Gannett Newspapers, heard about the work, said he'd always admired the conciseness imposed on the wartime British press by the shortage of newsprint, and that

Evans fellow should come to the United States for a few months to indoctrinate editors who'd hadn't realized they could tell more in less.

All these experiences were apprenticeships for accepting responsibility for the opinion and news columns of regional and then national newspapers. For fourteen years as editor of the *Sunday Times* (circulation 1.5 million), I pounded the typewriter to make sure the brilliant but complex work of the investigative team known as Insight—on thalidomide, the DC-10 disaster, the exposé of the espionage of Kim Philby[10]—could be understood by the man on the Clapham bus as clearly as it was by the lawyers who would be at our throats before the ink was dry.

I knew risks were embedded in every word from another learning experience at the *Sunday Times*. On vacation in Austria, I tried to ski. I couldn't do it. I blamed the complicated instructions about what to do with my knees and when, and having a care also for what I was doing with shoulders, arms, elbows, and hips while paralyzed by fear. The reputable book I bought left me giddier:

> The skier comes out of a traverse or a preceding turn, places increasing weight on the downhill ski, and tries to prepare for a stepping-off movement from the downhill ski by pressing his downhill knee forwards and uphill. Taking off with the help of a vigorous pole plant, he then steps his weight on the other ski and starts the next change of direction. As he turns, the ski which is now

---

[10] Described in *My Paper Chase* (Boston: Little, Brown, 2009).

weighted is edged on the other side and he steps up the ski from which he has taken off. The turn is controlled by the twisting movement of the legs, and a strong edging maneuver as well as the forwards and sideways movement of the upper part of the body.

Say again? From which ski am I to detach the upper body and hope the rest will follow? Brooding on the humiliation of being able neither to ski nor to understand the choreography led me to think what editing could do to make the instruction clearer. The following year I went back to the Alps with two similarly frustrated *Sunday Times* colleagues and tried again. We engaged a champion ski teacher, a Scottish disciplinarian, and talked enough of wild fondue parties to persuade a photographer and graphic artist to risk their necks. At night, we wrote up everything that had helped us get through the moguls in one piece, and everything that catapulted us into space. We all became good skiers, able to cope with any well-behaved mountain and stop with a decent flourish in front of the restaurant crowd. We were so exhilarated we wrote a book called *We Learned to Ski*.[11] That, too, was hard. We rewrote and rewrote, and rewrote. The three of us were haunted by the knowledge that the penalty for a clumsy sentence or badly labeled graphic prepared in comfort might be a skier with a sprained ankle, or worse, isolated on an icy mountain; risks multiplied when nearly a million learners took us at our word. It seems a good time was had by all. We had made ourselves clear.

---

[11] Harold Evans, Brian Jackman, and Mark Ottaway, *We Learned to Ski* (London: Collins, 1974).

In 1981, I became the editor of the *Times*, only the twelfth in two hundred years. It was the pinnacle of the profession. Abraham Lincoln had shaken the hand of its famous war correspondent John Russell in 1861 at the start of the Civil War: "I am very glad to see you in this country. The *London Times* is one of the greatest powers in the world—in fact, I don't know anything which has more power—except perhaps the Mississippi." I wrote policy editorials with Lincoln's words in my ear and the great thunderers Thomas Barnes, John Delane, and William Haley frowning over my shoulder. I was never allowed to forget that the Black Friars, the guardians of its literary traditions among staff and readers, were coiled to chastise any transgression of the Queen's English.

I had no trouble with the Black Friars, but I had hardly been installed when our cultured but combative columnist Bernard Levin shook everyone by insisting that one of his labyrinthine sentences should be published unchanged or he would write no more. It was 160 unbroken words. I loved reading Levin. He coruscated, but this passage stopped you dead. It was not clear. We were close to press time. I was told the *Times* had never before published such a long sentence. The Victorian tops were forty-five. I reckoned a cultural reference might persuade Levin to cooperate with his editor. I compared some of his sentences to the endless corridors of a Venetian palace: "You know there is something good at the end but your feet ache getting there." He was unmoved by metaphor. I appealed for compassion. A fair proportion of *Times* readers were elderly. No one had ever so tested their stamina. A full stop (U.S. period) in midpassage would give them a chance to catch a breath. He relented. The paragraph lit up, but it had been a close-run thing.

Subsequently, for seven years as president and publisher of Random House, U.S., in the nineties, I had to decide the level of financial and intellectual investment we would make in authors—we got it right with *Dreams from My Father* by a community organizer—but I still most relished line editing. I found working with celebrated authors and editors at Random House to be enjoyably instructive in the language and the varied approaches required of an editor in the foothills of Parnassus. I am proud of the bruises in linguistic encounters with Norman Mailer. Our prized novelist E. L. Doctorow had an answer when I asked where we were going with the narrative in *The Waterworks* (1994). "Writing a novel," he rejoined, "is a lot like driving a car at night. You never see further than your headlights but you can make the whole trip that way." Doctorow never needed roadside assistance, but as an editor I liked to know the route so I could always be at hand with a jack and spare tire.

Working comma by comma with the writers and the editors, I was entrusted with approving their work on the lethal complexities of nuclear treaties and the looming shadow of Chinese power, the brooding introspections of Marlon Brando, the hilarious concoctions of Christopher Buckley, the sardonic essays of Gore Vidal, the excitements of the life of Colin Powell, the outrages documented in Jonathan Harr's prizewinning legal thriller *A Civil Action,* and the forensic energies of Jeffrey Toobin and Lawrence Schiller writing independently on O.J.'s murder trial.

All very different in substance and writing style, all

meriting editing that respected their idioms and their nuances. Having grumbled about Twitter tantrums, I readily concede the value of Twitter as an alarm clock for news — opinion flashes, the swift formation of coalitions, and the instant exposure of absurdity. The *New York Times* Sunday magazine chose to feature a hairless egg-domed Hillary Clinton as a planet in the universe. Within seconds a whole universe of tweeters and parodists were flooding the zone, one of them describing the image of Hillary Clinton as a "sentient space testicle." Days into the row about the apparently vindictive closing of access lanes on the New Jersey side of the George Washington Bridge, Stephen Colbert said a lot in ninety-nine characters: "When Christie is President, he'll address our nation's crumbling infrastructure by making sure we stay off bridges."

This is Twitter at its best, but it's an elephant trap for loose writers. One moment of unwitting candor, one ambiguity, one misplaced pronoun, one misdirection, one errant syllable, and the trivia cops are on the case. Or worse. Jack Bauer had good reason for the insistent "Copy that" in the TV thriller *24 Hours*. In the Crimean War (1853–56), the British cavalry was sent to attack the wrong guns, a catastrophe memorialized by Lord Tennyson:

> "Forward, the Light Brigade!
> Charge for the guns!" he said:
> Into the valley of Death
> Rode the six hundred.
> ...
> Someone had blunder'd:
> Theirs not to make reply,

Theirs not to reason why,
Theirs but to do and die

Readers, like cavalrymen, deserve clarity. Writers may aspire to glory, but I hope this book can at least help you to say—whether in social media or published form—what you want to say concisely, without ambiguity, and without being put off by the mandarins in the corner fussing about "proper" English. May you be as braced for execrations about deviant tendencies in the deployment of *who* and *whom,* and *which* and *that,* as Churchill was for the impertinences of the vocative case. What really matters is making your meaning clear beyond a doubt. My aim is simple: to give you the tools so you can finish the job, first by describing the tools and then by applying them to lengths of knotty prose.

Do I make myself clear?

2

Use and Abuse of Writing Formulas

"*Sorry, but I'm going to have to issue you a summons for reckless grammar and driving without an apostrophe.*"

David Blundy, a reporter for the *Sunday Times* and the *Correspondent*, was at the front line of truth—not because he sometimes exposed himself to danger, but because he never ceased to expose himself to doubt. He used to hang his long frame over his battered portable typewriter and ask of himself and anyone within earshot in the newsroom, "Do you find a problem in getting the words in the right order? What's it all about?" He worried how faithfully he could portray what he'd just seen and heard on his varied assignments. What is the source of the fear on the streets of Belfast? How did an epidemic start in Haiti? And who is lying to him about the machine-gunning of El Salvador's peasants along the Sumpul River border with Honduras? He began his report:

> Lolita Guardado was awakened at about 4 am by a strange noise. There was the usual sound of persistent drizzle pouring from the roof of closely packed palm leaves and through the walls of mud and sticks. But outside across the Sumpul River she could hear men shouting. Groups of peasants gathered anxiously in the grey dawn to watch as Honduran soldiers formed a line on the far bank and ran to and fro carrying stones from the river bed. They built a low wall. Only later that day, after her family, friends and neighbours had been slaughtered, did she fully understand why the soldiers were there.

The Honduran soldiers were there to stop Lolita's family, and hundreds of Salvadoran peasants like them, escaping from a "border-cleansing operation" by El Salvador's army. Blundy's investigation exposed how the three hundred people killed at the river were innocent peasants, not the guerrillas El Salvador's army was hunting.

As his biographer noted,[1] Blundy's angst at the keyboard epitomized "every writer's eternal problem about getting the right words in the right order." The massacre was one of many perpetrated by a panicky right-wing government. The story could have been told any number of ways. ("El Salvador's army fired into hundreds of peasants," etc.) Blundy worried his way to telling it from the viewpoint of the peasants taken by surprise that morning. He adopted a narrative style. His first sentence raises curiosity about the strange noise, then carries us along to the shocking verb *slaughtered*. The end of this sentence leads us to the next paragraph. We are impelled to read on to find out what happened. (In the craft of journalism, the technique of holding the reader in suspense is called a *delayed drop*, apparently a term borrowed from parachuting.)

Ten years later, at the age of forty-four, Blundy had filed another dispatch on street fighting in El Salvador's continuing civil war, but wanted to make sure he had it right. He went into the barrio again for a last paragraph. He didn't write it. A random bullet took his life.

David Blundy at the Sumpul River had no literary pretensions. He had a story to tell. He wanted to get the words in the right order in the six sentences in this extract, and in the ones that followed it, so that nothing stood between the reader and a sense of the crime. He made himself clear. How did he do that? He used words within every literate person's vocabulary. They are mostly short, and they are concrete,

---

[1] Anthony Holden, ed., *The Last Paragraph: The Journalism of David Blundy* (London: Heinemann, 1990).

not abstract, so we can imagine the people in the scene. But the right words in the right order have to be corralled into some kind of sentence, the essential unit of English. This is where clouds form to obscure the view.

Ink for a hundred dictionaries has been shed defining a sentence. The angels dancing on a pinhead need not detain us. A sentence expresses a complete thought; we mostly write and read sentences defined as a meaningful collection of words ending at a full stop. (I prefer the unambiguous English *full stop* over the American *period,* a noun better busying itself as an expression of time.) There is no doubting the meaning of the single dot at the end of a sentence: you have said enough, now move to the next thought. The colon, a dot mounted on another dot (:), allows the thought to be continued or illustrated with an example. We know that one word between two full stops can express a thought. Nobody any longer fears arrest by the language police for sending a naked sentence into the world. Subject, verb, and predicate may be stripped off without loss of meaning even with an imperative — Women and children first! — and the surprise of a one-word staccato conclusion may wrap up an argument in the way President Lyndon Johnson did in grabbing the lapels of an objector. Bull! Microsoft Word's grammar and spell check is on sentry duty for verbless writing ("Fragment, consider revising"), but keep your temper if you feel like rejoining, "Up yours." It's worth being reminded that the verbless sentence, used too often, is like a mosquito buzzing in your ear.

Enough.

Blundy's apparently straightforward paragraph, as it

happens, comprises four structurally different sentences of graduating complexity. I illustrate with a rough sequence based on Blundy's narrative (but not his words).

1. The soldiers came to the river.

Simple one-clause sentence (one subject, one single-verb predicate)

2. The soldiers came to the river, and they built a low stone wall.

Compound—simple one-clause sentence linked to another by a conjunction.

3. Soldiers came to the river, where they built a low stone wall, watched by anxious peasants.

The complex sentence with one principal statement and one or more subordinate statements or clauses that modify or supplement the main statement.

4. Soldiers came to the river, where they formed a line on the far bank, and peasants watched them run to and fro carrying stones from the river bed to build a low stone wall. (34 words)

A compound-complex sentence where all the statements have one or more modifying statements.

Writers and editors are frequently enjoined to embrace

"simple" sentences. That's fine when it is understood to mean shedding adverbs, adjectives, and runaway subordinate clauses, less so if an editor of your work is incited to impose the grammatical definition of a simple sentence:

> Soldiers came to the river. They formed a line on the far bank. The peasants watched. The soldiers ran to and fro. They carried stones from the river bed. They used them to build a low stone wall. (38 words)

Even with the infinitive phrase (to build a low stone wall), the last sentence is still a simple sentence, one clause, one thought. A series of simple cat-sat-on-the-mat sentences provides monotonous clarity, which misses the point of being clear: we won't communicate anything if the sentences are so boring readers switch off. It's also wasteful to introduce a complete subject and predicate for each new idea. The compound-complex sentence flows better and it saves four words on the six simple sentences. The attraction of the simple sentence is that its one idea is more likely to stand clear, but complex sentences are not doomed to be unreadable. Later, we'll look at the architecture of some that don't collapse of their own weight. The longest Blundy sentence is thirty-two words. How long is too long? Could the average twelve-year-old read all the Blundy sentences with ease? The answer is yes. I can justify that assertion by inviting you to take a journey to the West of the United States—and then through time.

We land in Lincoln, Nebraska, in 1882, where the state university has just appointed to its chair in English a thirty-five-year-old Yale PhD who's been teaching Latin, Greek, and English at Hopkins Grammar School in Connecticut. Lucius Adelno Sherman (1847–1933), sadly widowed after a year of marriage, is the son of a Rhode Island carpenter and builder. He is to spend much of his forty-seven academic years investigating how the sentence developed clarity over a century. He is a daring young man. He has the nerve to apply metrics to art. His literary insights are acute; he has discerned how Shakespeare used the phrase as a special instrument of power, and then the clause. Sherman's heretical idea is that the elements of the prose of masters might be as susceptible to scientific study as the elements of chemistry. He plunges into counting the elements in works by Thomas Babington Macaulay, Henry James, Edmund Spenser, Ralph Waldo Emerson, Cardinal Newman, Thomas De Quincey, Thomas Carlyle—counting the number of words, prepositions, clauses, predications, abstract nouns, and so on. He will distill these laborious researches into a book of argument, tables, and graphs that is more readable than it sounds: *Analytics of Literature: A Manual for the Study of English Prose and Poetry*. Published in 1893, it documents how sentences sped up from pre-Elizabethan to Sherman's times. "Anyone acquainted with the Elizabethan or ante-Elizabethan prose-writers," he writes, "is well aware that their sentences are prevailingly crabbed or heavy and that it is often necessary to re-read, sometimes to ponder, before a probable meaning reveals itself." He found solace in discovering that from an early-sixteenth-century average of fifty words a sentence, the average fell to forty-five in the Elizabethan era, twenty-nine in the Victorian era, and twenty-three in the early twentieth century.

And with that compression, Sherman demonstrated, went greater clarity without loss of the inherent literary values.

Where did the easier reading come from? The clearer sentences weren't the result of some publisher's fiat that henceforth sentences should not exceed *x* number of words. Scrutinizing the great books, Sherman discovered that they got more concise because writers gradually dispensed with a feeling that every new thought had to be introduced as a package, a subject and a predicate made up of a verb and an object. He documented a "decrease in predication" over a century or so. His selected work by Chaucer had 5.24 predications in 480 words, Spenser 4.68, Bacon 3.12, Emerson 2.26, Macaulay 2.15. Two predications to a sentence became the new norm, and with that a 33 percent increase in the proportion of simple sentences. Think of it as reducing the baggage a sentence was expected to carry. The invention of subordinate clauses relieved the burden, and then phrases supplanted the clauses. It was all a natural organic consequence, an effect, not a cause.

Sherman attributed the faster concrete sentences as an adaptation of prose to the directness of speech. There must be something to this. Any number of authors testify that reading aloud strips the veneer from sentences that look polished in print. I cherish the image of Flaubert declaiming, before his ink had dried, parts of *Madame Bovary* to his friends or, if there were none around, to himself. "Night after night," writes Eric Ormsby, "he would shout his sentences to the stunned flowerbeds and dumbstruck nightingales in his Croisset garden."

Sherman reported that his numerate literature course roused enthusiasm for reading among his students and claimed that those accustomed to write in "a lumbering awkward fashion began to express themselves in strong, clear phrases and with a large preponderance of simple sentences." Students—with no computers then—must have found it tedious to count the words in 100,000 sentences by seven authors; one of the class rebelled. The teenage Willa Cather (1873–1947) was to become an admired novelist of the western plains but a satirist of her teacher's method. She wanted literature to make her "feel the hot blood riot in the pulses" rather than have to ponder "the least common multiple of *Hamlet* and the greatest common divisor of *Macbeth*." Her deflation of magic-from-metrics has not deterred scholars at Nebraska. In 2006, Andrew Jewell, the editor of the Willa Cather archive, suggested "digital Americanists" might infiltrate the Cather archive to detect language patterns in her fiction. "Perhaps one could even find the least common multiple of *Death Comes for the Archbishop*."

The arguments may seem esoteric, but Sherman achieved something significant a century before the digerati took over the world. For his initiative in bringing forth reasoned facts, Mark Liberman, professor of linguistics at Penn, suggests the accolade "the first digital humanist *avant la lettre*." The Nebraskans scanning the Cather sentences in the archive today acknowledge that any quantitative analysis risks an assault to literature-loving sensibilities. One of Sherman's notions was to assess the power of passages by means of a "force-ratio," which meant assessing the number of emphasized words in relation to the total. "In the prose passage from Carlyle, there is more than seventy percent of emphasis but the force-ratio of the present paragraph and the next is 25:45, or only fifty-five percent." That rates a giggle, but the importance of Sherman's work is real and well summarized by William DuBay:[2] "Sherman's work set the agenda for a century of research in reading." DuBay is an authority in "readability." That's not a subjective judgment on whether the latest Stephen King is a good read. Readability isn't a literary or legibility issue. It's a dispassionate, objective measure of whether a selection of words and sentences will be understood by the intended audience. Comprehension comes before enjoyment; you can't be gripped if you can't follow the narrative. (Nor can you if the typography is anything as illegible as *Wikipedia*'s 250 characters to a line.)[3]

Mark Twain, J.R.R. Tolkien, Jane Austen, Louisa May Alcott, Harper Lee, Arthur Conan Doyle, J. D. Salinger, Norman Mailer...which of their books can be assigned to twelve-year-olds and which only to high-schoolers? You can guess, but getting it wrong for thousands of schools is expensive and seeds, in the uncomprehending, a hatred of high-falutin literature. Educators had questions that could be answered only by embracing Sherman's empiricism, testing selections of representative text on large numbers of targeted readers, and correlating the results. The impetus for objective readability research gained force through the 1920s, initially to find reader-friendly texts for immigrants and then

---

[2] DuBay edited the seminal collation of readability studies *Unlocking Language* (Costa Mesa, CA: Impact Information, 2007).

[3] Harold Evans, *Text Typography* (London: Heinemann, 1972).

servicemen. In 1931, William Gray and Bernice Leary in Chicago identified 228 elements that affect readability, a total guaranteed to multiply the number of Depression-era authors suffering writer's block. Gray and Leary boiled down their variables to five because for all the extra counting, there was little payoff in accuracy.

Out of all this work came readability formulas to count the prevalence or absence of variables associated with reading difficulty, basically syntactic (sentence structure) and semantic (vocabulary).

Rudolf Flesch galvanized the effort. He had thought he would have a successful career as a lawyer in Vienna until the Nazis marched in. He came to the United States in 1938 as a refugee, found his law degree not recognized, worked in a book-shipping department, got a scholarship to Columbia, and in 1943 publicized the first way to measure what the average American adult could read and, therefore, how authors should write if they were to have any hope of bestseller success. He wrote *The Art of Readable Writing* and nineteen other popular primers, inspired Dr. Seuss to write *The Cat in the Hat,* campaigned for the phonic teaching of reading, and bequeathed us the Flesch Reading Ease index. It's a simple calculation of complexity judged by the average length of sentences and the number of syllables per hundred words. He urged writers to *average* eighteen words a sentence. In his 1949 book, still available, the endpaper is a nomograph, three columns scored like thermometers, one on the left for words per sentence, one on the right for syllables per hundred words, and one in the middle. The writer places a ruler to run from the word total on the left to the syllable total on the right. The intersection with the center Reading Ease column yields the score: 100 for a child's primer, 0 for an academic paper. Like the typewriter, the nomograph is a curiosity.

Your laptop can do the analysis before you can check *nomograph* in the dictionary—and the Flesch test is free online. So are a number of later formulas I list in the bibliography. In 1975, a U.S. Navy educationist, J. Peter Kincaid, related the Flesch Reading Ease index to grade levels. Ten years after Flesch, Robert Gunning created the fog index. Working with newspapers and business corporations, he identified seven measurable factors that affect reading: average sentence length in words; percentage of simple sentences; percentage of strong verb forms; proportion of familiar words; proportion of abstract words; percentage of personal references; percentage of long words. He simplified his prescription for writers: If you want to be clear, count the average number of words in your sentences, count the number of words of three syllables (the percentage of hard words), total the two, and multiply by 0.4. The lower the ranking on the fog index, the easier the reading, so a 6 index is material for grades six and seven. "If your copy tests 13 or more...you are writing on the college level of complexity and your reader is likely to find it heavy going, even though he is paying close attention. Copy with a fog index of 13 or more runs the danger of being ignored or misunderstood." Edgar Dale, professor of education at Yale, and Jeanne Chall, later at Harvard (consulted by *Sesame Street* producers), concentrated on vocabulary. Their formula bases readability on the number of hard words—that is, words that are not in a basic vocabulary of three thousand easy words. William DuBay judges the Dale-Chall index "the most reliable of all the readability formulas." A score of 8 to 8.9 on Dale-Chall is readable by eleventh-graders; 9 is a college reading level; 10 or over is a college-graduate level.

The assertion I made early in this chapter that the average twelve-year-old could understand the opening paragraph by David Blundy was based on testing it against a number of readability indexes.

I called up Count Wordsworth, alias Joseph Rocca of Auteuil, who maintains "an (unnecessarily) elaborate enquiry into the statistics of prose." The Count spares me the arithmetic of reckoning the average number of words in the Blundy sentences. It is 15.29. None of the sentences is longer than thirty-two words. None of the words is longer than ten characters; the average number of syllables per word is two. The paragraph about Honduran soldiers I wrote following Blundy's (page 31) has similar characteristics. But most helpful is the comparison with readability formulas, provided you understand that a high score on Flesch means easy reading, whereas a high score on Dale-Chall means hard. Here is Count Wordsworth's analysis of four indexes. All four give roughly the same signal of relatively easy reading for a twelve- to thirteen-year-old.

Readability Scores

Flesch Reading Ease index	69.56
Flesch-Kincaid grade level	7.35
Dale-Chall Formula	8.23
Gunning fog index	6.49

A low score for readability that surprises you may be due to a few knotty tangles of sentences or a bunch of clichés you overlooked in a hurry and can fix. The digital analysis enables you to see how you construct your work. It puts you, the word mechanic, in the position of the auto mechanic who makes sense of the connections under the hood. The indexes may vary in their scores but not by enough to make a difference. Readabilityformulas.com and Readability-score.com will give you individual results or a consensus of seven or more analyses.

Arithmetic can't write. I am not advocating an abacus at every desk. Clear writing meets the judge's definition of *porn:* I know it when I see it. But the formulas will give you a clue whether your assumptions are right about the comprehension of your likely readership. Bureaucrat, meet the baffled person who would receive a benefit if he could understand how to claim it. Company chairman, meet your shareholders. Tycoons and their henchmen need as much help as they can get. The *Financial Times* columnist Lucy Kellaway has been the dragon slayer of jargon. Her Golden Flannel Awards go to masters of the universe who use guff for exaggeration, euphemism, and obfuscation and encourage marketing people to "turn something that we need into something entirely baffling." To test the acumen of Readabilityformulas.com I fed it four separate Golden Flannel sentences[4] from Ms. Kellaway's absolutely indispensable

---

[4] I removed brand names because they would distort the readability scores.

branded corrective product. Sorry, no money back if you gag in the course of ingestion:

(1) As we iterate on the logged out experience and curate topics, events, moments that unfold on the platform, you should absolutely expect us to deliver those experiences across the total audience and that includes logged in users and users in syndication.

(2) As brands build out a world footprint, they look for a no-holds-barred global POV that's always been part of our wheelhouse.

(3) In the wholesale channel, we exited doors not aligned with brand status and invested in presentation through both enhanced assortments and dedicated customized real estate in key doors.

(4) Going forward, we are focused on aggressively managing short-term challenges and opportunities and we remain committed to delivering our mid-decade plan and serving a growing group of customers.

All the readability formulas spat out the same verdict: difficult to read, only for college graduate and above. But the algorithm's vindication of Ms. Kellaway's judgment misses the comic pretension of the flannellers. Were they fed on cotton wool as babies?

None of the measurements should be regarded with reverence. The readability experts George Klare and Byron

Buck crystallize the point: "Formulas are *rating* tools, not *writing* tools."[5] Reflect on the red flag for the long sentence or unusual word, but don't be browbeaten. Formulas don't worry about the right words in the right order as David Blundy did. They are blind to meaning, to the progression of an argument. You can write illogical nonsense and get a good score of readability; the classic proof is that if you enter your sample from the last word to the first, you get the same score. Metaphor, analogy, and satire are unrecognized, wit unappreciated. The formulas have tin ears for the rhythm of sentence variety, for word choice, for the energy in the writing.

These are qualities in the best reporting, commonly written against the clock and sometimes at risk. In the Mexican Revolution of 1913–1914, a would-be war reporter from New York in search of the rebel patriot Pancho Villa had to ask permission to cross the Rio Grande. The federal general Pascual Orozco made himself clear: "Esteemed and Honored Sir: If you set foot inside of Ojinaga, I will stand you sideways against a wall, and with my own hand take great pleasure in shooting furrows in your back."

The reporter took a chance; he found a spot where he could wade across with a dry notebook and timed it for when the sun was high and the sentries would be taking their siesta on the shady side of adobe walls. The adventurous gringo John Reed, twenty-seven, rode four months with Villa and his guerrilleros before heading off to another revolution, in

---

[5] George Klare and Byron Buck, *Limitations of the Readability Formulas* (New York: Hermitage, 1954), 136–51.

Russia; Warren Beatty played him in the movie *Reds*. Reed's Mexican reports, telegraphed from dusty townships to New York's *Metropolitan Magazine*, came to be eclipsed by his better-known reports from the Bolshevik Revolution, published in his book *Ten Days That Shook the World*. His earlier book, *Insurgent Mexico*,[6] was out of print for decades, but the sentences throb with drama as he rides to battle with the guerrillas, "readier to lend their woman than their horse," but also too ready to "please the trigger finger."

The drunk pockmarked officer who bursts into Reed's small-town rented room says, "I am Lieutenant Antonio Montoya, at your orders. I heard there was a gringo in this hotel and I have come to kill you. My only difficulty is to determine which revolver I shall use."

Reed trades his wristwatch for his life. He is a portrait artist and a muralist. His sentences reflect the rhythms of his experiences. The long first sentence in the following paragraph would set off the alarms on the readability formulas[7]—it is 77 words, 153 syllables—but the progression is easy to follow, each of the five phases of deployment marked by a comma, the unwinding finally marked by a semicolon. The words are concrete, as with Blundy:

> At Santa Clara the massed columns of the army halted
> and began to defile to left and right, thin lines of troops
> jogging out under the checkered sun and shade of the

---

[6] John Reed, *Insurgent Mexico* (New York: International Publishers, 1969).

[7] The Gunning fog index is 31.2 (postgraduate); Flesch is 12.22 (from the 100 scale of easy reading).

great trees, until six thousand men were spread in one long single front, to the right over fields and through ditches, beyond the last cultivated field, across the desert to the very base of the mountains; to the left over the roll of flat world. The bugles blared faintly and near, and the army moved forward in a mighty line across the whole country. Above them lifted a five-mile-wide golden dust-glory. Flags flapped.

We see it all.

3

~~~

The Sentence Clinic

"This is going to be a little invasive."

The joyously dim Emperor Joseph II complains to Mozart in the movie *Amadeus,* "Too many notes.... There are only so many notes an ear can hear." To which Mozart asks which ones the emperor would like cut. It's a fair question. Every day I stumble on long sentences I have to read twice. I set them aside in the sentence clinic so I can attempt a diagnosis at leisure—maybe the difficulty is not so much in the number of notes, but the way they are organized. Or maybe I will conclude that the fault is not in the syntax but in myself. And I do, indeed, suffer from a chronic condition of editor's reflex, my attention too easily diverted from the thread of the argument or narrative to find out what stands between me and the sense the writer wants to share. I don't get mad. I enjoy finding the clues, the footloose modifier, the duplicitous pronoun, the subject in search of conjugation with a friendly verb. It always helps to find where the writer has hidden subject and verb. The family of subject, verb, and object that should stick together frequently becomes separated on a crowded thoroughfare—where's Junior? Or there may be something else I can't quite fathom that has made the sentence a Rubik's Cube of words. A useful habit is to ask dumb questions of writer or text. What follows here is a ragbag of sentences that had passed some kind of editorial scrutiny before I seized them as examples of the unclear. They may be grammatically flawless, so what is it that makes them hard to follow? I offer them as editing exercises because I think it's good for writers to come into the engine room where the pipes hiss and clang; I suggest correctives but with every one you're welcome to take a wrench and do your own repair. I don't name the authors of the errant sentences; they represent us all.

The commonest case in the clinic is the overcrowded sentence. Take a moment's break and watch a fragment of the video I've footnoted[1]—then come back! It's a video of "pushers" in Japan trying to cram people into packed subway cars;

---

[1] https://www.youtube.com/watch?v=KM5qlOWqdWI

they are doing what journalists do, notably in oversourcing an introduction to a good story; what lawyers do in shoving in clauses to catch every imaginable contingency; what office seekers on the stump tend to do. Winston Churchill discerned it in Ramsay MacDonald as "the gift of compressing the largest number of words into the smallest amount of thought." Here as a warm-up is a bureaucratic masterpiece, a sentence from a federal regulation typical of the abuse regardless of an administration's political party:

> Whenever the Commission shall be of opinion that any change, classification, regulation or practice of any carrier or carriers is or will be in violation of any of the provisions of the chapter, the Commission is authorized and empowered to determine and prescribe what will be the just and reasonable charge or the maximum and minimum charge or charges to be thereafter observed, and what classification, regulation or practice is or will be just, fair, and reasonable to be thereafter followed, and to make an order that the carrier or carriers shall cease and desist from such violation to the extent that the Commission finds that the same does or will exist, and shall not thereafter publish, demand, or collect any charge other than the charge so prescribed, or in excess of the maximum or less than the minimum so prescribed, as the case may be, and shall adopt the classification and shall conform to and observe the regulation or practice so prescribed.

What a monster, a boa constrictor of a paragraph. How to grapple with it? In editing, I searched for the verb that drives the sentence. There—after 35 prefatory words—we have a cluster, *is authorized and empowered to determine and prescribe.* We can then more or less follow the author, a lawyer with hiccups. The tedious repetitions add up to a blanket authority. The sense of it all can be rendered in 29 words instead of 165:

> The Commission has the authority to act against any violation of the provisions of this chapter. It may prescribe charges and practices it judges to be fair and reasonable.

BEWARE THE PREDATORY CLAUSE

"Write shorter sentences" is the standard imprecation in advice on writing. Count me in, but note that I closed the last chapter with a long quote from John Reed. His description of the massing of the army columns in Mexico was 77 words, but it could be read and enjoyed. Why? In my experience, writers and editors alike miss or understate another source of mystification in the way a sentence is put together. We see it in the first 35 words of the Commission's sentence. You could say it takes too long to get to the point. True, but the source of the reader's exasperation is the bureaucrat's long opening conditional clause before unveiling the ideas in the main clause. The more we delay linking subject to verb, the more the reader wonders what the hell we are on about. We can grasp the meaning in a long sentence when we read a concise introduction of the subject ("the massed columns of the army") and an early verb ("halted"). The connection between subject and verb is crucial.

I call the overweening prefatory element *predatory* because it steals the reader's attention and clogs cerebral arteries. It's the hydrogenated fat of prose. It's why David Crystal is justified in this, as much else, when he writes, "The longer the subject gets, the more uncomfortable we feel." In umpteen practical editing experiences in journalism and publishing, I struggled to save sentences from suffocation by a predatory clause, and must have written quite a few. As writers, we set out to seize attention with a bold declaratory sentence, but before we get to the main idea that excited us, we think of a detail or qualification and plonk it in. Ambition should be made of sterner stuff. What seems to be a neat and economical way of speeding up the story—two ideas for the price of one—imposes a burden on the reader's short-term memory and concentration. The predatory clause is more a threat to clarity than footling prescriptive consternation about *that* or *which* or *who* and *whom*.

The predatory clause ought to have expired of its own weight long ago. Nearly two centuries ago Thomas De Quincey (1785–1859), author of *Confessions of an English Opium Eater*[2] was clear enough about what he called the "hypothetic" effect of opening with a subordinate clause.

A sentence, for example, begins with a series of ifs; perhaps a dozen lines are occupied with expanding the conditions under which something is affirmed or denied...all

---

[2] A fine essay by Colin Dickey is at http://www.laphamsquarterly.org/roundtable/addicted-life-thomas-de-quincey

is suspended in air. The conditions are not fully to be understood until you are acquainted with the dependency; you must give a separate attention to each clause of this complex hypothesis, and yet, having done that by a painful effort, you have done nothing at all; for you must exercise a reacting attention through the corresponding latter section.

He has a metaphor for the damage inflicted by the predatory clause (though he does not use my term).

Each separate monster period is a vast arch, which, not receiving its keystone, not being locked into self-supporting cohesion until you nearly reach its close, imposes of necessity upon the unhappy reader all the onus of its ponderous weight through the main process of its construction.

The young English philosopher Herbert Spencer (1820–1903) buttressed De Quincey's argument. Spencer — creator of the phrase "the survival of the fittest" — was thirty-two when he published *Philosophy of Style,* in which he visited the disdain of Victorian morality on writers whose "labyrinthine complexities" demand a great expenditure of mental energy with a result "that tallies ill with the pains taken." Yet it has proved hard to extinguish the predatory clause, as hard as getting rid of the central character in a Gothic novel invented by another Victorian writer, Bram Stoker (1847–1912), author of *Dracula.*

WHO'S FOR SLAVERY?

Colorado citizens voting in 2016 were invited to accept or reject a constitutional amendment. As Peter Hessler recounted in *The New Yorker* (November 21, 2016), he stood in a voting booth in the Ouray County Courthouse, at an elevation of 7,792 feet. He could cope with the thin air, but experienced a sensation of vertigo trying to find a way to oxygen through language shrouded in clouds of unthink. It helps to clarify one's own writing to ask questions of a muddled sentence. This was the enigmatic proposition:

> Shall there be an amendment to the Colorado constitution concerning the removal of the exception to the prohibition of slavery and involuntary servitude when used as punishment for persons duly convicted of a crime?

The bad writing begins with the inert, negative construction *Shall there be an amendment concerning the removal?*, which means "Shall we amend the constitution to remove an exception?"

What exception? An exception to the general rule that the state of Colorado prohibits slavery and involuntary servitude. The exception allows slavery and involuntary servitude as punishment *for people convicted of a crime*. So all the verbiage comes down to: Shall we keep slavery and involuntary servitude as punishment for criminals? Eleven words against the 34 in the state's question.

Just over half the 2.2 million voters voted not to remove the exception, meaning it remained legal for the state to refuse pay or restitution for work done by prisoners. Mr. Hessler says, "I honestly cannot remember whether I voted for or against slavery." Who can blame him?

UNDERSTANDING AN ECONOMIST

A leading economist writes on the prospects of a collapse of the eurozone:

> Finally, because neither restructuring of insolvent sovereigns, nor recapitalization of zombie banks, nor ring fencing of those sovereigns that are most likely solvent, but vulnerable to illiquidity ambushes have been addressed decisively and completely, tight financial conditions and intensifying fiscal austerity will contribute to a European recession in 2012 and possibly beyond. (52 words)

Even for the reader familiar with the terms, the structure of the sentence is confusing for two reasons. This is a fifty-two-word sentence with the essential warning message in ten words at the end. What are the preceding forty-two words doing? They give the economist's reasoning. It is akin to someone rushing into a building saying he's sorry to interrupt the meeting, but it's important that, for a number of reasons too complicated to explain at this moment, everyone there should be good enough to pack up their stuff and leave in haste *because the building is on fire.*

The forty-two words are meaningless until we get to the end. We are expected to carry this mental baggage all that way but when we think we see light at the end of the tunnel, we are trapped by the second obstacle, a *neither/nor* construction. We can usually follow one *neither/nor,* but here we have another *nor,* too. The point is that a leading economist is trying to warn the eurozone countries of the dangers of a recession in 2012. No wonder they got one.

How do we disentangle? It's okay to talk to ourselves again.

Q. What is the core message?
A. There is a risk of a recession in Europe in 2012 and possibly beyond.

Okay. Well. Let's say that.
Next questions:

Q. Why is there a risk?
A. Because credit will be tight and the authorities are also intensifying deficit-cutting austerity programs.

Q. What should they have done? In what ways have they failed?
A. They should help solvent countries restructure their balance sheets so they can pay their debts on demand and protect countries presently solvent but with too little cash to meet a sudden demand for redemption. They should insist that banks with big debts— zombies—get more capital.

So now let's have the economist make himself clear in two sentences in the active voice, with subject, verb, and object close by. We can deploy two semicolons, not commas, to put a little more air between the related facts:

> Europe will suffer a recession in 2012 and possibly beyond because of tight credit and intensifying austerity programs. Insolvent countries have failed to restructure their balance sheets; the authorities haven't ring-fenced countries which can presently pay their debts but are vulnerable to liquidity ambushes; and there are still too many "zombie" banks with insufficient capital. (55 words)

TV DOCTORS

Here is a published report that set out to clarify how far the law restricts doctors who want to puff a commercial product. Laudable ambition, lamentable execution:

> Even if the doctors are not reimbursed and it is not advertising, if their recommendations imply or include the purchase of their endorsements, then it constitutes "commercial speech," which the Supreme Court defined as "speech that proposes a commercial transaction" in *State University of New York v. Fox* and receives "lesser protection to commercial speech than to other constitutionally guaranteed expression," as the court found in *United States v. Edge Broadcasting.* (71 words)

Once again, we have a predatory clause of qualification before we know what is being qualified and, as a further aggravation, we have two negatives (*not reimbursed* and *not advertising*) and the mischief-making relative pronoun *which*. Here it opens the door for a clause that overstays its welcome, confounding us with forty words of detail when we are still reeling.

Rewrite:

> Doctors who endorse products on television are engaging in "commercial speech" even if they are unpaid and their programs are not advertising. "Commercial speech," defined by the Supreme Court as "speech that proposes a commercial transaction" (*State University of New York v. Fox*), has lesser protection than other constitutionally guaranteed expression, as the court found in *United States v. Edge Broadcasting.* (61 words)

A GAZA CONUNDRUM

In the summer of 2014, Israel and Hamas, the Palestinian resistance movement, fought for seven weeks over the Gaza Strip, initially by barrages of rocket fire from Hamas and air strikes by Israel, followed by an Israeli invasion. In September, the United Nations Human Rights Council authorized an independent commission of inquiry to investigate "all violations of international human rights law." On June 22, 2015, the commission reported that it had found credible allegations of war crimes by both Israel and Hamas.

This important report is a mess. To make it simpler to follow, I analyze the opening clause, 221, in two sections. The first misstep is easier to fix than the second.

Misstep No. 1

> 221. Given the delays in setting up the Secretariat, the lack of access to Gaza, Israel and the West Bank, the obstacles to freedom of movement for the people in Gaza, and the importance of prioritizing the documentation of possible violations, the commission ultimately decided to focus on conducting individual meetings and interviews with victims and witnesses and issuing a public call for submissions.

Rewrite:

> The commission was hampered by delays in setting up the Secretariat, by lack of access to Gaza and the West Bank, and by obstacles to free movement for the people of Gaza. It put a priority on the earliest documentation of alleged violations by interviewing victims and witnesses and inviting public submissions.

My edit of the commission's opening paragraph is in two sentences and goes right to the point, without all the cumbersome "Given the delays," etc. The rewrite is fifty-two words, eleven fewer words and right away easier to understand.

Misstep No. 2

We are now confronted with language detached from thought, words adrift in the ether. Suit up; this is what an astronaut feels like on taking the first step free of gravity.

221. Given the absence of information suggesting in each case that the anticipated military advantage at the time of the attack was such that the expected civilian casualties and damage to the targeted and surrounding buildings were not excessive, there are strong indications that these attacks could be disproportionate, and therefore amount to a war crime. (55 words)

Read it once, read it twice, read it as long as you like, it remains incomprehensible. Note that the floundering writer has to reach for *therefore*. It's a confidence trick, the word for intimidating a reader who is beginning to suspect an argument does not make sense. At first reading, the sentence is illogical gibberish. "The attacker could be guilty of a war crime because there is no evidence." *Or is some glimmer of reason hiding in this rendering?*

The attacker could be guilty of a war crime because there is no information that the damage to civilians and surrounding buildings was "not excessive."

Let's take this second misstep apart to see if we can find the fault line:

Given the absence of information...

Dumb question: Does it mean the attacker was denied some information? Or that he didn't know the military advantage he saw would yield extensive civilian casualties and damage to the targeted and surrounding buildings? Or does it mean the opposite, that the civilian casualties and damage to targeted and surrounding buildings would be "not excessive"?

The head spins. Let's shed the giddy predatory clause and attempt to find solid ground, moving from the vague concept of an "absence of information" to the particular. Who didn't know what? The report talks of "the attacks," which I have personified as "the attacker," either Israel or Hamas. So it is *the attacker* who is affected by the "absence of information" in certain cases. Next, let's convert the confusing negatives to positives ("absence" and "not excessive"). What did the attacker not know? He lacked the information to judge whether his attack would be excessive in terms of civilian casualties and damage to buildings. But he went ahead anyway. Okay so far? Then this is what you get:

> The attacker saw a military advantage in each case. He went ahead even though he didn't know if the civilian casualties and damage to the targeted and surrounding buildings would be excessive. These are strong indications that the attacks could be disproportionate and that would mean they were war crimes. (50 words)

Three direct sentences, easily understood, positive, and six words shorter. But we haven't finished with subordinate clauses making us feel clueless in Gaza. Three Israeli teenagers were abducted on the West Bank on June 12, 2014, one of the provocations for Israel's war on Hamas in Gaza. Consider the bewildering effect of reading a *Wikipedia* entry on the abduction. The writer tries to embrace too many ideas at once with a predatory clause and a misplaced modifier and meets himself coming back:

> Withholding evidence in its possession suggesting that the [Israeli] teens had been killed immediately until July 1 Israel launched Operation Brother's Keeper, a large scale crackdown of what it called Hamas's terrorist infrastructure and personnel in the West Bank, ostensibly aimed at securing the release of the kidnapped teenagers. (49 words)

Rewrite:

> Israel launched Operation Brother's Keeper ostensibly to secure the release of the three teenagers kidnapped on June 12, but did not reveal until July 1 that it already knew they'd been killed. (32 words)

ORGANIZING A LIST

Be up front about it if you want to present us with a list of causes or consequences. We can cope with a long list if we are prepared for the journey. Here the writer is eager to examine the causes (plural) of a currency crisis. He fails to alert us to the oncoming torrent of words in a sentence bereft of an organizing principle.

> But if we examine the true, root causes of the crisis, the dollar's (and to a lesser extent the euro's) role as the world's reserve currency and the build-up of reserves by Asian central banks, budget deficits across Western

countries that are growing at or near their potential, inappropriate exchange and interest rates imposed on the lesser-developed peripheral economies of Europe, the implicit government-sponsored entities, and so on, we find not greedy capitalists but government and central-bank actions that led to massive distortions in the price and availability of credit, i.e., a bubble. (93 words)

Rewrite:

But if *we examine* the root causes of the crisis, *we find* not greedy capitalists but government and central bankers. They presided over massive distortions in the price and availability of credit through mismanagement of the dollar's role as the world's reserve currency and to a lesser extent the euro's; *by Asian* central bankers building up reserves; *by Western* countries accepting budget deficits at or near potential; *and by inappropriate* exchange and interest rates imposed on the lesser-developed peripheral economies of Europe. In short, the formula for a bubble. (89 words)

The unedited version requires the reader to carry fifty-six words in his head without knowing where it is all leading. We are more likely to understand the argument if we know where we are heading. The writer may have been attempting to build to the climax of the "bubble" payoff line at the end ("government and central-bank actions that led to massive distortions in the price and availability of credit, i.e., a bubble").

It does not work. The answer is to bring together the two

verbs (*examine* and *find*) in three sentences, not one, and use the semicolon to organize the list of causes instead of meandering through a shower of commas. It helps the thread between the semicolons if we continue the list of causes with the same insistent *by*. And we can still end the sentence with the strong noun *bubble*.

INFLAMMATION OF THE PARENTHESES

This is one sentence from an opinion article about the welfare program in the Gaza Strip, run by the United Nations Relief and Works Agency (UNRWA).

> With the agency handling household chores, Hamas—especially since its bloody takeover of Gaza in 2007, ousting the Palestinian Authority's Fatah—has found the time and resources to amass rocket arsenals (UNRWA last month reported finding rockets stashed in three of its vacant schools) to bombard Israel (sometimes in close proximity to UNRWA premises), and to build miles of concrete-reinforced tunnels extending into Israel for terrorist attacks. (67 words)

The writer of the predatory opening phrase is in a tizzy whether to take the story forward or back and tries to cram in parenthetical comments and asides between dashes. Before we learn what Hamas has "found the time" to do, we are dragged back to 2007 and then invited into a bracketed sentence with its own incoherent parentheses. This is sadism of high order.

Here's a rewrite in three sentences. It has a six-word prefatory phrase that's short enough not to be predatory:

With the agency handling household chores, Hamas has found the time and resources to amass rocket arsenals and build miles of concrete-reinforced tunnels extending into Israel for terrorist attacks. This tactic has been marked since Hamas ousted the Palestinian Authority in 2007. UNRWA last month reported finding rockets for bombarding Israel stashed in three of its vacant schools. (59 words)

A BRACKET TOO FAR

A famous writer roused my interest via the sardonic opening of his column on a change in California voting law: "Under the current imperfect administration of the Universe, most new ideas are false, so most ideas for improvements make matters worse."

Neat. What gave me pause was not the sentiment but his summary of the proposal California voters passed:

Proposition 14 is an attempt to change government policies by changing the political process. Henceforth, in primary elections that select candidates for most state and federal offices — including almost one eighth of the US House of Representatives — all voters, regardless of party registration, or those who "decline to state status" (no party identification — 20.2 percent of Californians), will receive the same ballot.

He continues:

> All candidates for an office would be listed, regardless of party affiliation, if any, which they may choose to state or not. The two receiving the most votes will be on November ballots, regardless of the desires of the parties the nominees may choose to represent. (108 words)

Who does what to whom? The trouble begins with a predatory clause.

"Henceforth, in primary elections…"

We have to traverse a gap of 23 words before we get a grasp of the sense that this has to do with "all voters," and then we have to read another 20 words to learn what all voters will receive. If you don't find the detailed diversions maddening, congratulations. You have superior powers of concentration.

It's no different from the common experience of driving or walking somewhere new. You ask a loquacious bystander for directions. Ten minutes later you find yourself back where you started. There were just too many side roads to remember whether this crossroads was where you should turn left or right. You've had to absorb too much information. Same with the diversions in this passage of prose.

First, you take in a fact that primary elections "select candidates for most state and federal offices…"

Okay, got that, thanks. Now you are in a cul-de-sac, distracted this time with detail marked off by dashes ("including almost one eighth of the U.S. House of Representatives").

You get back on track with "all voters," but again you get

overloaded, this time by 14 words of qualification "regardless of party affiliation, or those who 'decline to state status' (no party identification)…"

This is where you scream for help.

The key connection here is *voters*. Start the sentence with the subject noun (*voters*) and marry it to the verbal phrase "will receive the same ballot." The fat falls away. We can cope with the detail because we know where we are. The phrase "primary elections that select" is a roundabout way of getting to the point that party affiliations won't automatically be on the ballot.

> Proposition 14 is an attempt to change government policies by changing the political process. Voters in primary elections for most state and federal offices, including one eighth of the House of Representatives, would receive the same ballot. No party affiliation would be indicated unless the candidate chooses: 20.2 percent of Californians decline to state party affiliation. The two candidates receiving the most votes would be on November ballots, regardless of the desires of the parties the nominees may claim to represent. (81 words)

DASH RASH

Michael B. Mukasey, former U.S. attorney general, on Hillary Clinton's emails:

> The simple proposition that everyone is equal before the law suggests that Mrs. Clinton's state of mind—whether

mere knowledge of what she was doing as to mishandling classified information; or gross negligence in the case of the mishandling of information relating to national defense; or bad intent as to actual or attempted destruction of email messages; or corrupt intent as to State Department business—justifies a criminal charge of one sort or another.

There are forty-eight words in between the dashes. Few readers will remember Mr. Mukasey's simple proposition by the time they get through forty-eight words to "justifies a criminal charge." Simple to fix:

Assuming everyone is equal before the law, a criminal charge of one sort or another is justified against Mrs. Clinton. Mere knowledge of what she was doing as to mishandling classified information would be enough. She could also be accused of gross negligence by mishandling of information relating to national defense; or bad intent as to actual or attempted destruction of email messages; or corrupt intent as to State Department business.

SAWDUST AND BUBBLE WRAP

Academic writers outlining a nonprofit seminar program often strive to sound impressive. The temptation is to wrap the offering in worthy phrases—conference-speak. This one for a seminar panel has 127 words of Bubble Wrap and sawdust, identified by my italics. Remove the packing and you have 38 words of substance:

It is increasingly recognized that investing in girls and women not only empowers communities but strengthens the global economy. For example, if empowered with appropriate job skills, girls could increase global GDP by as much as 5.4 percent. *Creating the conditions to unlock their full potential, however, requires greater advancement in terms of education health care and safety worldwide. To further the agenda for girls and women,* this Topic Dinner will feature three global advocates *who will share their perspective on current programs and multi sector partnerships that focus on* family planning, gender-based violence, health challenges, economic development and education. Participants will discuss how to overcome *existing barriers and also innovate solutions that create pathways so that girls and women can not only improve lives,* but thrive. (127 words)

First, I removed the sawdust.

Now nothing stands in the way of letting the reader in on the secret that the subject is *girls,* a single word guaranteed to raise more interest than the wordy abstractions in the italicized lines I deleted.

Rewrite:

Girls could increase global GDP by as much as 5.4 percent. In this Topic Dinner, three global advocates discuss how it could be done through education, job training, family planning, and protection from gender-based violence. (35 words)

DISCONNECTIONS: PESKY PRONOUNS
AND PERILOUS PREDICATES

Some of the incoherence of the exchanges in the 2016 Republican primary debate seeped into the reporting.

> As Mr. Romney amplified his pleas on Friday, Mr. Trump snubbed a major meeting of Republican activists and leaders after rumblings that protesters were prepared to demonstrate against him there in the latest sign of Mr. Trump's break from the apparatus of the party whose nomination he is marching towards. (50 words)

Who is the "him" and who are the protesters — Trump's supporters or Romney's?

Rewrite:

> As Mr. Romney amplified his pleas on Friday, Mr. Trump snubbed a major meeting of Republican activists and leaders on hearing that he could expect to encounter demonstrations against his break with the apparatus of the party whose nomination he is seeking. (42 words)

A witty opening sentence in a 2014 *Wall Street Journal* article can't rescue the paragraph from difficulty. Is "interview" a noun or a verb? The paragraph has a hole in the middle and an infelicitously divided predicate ("let David Remnick...know").

Benghazi isn't distracting Congress because they are not doing anything.

The president, detached and defeatist when he isn't in your face and triumphalist, let David Remnick, in the *New Yorker* interview people keep going back to as the second term's Rosetta Stone, know that he himself does not expect any major legislation, with the possible exception of immigration, to get done.

Rewrite:

The president, detached and defeatist when he isn't in your face and triumphalist, suggested, in a David Remnick interview in the *New Yorker,* that he does not expect any major legislation to pass, with the possible exception of immigration. People have viewed the interview as the Rosetta Stone of the second term.

A FATAL SWITCH: TOO MANY IDEAS

A faulty ignition switch in millions of General Motors cars led to the deaths of 124 people over eleven years. I will examine the investigation by Anton Valukas in chapter 10, but this paragraph in a *Wall Street Journal* summary of the Valukas report is a muddle:

Why did GM engineer Ray DeGiorgio—who by all accounts feels awful about what happened and is becoming the fall guy—approve a below-spec switch in the first place and then order a fix in 2006 without filing a new part number, thus inhibiting GM's discovery of a link between the original switch and fatal accidents in which air bags didn't deploy? Mr. Valukas contents himself with saying "whatever DeGiorgio's reasons for not changing the part number," serious consequences followed. (80 words)

The mistake is cramming too many ideas into one sentence. The intrusion about Ray DeGiorgio impedes understanding. It belongs after his role has been identified.

Rewrite:

Why did GM engineer Ray DeGiorgio approve a below-spec switch in the first place and not file a new part number for the fix he ordered? By all accounts, he feels awful about what happened and is becoming the fall guy, but that failure frustrated GM's discovery of a link between the original switch and fatal accidents in which airbags didn't deploy. Mr. Valukas contents himself with saying "whatever DeGiorgio's reasons for not changing the part number," serious consequences followed. (80 words)

LONELY MODIFIERS

Divorce is unfortunate in life—and in language. Let no one lightly put asunder a verb and its modifier. Any number of writers should flinch at the criticism Clive James made of President George W. Bush: "Every sentence he manages to utter scatters its component parts like pond water from a verb chasing its own tail." Here's a lapse by the *New York Times* in a report on a rescue of Yazidis besieged by ISIS in northern Iraq:

> The news took the far-flung advisers who were in the videoconference—including Secretary of State John Kerry, who was in Hawaii; Defense Secretary Chuck Hagel, on a plane over the Rockies; and the national security adviser, Susan E. Rice, who was with the president on Martha's Vineyard—by surprise.

Rewrite:

Move the misplaced modifier *by surprise* to hug its verb and any number of advisers can be flung far:

> The news took *by surprise* [or *surprised*, or *was a surprise for* or *to*] the advisers who were in the videoconference—including Secretary of State John Kerry, who was in Hawaii; Defense Secretary Chuck Hagel, on a plane over the Rockies; and the national security adviser, Susan E. Rice, who was with the president on Martha's Vineyard.

BOSTON MARATHON BOMBING

An Associated Press report didn't intend to implicate the Boston police; only the caption writer did that:

> Monday, April 15, 2013, photo, taken approximately 10–20 minutes before the blast, shows Tamerlan Tsarnaev, center-right, who was dubbed Suspect No. 1 and Dzhokhar A. Tsarnaev, center-left, who was dubbed Suspect No. 2 in

the Boston Marathon bombings by law enforcement. (42 words)

Rewrite:

Again, hug the verb:

> Monday, April 15, 2013, photo, taken approximately 10–20 minutes before the blast, shows Tamerlan Tsarnaev, center-right, who was dubbed by law enforcement Suspect No. 1 in the Boston Marathon bombings, and Dzhokhar A. Tsarnaev, dubbed Suspect No. 2. (38 words)

CRUELTY TO COMMAS

The *New York Times* columnist severed the verb and expected the humble comma to come to the rescue.

> Obama has told Israel, when it has threatened to go it alone on striking Iran, to back off, guaranteeing the U.S. would use force if necessary to prevent Iran from getting a nuclear weapon. (34 words)

Choice of edits:

> 1. Obama has told Israel to back off threatening Iran because the U.S. itself will attack if Iran does get close to having a nuclear weapon. (26 words)

> 2. Obama has told Israel not to go it alone to keep Iran from getting a nuclear weapon because if Iran gets close, the U.S. itself will attack. (27 words)

PESKY PRONOUNS

Abbott and Costello remind us that proper nouns can be mischievous,[3] but pronouns are treacherous. There is no such thing as a tame pronoun. I get a whiff of paranoia when I reread something I've just written and find, all too often, that the pronoun I summoned, sure of its identity, belongs to someone else. This sentence is from a trial case to decide whether a catchphrase from the TV show *Seinfeld*—"Not that there's anything wrong with that"—could be interpreted as a homophobic taunt.

> Attorney David Albert Pierce is fighting a $1 million defamation lawsuit filed by Kenny Kramer against his client comedian Fred Stoller.

Whose side is the attorney on? Fans of *Seinfeld* may remember, but others have to guess. Is Fred Stoller upset with his, Kramer's, client? It is easy enough to reorder, once you know:

> Attorney David Albert Pierce is fighting a million-dollar lawsuit filed by Kenny Kramer against a Pierce client, the comedian Fred Stoller.

Where you have two or three names in a sentence with accompanying pronouns, leave not a scintilla of doubt who is represented by each pronoun. Better to repeat a name.

---

[3] https://www.youtube.com/watch?v=kTcRRaXV-fg

THE POPE AND A PRONOUN

During the 2016 presidential campaign, Donald Trump, presumptive builder of a wall between Mexico and the United States, squared off for a word war with the pope, who said that anyone who obsesses about building walls to keep people out "is not Christian." Then Trump thought better of it: "It was probably a nicer statement than was reported by you folks in the media." Of course, the media is to blame just for reporting what the candidate said, but a fine columnist, commenting on Trump's soft soap, should not have left us uncertain whether His Holiness enjoyed his Big Mac:

> Now, you could see how he might have jumped to the wrong conclusion if somebody had yelled, "Hey, the pope thinks you're not acting like a Christian!" while he was walking into McDonald's for lunch.

Let's make it clear who was walking into McDonald's.

> Now, you could see how Trump might have jumped to the wrong conclusion if, while he was walking into McDonald's for lunch, somebody had yelled, "Hey, the pope thinks you're not acting like a Christian!"

THE EVANS COROLLARY

Murphy's Law—anything that can go wrong, will go wrong—is vindicated every day. I propose the Evans Corollary: anything that goes wrong will always be wordier than anything that goes right.

> The lack of people in the [department] with a sufficiently high level of skill in infectious disease control, microbiology, epidemiology, outbreak management, etc. and indeed, in project administration, plus the poor level of motivation caused by low financial rewards offered to staff employed by the civil service, were an impediment to managerial and work efficiency. (55 words)

Rewrite:

> Work in the department suffered for two reasons. Few if any of the staff had high skills in infectious disease control, microbiology, epidemiology, outbreak management, etc. and, indeed, in project administration. Second, they were dispirited by low civil service pay. (40 words)

And that's final...we think.

I am not so cynical as to believe government agencies are in conspiracy against the common man. I just wish they spoke the same language as the rest of us. The U.S. Department of the Environment betrays its high sense of purpose with stuff like this:

> The agency need make the finding of "no significant impact" available for public review for thirty days before the agency makes its final determination whether to

propose an environmental impact statement and before the action may begin only in one of the following limited circumstances. (45 words)

Rewrite:

The agency must give the public thirty days to review any finding of "no significant impact" before it decides whether to write an environmental impact statement. Work may begin only in one of the following limited circumstances. (37 words)

WHERE ANGELS FEAR TO TREAD

Jane Austen's novel *Pride and Prejudice* is such a joy, it seems churlish to mention a paragraph that has to be read twice. There is nothing grammatically wrong with the following sentence describing Elizabeth Bennet's misgivings about Darcy, but it's overloaded, a misstep in a classic:

The vague and unsettled suspicions which uncertainty had produced of what Mr. Darcy might have been doing to forward her sister's match which she had feared to encourage as an exertion of goodness too great to be probable, and at the same time dreaded to be just, from the pain of obligation, were proved beyond their greatest extent to be true. (61 words)

What is Jane Austen saying? What had Elizabeth feared to encourage, her suspicions or the match itself? The paragraph can be made clearer in nine brutally simple sentences but they add up to ninety words about as readable as a time-table and barely cope with the thoughts:

> She had vague and unsettled suspicions. These suspicions had been produced by uncertainty. She did not know what Mr. Darcy had been doing to forward her sister's match. She feared to encourage these suspicions. She had two reasons. It was very good of Mr. Darcy to help if he was helping. She doubted if anyone could be so good. She would then have a debt to him. In the event, her suspicions were proved to be true.

Properly constructed complex sentences can make assertions about a subject more clearly and economically without losing the flavor. This version splits the thought into four groups and deals with these in the four varied sentences:

> She had been filled by vague and unsettled suspicions about what Mr. Darcy might have been doing to forward her sister's match. She had not liked to dwell on these. Such an exertion of goodness seemed improbable, yet she had dreaded the idea that the suspicions might be just, for she would then be under obligation to him. Now the suspicions were proved beyond their greatest extent to be true.

COME AGAIN

Opening a sentence with a short phrase can be useful, but it must march in the same direction as the rest of the sentence.

The writer or editor of a potted biography or obituary has to assemble a lot of facts and is soon exporting non sequiturs. None of the three variations is any good; each suggests golf has something to do with having been a father:

> A keen golfer, he leaves three children.
> Leaving three children, he was a keen golfer.
> He leaves three children and was a keen golfer.

Likewise:

> He was born in Alabama and always arrived punctually
> at work.

This statement gives the impression that there is some connection between the birth in Alabama and the timekeeping. There isn't. The reader has been misled. The needlessly linked sentences divert the mind to speculation. There should be two sentences, but this, too, can be awkward:

> He was born in Alabama. He always arrived punctually
> at work.

Adjoining sentences need some linking thought, as in this example:

> He was born in Alabama when racial segregation was the
> law. His father got in trouble for employing a black errand
> boy in his pharmacy.

The last word on prefatory elements must go to Marc Rose, a *Reader's Digest* editor who complained to the *New York Times:*

Born in Waukegan, Illinois, I get damn sick of the non-sequiturs.

4

Ten Shortcuts to Making Yourself Clear

*"O.K., but change 'Her tawny body glistened beneath the azure sky'
to 'National problems demand national solutions.'"*

Bet you're glad to get out of the sentence clinic. You may wish to
endorse Hemingway's observation that there is nothing to writing. ("All you do is sit down at a typewriter and bleed.") Well,
you're now in the kinder, gentler rehab center where we establish
principles for a better class of prose by light routines of stretches

and calisthenics with words (beauty plus strength). Core princi-ples, I'd say, if *core* didn't suggest high-rep workouts of crunches, lunges, squats, pull-ups, curls, and similar unpleasantness. All you're expected to do in this program is keep ten shortcuts in mind when you write and edit: Your very own Listicle. The bullet points are mainly intended to help a writer convey meaning, and shades of meaning; help an editor engage with piles of dross to produce concise, direct English any reasonably literate person can understand; and help a reader unravel spaghetti.

But—and there's always a *but*—I wouldn't want to dis-courage literary excursion, within the bounds of nonfiction. I weighted the ten injunctions for conciseness and clarity, rather than literary effect, because windiness is the prevailing afflic-tion. We savor Scott Fitzgerald as well as Hemingway. I follow the Listicle with instructive passages where the writer has sum-moned observation, the color of metaphor and simile, the sly art of equivocation, the martial art of polemical opinion, and the gentle art of persuasion. Ambiguity has its claims. Who would expunge a pun in Shakespeare? Who hasn't evaded a direct statement, for motives good or bad? Precision may not be a blessing where emotions flare. "No compromise! No sur-render!" says board chairman John Anthony in John Galswor-thy's play *Strife*. "No compromise! No surrender!" says union leader David Roberts. And look where that gets them. Clarity gives way to assertion, a dead end. Two parties to a political or industrial conflict, if they are not Tea Party clones of Galswor-thy's Anthony and Roberts, may have enough in common to prefer patching the cracks to slogging out to gridlock.

How far indirect language may be a benign agent has to be a judgment case by case. Barton Swaim, a speechwriter for former governor Mark Sanford of South Carolina, cares as much for language as anyone, but suggests that being concise might be taken as being cold. "Sometimes what you want is feeling rather than meaning, warmth rather than content. And that takes verbiage."

Roya Hakakian, the Iranian-born author, tells me the simple direct prose admired in the West is abhorred in Persian writing.

> Persian literature is rife with deceptive language....Most of the deception manifests itself in outright ambiguity of meaning. For instance, Muhammad Rumi, the 13th-century Persian poet, is the best selling poet in Iran, but also in America where he is the idol of the gay community. How is that possible? Well, it's simple really. Because Persian is a gender neutral language, meaning the third-person pronoun is the same for *he* and *she,* in Iran the tenor person in Rumi's poems is deemed to be Allah. In the west, we know it is a lover who happens to also be a man. Blasphemous!

Roya suggests that the habit of deception in literature seeps into prose. "Because censorship has been a perennial threat, the deception in Iranian writing is considered a virtue. This explains a lot about why negotiations with Iran never go anywhere and why all reporters find Iran 'enigmatic.'"

So now we know.

I. GET MOVING

We've seen how even writers of renown try to squeeze in more words than the structure can accommodate. That confusion advertises itself. More insidious is the passive voice that so often sneaks past usage sentries. It robs sentences of energy, adds unnecessary words, seeds a slew of wretched participles and prepositions, and leaves questions unanswered: *It was decided* to eliminate the coffee break. Which wretch decided that?

Vigorous, clear, and concise writing demands sentences with muscle, strong active verbs cast in the active voice.

Active voice:

The pope kissed a baby on the forehead, leading the crowd of thousands to erupt in cheers and praise. (19 words)

Passive voice:

A baby was kissed on the forehead by the pope, leading the crowd of thousands to erupt in cheers and praise. (21 words)

In the active voice, the subject (the pope) is the actor; the receiver of the action (the baby) is the object. The verb (*was kissed*) is being used transitively because you can't just leave it at "The pope kissed"... who or what? The verb *kissed* requires an object, the baby. In the passive voice, the *was kissed* verb, with its object turned subject, lacks vigorous agency.

When you write in the passive voice you can't escape adding fat any more than you can escape piling on adipose tissue when you grab a doughnut.

Let's visit a few sentences to see the effect.

Doughnut:

The Great Wall of China has been walked by millions of people. (12 words)

Active:

Millions of people have walked the Great Wall of China. (10 words)

Strengthen sentences by switching from the passive voice's reliance on the colorless *be* verbs (*is, are, am, was, were, has been, had been, have been, will be, will have been, being*).

Doughnut:

There were riots in several cities last night in which several shops were burned.

Active:

Rioters burned shops in several cities last night.

The active version has eight words, and it is more direct than the doughnut's fourteen. Give thanks to how small changes in English, like laundry detergent, can add brightness to lightness and cost you less.

Doughnut:

A petition by 31 householders requesting a reduced speed limit in Clay Road, between Jefferson and Calkin Roads, was presented to the Henrietta Town Board last night. (27 words)

Active:

Thirty-one householders petitioned the Henrietta Town Board last night for a lower speed limit in Clay Road, between Jefferson and Calkin Roads. (22 words)

Doughnut:

The creation of a national organization to assist a variety of local authorities and voluntary societies and to bring a sense of urgency to the coordination of rescue work around the coast of Britain was urged by the Medical Commission on Accident Prevention. (43 words)

Render the sentence in the active voice and it remains dull: "The Medical Commission on Accident Prevention urges local authorities and voluntary societies to coordinate rescue work around the coast of Britain." Better:

Active:

People will drown off the coasts of Britain unless a national body coordinates rescues by voluntary societies and local authorities, said the first report of the Medical Commission on Accident Prevention. (31 words)

The passive voice is preferable if not inescapable in four categories:

(i) *When the doer of the action is not known:*

The lease was sent back to us without a signature.

(ii) *When the receiver of the action merits more prominence than the doer:*

A rhinoceros ran over Donald Trump today.

That is active (and news). But there is a case for believing that more people are interested in Mr. Trump than a bad-tempered rhino:

Donald Trump was run over by a rhinoceros today.

Again, the emphasis or urgency of a news point can make the passive voice preferable to the active:

Ebola was detected.

Rather than:

A laboratory detected Ebola.

(iii) *When the doer of the action is known but tact or cowardice imposes reticence:*

Your application is denied.

The last of the chocolate ice cream was eaten.

Author Edward Johnson[1] neatly labels such cop-outs as the *pussyfooting passive*. Legal inhibitions — or cowardice — may require the *prudent passive:*

Methylamines found in air samples were judged the source of the malodorous mists enraging people in townships across the valley.

Note that we are not told who did the judging.

(iv) *When the length of the subject delays the entry of a verb:*

The complexity of designing an aerial propeller when none had ever existed, marine propellers having simply to displace water and not cope with the complex aerodynamics of flight, *troubled* Wilbur. [active voice]

---

[1] Edward Johnson, *The Handbook of Good English* (New York: Facts on File, 1983).

Better:

> The complexity of designing an aerial propeller *was troubling* Wilbur since none had ever existed, and marine propellers had simply to displace water and not cope with the complex aerodynamics of flight.

(v) *When the active voice creates ambiguity:*

> The crisis began in November when a Stockholm daily newspaper published accusations of a long history of sexual assaults by Jean-Claude Arnault, a French-Swedish photographer.

The unfortunate "by." Did Mr. Arnault publish the accusations, or was he the person accused? The identity is clearer in the passive voice:

> The crisis began in November, when the French-Swedish photographer was accused of a long history of sexual assaults.

With those exceptions, sentences in the active voice should be favored by writers and editors—or, rather, writers and editors should favor sentences in the active voice. Bureaucrats, lawyers, business executives, and academics are recidivists, habitual perpetrators of the passive without plausible excuse. Their sentences raise the white flag of subterfuge at the start: "It was felt necessary"; "In the circumstances, it is considered inadvisable"; "The visitor might be reminded";

"It should perhaps be pointed out"; "It cannot be denied"; "It will be recognized"; "It should be kept in mind"; "Our attention has been drawn." British officials, with or without umbrellas, never get rained on. Precipitation is experienced. Higher levels of administrators learn how to couple the passive with the conditional so that, as Robert Graves and Alan Hodge remarked,[2] the decision is "translated from the world of practice into a region of unfulfilled hypothesis." "The Minister would find it difficult to agree if the facts were to be regarded in the light suggested." I guess it's empowering to imply that deliberations emanate from some central intelligence uncorrupted by human prejudices, documents handled only with gloved hands, or these digital days from some algorithm no one dare argue with. Bureaucrats are happy to borrow a halo from science journals and reports where the passive voice has been standard to forestall ego trips and any suggestion of subjectivity. "A quantity of germanium was obtained"; "a comparison was made"; "a conclusion was arrived at." But I don't see why an individual researcher or team can't report in the active voice with as much or little personal identification as suits the circumstances.

According to the reliable Writing Center at the University of North Carolina at Chapel Hill, the trend in current editions of scientific style guides is away from the passive voice because the active voice is more likely to bring subject and action together so readers don't drown in a sea of prepositional phrases. The center offers in evidence a fragment

---

[2] Robert Graves and Alan Hodge, *The Reader over Your Shoulder* (New York: Random House, 1979).

held together by no fewer than eleven prepositional phrases. Is this a record?

> ...to confirm the nature of electrical breakdown of nitrogen in uniform fields as relatively high pressures and interelectrode gaps that approach those obtained in engineering practice, prior to the determination of the processes that set the criterion for breakdown of the above-mentioned gases and mixtures in uniform and non-uniform fields of engineering significance.

In *They Made America* I used both passive and active voice in exploring how Herbert Boyer and Robert Swanson made possible genetic engineering with human DNA:

> The cells were sent down to City of Hope, where they were broken apart, the methionine dissolved, and the protein collected and purified.

But also:

> Boyer's team connected the somatostatin gene to the comparatively enormous beta-gal gene.

Prolonged exposure to business and official documents will give anyone a more intense aversion to the passive voice than generally expressed in grammars, stylebooks, and tutorials. While all duly mention its weakness, I froth at the mouth. In 1978, Jefferson D. Bates, charged with rewriting

U.S. Air Force regulations, manuals, and reports, got so mad about his immersion in passives he dared to strafe "most of the experts — Strunk and White, Gunning, Flesch and all the rest, for not making the active voice Rule No. 1 for conciseness, readability and precision." A generation later I think he would have exempted the word warriors William Zinsser and Richard Mitchell; Zinsser regarded the difference for a writer between the active-verb style and a passive-verb style as "the difference between life and death." Mitchell excoriated the passive and pretentious in academic writing. I would like to have heard them on *The Cambridge Grammar of the English Language,* a collation by Rodney Huddleston and Geoffrey K. Pullum (2002). It describes itself as a "synchronic, descriptive grammar of general purpose, present-day international Standard English." It's comprehensive, supposedly averse to prescription, but the authors cannot contain their rage at advocacy of the active voice. They describe Strunk and White "as a pair of authors so grammatically clueless that they don't know what is a passive construction and what isn't." The ill temper has affected lesser pretenders to linguistic authority; I have no such pretensions.

For me, the offense of the passive that most rankles is the escape hatch it offers to shuffle off responsibility. In chapter 9, I edit an Obama administration document on national security, riddled with cover-your-ass passives. If after all this hectoring from me, you or your editor still find inexcusable passive sentences lying prone in your paragraphs, post this one on your screen: *The moon was landed on by Neil Armstrong today.*

2. BE SPECIFIC

Significant details of human life illuminate great writing and in simple, concrete terms. How we relate the detail to general description is an art writers must master. We are indebted to S. I. Hayakawa (*Language in Action,* 1939) for the concept of how we may move from detail to hypothesis and the glory of truth. I devote much of my Afterthought to his ladder of abstraction, but overworked abstract nouns are the condensed water droplets hanging in the atmosphere at the surface of the earth—the fog of *Bleak House.* You cannot make yourself clear with a vocabulary steeped in vagueness. Comb through passages you are writing or editing for the opaque obscuring the view:

> amenities, activities, operation, purpose, condition, case, character, facilities, circumstances, nature, disposition, proposition, purposes, situation, description, issue, indication, regard, reference, respect, connection, instance, eventuality, neighborhood, satisfaction

Words like these squeeze the life out of sentences, a subject for elaboration in the next chapter, "Please Don't Feed the Zombies, Flesh-Eaters, and Pleonasms." The great escape should be made from "mere intellectualism with its universals and essences to concrete particulars, the smell of human breath, the sound of voices, the stir of living."[3] Chase out most abstract words in favor of specific words. Sentences should be

---

[3] C. E. Montague, *A Writer's Notes on His Trade* (London: Penguin, 1952), 147.

full of bricks, beds, houses, cars, cows, men, and women. On TripAdvisor.com, an online travel guide, I read:

> Mombasa is well known among travelers as a place to buy traditional Kenyan crafts and clothing. The city is full of markets that have been operating in the same way that they do today for hundreds of years. These markets are attractions in themselves, as well as places to shop, as they give visitors a genuine taste of Mombasa.

Fair enough, but the market for specifics thrives when you go shopping with Martha Gellhorn, who arrived in Mombasa to set up house in 1964:

> We shopped ourselves blind. It is never heart-lifting to concentrate on garbage cans, pillow slips, knives, forks etc. But there were compensations. Between the bath-towel store and the frying-pan emporium, one passed on the Mombasa streets a whole exotic world. Sikhs with their beards in hair nets, Indian ladies wearing saris, caste marks and octagonal glasses. Muslim African women, enormous and coy, hidden except for their eyes in black rayon sheets, tattooed tribesmen loading vegetable trucks; memsahibs driving neat cars filled with groceries and blond children; bwanas in white shirts and shorts and long white socks, hurrying to their offices.... Bicycles zoomed in like flies.[4]

---

[4] Martha Gellhorn, *The View from the Ground* (New York: Atlantic Monthly Press, 1988), 261.

The scene is alive. The English philosopher Herbert Spencer argued that the superiority of specific expression is due to the saving of effort required to translate words into thought. "Whenever any class of things is referred to, we represent it to ourselves by calling to mind individual members of it; it follows that when an abstract word is used, the hearer or reader has to choose from his stock of images, one or more by which he may figure to himself the genus." Spencer concocted a generality, often quoted, to dramatize how abstraction sandbags literature.

Vague:

In proportion as the manners, customs, and amusements of a nation are cruel and barbarous, the regulations of their penal code will be severe.

Spencer specific:

In proportion as men delight *in battles, bull fights and combats of gladiators,* will they punish by *hanging, burning and the rack.*

Orwell's diagnosis is as valid as when he wrote this sentence in *Politics and the English Language:*

As soon as certain topics are raised, the concrete melts into the abstract and no one seems able to think of turns of speech that are not hackneyed: prose consists less and less of *words* chosen for the sake of their meaning, and more and more of phrases tacked together like the sections of a prefabricated henhouse.

Enrich your vocabulary by noting the devices of simile and metaphor, the shock of unexpected marriages. In my days organizing coverage from the cauldron of Northern Ireland in the seventies and eighties, I was haunted by Yeats's poem "The Second Coming":

> Mere anarchy is loosed upon the world,
> The blood-dimmed tide is loosed, and everywhere
> The ceremony of innocence is drowned

The genius of *mere!* To all but Yeats, *anarchy* would be accompanied by hyperbolic adjectives—*terrible, ugly, violent, disastrous*—none to flutter an eyelid, none to express the futility of the void.[5]

3. RATION ADJECTIVES, QUESTION ADVERBS

In World War II Britain, posters interrogated travelers waiting for a train: *Is Your Journey Really Necessary?* Subject your sentences to the third degree: Is your adjective really, really necessary to define the subject of your sentence, or is it there for show? What exactly, precisely, does your adverb add to the potency of this or that verb or adjective?

---

[5] The *Paris Review* calls "The Second Coming" "the most thoroughly pillaged work of literature in the English language," so take this as a cue to read the twenty-three lines of the masterpiece again.

You can see we are in trouble already. *Really, exactly,* and *precisely* have elbowed in. Adverbs modifying verbs and nouns and adjectives have the excuse that they tell us *where, when,* and *how* or *how often,* and they do essential work. A theater can be *almost* empty. It was economical for the British department store John Lewis to claim it was never *knowingly* undersold. But too often (adverb of frequency) they are redundant, as in my extrapolation of the wartime message: *exactly, precisely, really, really* are passengers. The first *really* is for stress. It's a raised voice and as a wartime traveler on packed trains I can say I heard it loud and clear. It made me think twice. But I don't think twice about getting rid of adverbs hitching a ride on a verb to tell us what we already infer: brides coming *very* happily from weddings, thieves running speedily, children lagging wearily, fists shaken angrily, burgers eaten hungrily. These low-information adverbs of manner ending in *ly* don't enhance. They enfeeble. A report from Saudi Arabia tells us, "The government has yet to *actually* seize many of the assets" of certain princes. *Seize* is a powerful verb, watered down, humiliated, by the wimpy adverb *actually.* So we must conclude the assets had not been seized before—surrendered, forfeited, given up, yielded possession of. We can only guess. We will probably never rid ourselves of the intensifiers "absolutely true," "completely true." Eventual*ly,* nobody will be believed unless they swear on their honor that a statement is absolutely, completely, certifiably, undoubtedly, verifiably true, meaning that all preceding statements were dishonest, lying, cheating, ignominious fabrications, outrageous falsehoods. If you are inclined, judgmental*ly* to challenge the assertions, I will ask Stephen King to terrify you with his story of dandelions growing sinister*ly* in a lawn. The author of the sentence "I believe the road to hell is paved with adverbs" feels strong*ly*.[6] Alternative*ly*, you could use the Adverb Annihilator, free on any laptop or mobile. Just type in *ly* and interrogate any *ly* adverb that pop ups like a knee-jerk. Purely for mischief, I just counted the adverbs in the extracts of expansive writing I selected (124–138). Gratifyingly few—five in fourteen pages.

Adjectives are more seductive. As a young reporter assigned to cover a few soccer matches, I was checked in admiring my colorful writing by a stylebook chastisement: "Genesis does not begin 'The amazingly dramatic story of how God made the world in the remarkably short time of six days.'" The best of the good sportswriters today have lean prose and narrative excitement. George Orwell's distemper with sportswriting lay in his detestation of international team sports as fomenters of nationalism, but this World Cup collation of adjectives and adverbs in a single report for the *Sunday Times* would have been a target:

> Magnificent...out of this world...their glowing skills and unflinching bravery...this man of magic. The thunder of exultant...rejoicing thousands; raked *relentlessly* through a shattered defence....An athletic immortal in his own golden age flicked in a shot that was a gem, a jewel of gold—no, a Crown Jewel...the golden dream subdued and well-thrashed...so gallant and *knightly;* the red-and-white cauldron of Wembley bubbled *joyously*... the honest joy gleaming.

---

[6] Stephen King, *On Writing: A Memoir of the Craft* (New York: Scribner, 2000).

Relentlessly detracts from the strong verb *raked;* the pre-emptive *joyously* has no business butting in on *honest joy gleaming.* And beware of superlatives. Rinse them through a sieve for accuracy. The biggest, tallest, fastest, richest so often turns out to be the second biggest, second tallest, second fastest, and nowhere near the richest.

Travel writers should be inoculated before being asked to risk their muscular prose in areas of Europe where even the young Mr. Samuel Clemens succumbed to superlatives.

If something is amusing or sensational there is no need to tell us it is amusing and sensational. Just describe the incidents that amused or shocked and we'll do the laughing and the grimacing. Gretel Ehrlich let us do that in a taut paragraph of action and thought from her long dog-sledge ride with Inuit subsistence hunters in Greenland. This is the moment the men corner a polar bear and her cubs.

> The bear's nose, eyes, and claws are black dots in a world of white, a world that, for her, holds no clues to human ambivalence. She gives me the same hard stare she would give a seal.
>
> The bear's fur is yellow, and the ice wall is blue. The sun is hot. Time melts. What I know about life and death, cold and hunger, seems irrelevant. There are three gunshots. A paw goes up in agony and scratches the ice wall. She rolls on her back and is dead.

Ehrlich is confident enough as a writer to know that strong nouns should be left to stand on their own, not weakened by modifiers. Danger is danger. Its force is diluted when it is prefaced by *really serious* and *real*. The scriptwriters for Harrison Ford, Liam Neeson, or Tom Cruise screw up the tension from one peril to another with imaginative new threats, but the unadorned adjective *dangerous* describes every one of them. *Real* may be justified if an imaginary danger is contrasted; but whoever heard of an unserious danger? Sir Ernest Gowers,[7] in his admirable book for civil servants, nailed another abuse in the modifiers *due* and *undue*. "The tenants were asked not to be undu*ly* alarmed." As Gowers says, it differs little from "there is no cause for alarm for which there is no cause," and that hardly seems worth saying.

So strike out meaningless modifiers. You risk bloat and nonsense if you mess with adjectives that express absolutes. There is no such condition as *nearly* unanimous. The vote is either unanimous or not. Adjectives that should rarely by modified are: *certain, complete, devoid, empty, entire, essential, everlasting, excellent, external, fatal, final, fundamental, harmless, ideal, immaculate, immortal, impossible, incessant, indestructible, infinite, invaluable, invulnerable, main, omnipotent, perfect, principal, pure, round, simultaneous, square, ultimate, unanimous, unendurable, unique, unspeakable, untouchable, whole, worthless.*

Well, you may say, do not Americans revere the "more perfect union" in the Constitution? "We the People of the United States, in Order to form a more perfect Union, establish Justice, insure domestic Tranquility, provide for the common defense."

---

[7] Sir Ernest Gowers, *Plain Words: A Guide to the Use of English,* revised and updated by Rebecca Gowers, his great-granddaughter (London: Particular Books, 2014).

Grammar can't extinguish the claims of history or poetry, but we can regard the "more perfect union" as implying "moving toward a perfect union" from the imperfect union of thirteen states governed by the Articles of Confederation of 1777. The following decade demonstrated the need for a federal structure with executive power, courts, and taxes. So, too, the Constitution of the United States in 1788, and the inauguration of the first president in New York on April 29, 1789.[8]

4. CUT THE FAT, CHECK THE FIGURES

Simply shedding fat does wonders for sentences. Down with bloat. "The test of style is economy of the reader's attention" (Herbert Spencer). "If it is possible to cut a word out, always cut it out" (George Orwell). "Murder your darlings" (Arthur Quiller-Couch). "Read over your compositions, and wherever you meet with a passage which you think is particularly fine, strike it out" (Samuel Johnson). It would spare editors the tedium of nouns acting as magnets to every passing iron filing. Strunk's words in *Elements of Style* should be chiseled in marble:

> Vigorous writing is concise. A sentence should contain no unnecessary words, a paragraph no unnecessary sentences, for the same reason that a drawing should contain no unnecessary lines and a machine no unnecessary parts. This requires not that the writer make all his sentences short, or that he avoid all detail and treat his subjects only in outline, but that every word tell.

---

[8] Harold Evans, *The American Century* (New York: Knopf, 1998).

How many of us, writing that paragraph, would have ended the last sentence *but that he make every word tell?*

You will note that *unnecessary* is repeated four times, but they are necessary *unnecessarys* for emphasizing the comparisons. You should be careful not to delete a word that supports a structure, but it is a lesser danger than tolerating parasites. The following message of 108 words, which I received from a large corporation, is not a monster; just normal flatulence with a polite dash of diffidence.

If you would like to opt out from receiving hard copy reports and in future receive written notification of when the report is available to view on line, please sign and return the attached form.

We would like to take this opportunity to thank you for your continued investment.

If you have any questions, would like to learn more about our product range or require a hard copy of the Annual Report and Accounts (Long Report), please contact us on the details provided above. Our offices are open Monday to Friday 8.30 am until 5.30 pm UK times.

Telephone calls may be recorded for monitoring and training purposes. (108 words, 506 characters)

It took a minute of my time, double what it would have taken if written concisely, as in:

Thank you for investing with us. If you prefer hard copy reports instead of online, please sign and return the attached. We are glad to answer questions on our products or post a hard copy of the Annual Report and Accounts (Long Report). Office hours are 8.30 am to 5.30 pm UK time. We may record and monitor calls. (59 words, 41 words saved, 259 characters)

That would have been a tiny thirty-second saving of my time, but cumulatively the office of circumlocution robbed five hundred thousand people of eight hours. That's the hidden arithmetic of verbosity.

In researching *They Made America,* I was entranced by the story of John D. Rockefeller watching a machine seal lids on five-gallon cans of kerosene for export. It used 40 drops of solder. He asked, why not 38 drops? Some fraction of the cans still leaked. "Try 39!" None leaked. Said Rockefeller: "That one drop of solder saved $2,500 the first year, but the export business kept on increasing after that and doubled, quadrupled—became immensely greater, and has amounted since to many hundreds of thousands of dollars."

I can't guarantee you'll make a fortune saving words, but here's a declension of characters in a routine business notice.

A meeting will be held by the board of directors next week. (59)

The board of directors meets next week. (39)

The directors meet next week. (29)

The board meets next week. (26)

In business reporting we get *in the majority of instances; in a number of cases; a large proportion of.* Avoid these prolix forms. Question modifying and deprecating phrases—

unduly, relatively, comparatively, in more or less degree, some-what, to a certain extent, to a degree, small in size, quite. Often there is nothing to compare, and the qualification is mean-ingless as well as space-consuming. Check: Is there a real com-parison in the story? If there is not, out with it. Delete that news accretion *mark:* "The death toll has topped the 300 mark." Why *mark?* We don't want the embroidery. It's not some form of competition; "more than 300 have died" is bad enough.

But spare the ax when numbers are the crux of the mat-ter, as they often are in arguments. It is convenient to sum-marize with the adjectives and adverbs *some, often, many, few, large, high proportion,* and I can't bear to count how many times I have used them in this book. But consider how clarity is clouded by fear of figures. How many failures con-stitute "a large percentage of failures"?

An American is more likely to die from guns than a citi-zen of 22 other countries of comparable population and wealth. By 1969, more Americans had died from gunfire than in all the wars in American history.

Nothing wrong with the grammar, but statements like this invite more questions. How much more likely? How many were suicides? How many were homicides? How many were accidents? How many were shot by police? Did police hold back enforcing the law after the outcry over the shoot-ing of an unarmed black man in Ferguson, Missouri? Was there a "Ferguson effect"? The Brennan Center for Justice attempted to answer that question by counting homicides in twenty-five of the thirty biggest U.S. cities from January 1 to

October 1 in 2015, and comparing the figures to the same period in 2014. They projected the full year of 2015 would show 11 percent more homicides. The *Atlantic* magazine, *Vox* website, and John Jay College of Criminal Justice all left themselves open to the accusation[9] that they—and "progressives and their media" allies—had played down Brennan's predicted jump in homicides.[10] The *Atlantic* article "Debunking the Ferguson Effect" didn't give the figures. It said the homicide increase was "slight," John Jay called it "moderate," and *Vox* said it was "bunk." None of them gave the figures.

Economy challenge: Go back over your last five hundred words and save fifty. You'll get to be jealous of every syllable.

5. ORGANIZE FOR CLARITY

In the first of this list of ten imperatives, shortcuts to good writing, I emphasized the value of the active voice, but also identified four occasions where the passive voice may be preferred. I resorted to a parallel structure, imposing the same grammatical structure on the four exceptions favoring the passive voice by starting each exception with the same insistent word (*when, when, when*). Again, in the following passage, I repeat the word *wing* to stress the continuity of Wilbur and Orville Wright's experiments:

---

[9] Adapted from a contribution by Heather MacDonald, Thomas W. Smith Fellow at the Manhattan Institute, for a *Wall Street Journal* op-ed, December 26–27, 2015.

[10] Ibid.

Over two months, they stood stock still in the same place, held their breaths, and turned on the fan to test *wing* after *wing* with a wide range of design variables: they tested 200 *wings* of subtly different varying cambers, *wings* with pointed tips, rounded ends, tapering sharply or slow, *wings* with sharp leading edges and *wings* whose front edges had been thickened with layers of wax or soldered tin, *wings* in monoplane and biplane configurations.

For his second inaugural address, President Obama might have said:

My fellow citizens, I stand here today humbled by the task before us, because you have put your trust in me and I am well aware of the sacrifices borne by our ancestors.

It would have been a serviceable, if prosaic, sentence. Instead, he chose a more poetic expression, an appealing rhythm in parallel repetition:

My fellow citizens: I stand here today *humbled* by the task before us, *grateful* for the trust you have bestowed, *mindful* of the sacrifices borne by our ancestors.

A parallel sentence from *Pride and Prejudice:*

She was a woman of mean understanding, little information, and uncertain temper.

Parallelism for lists

As I mentioned in the sentence clinic, writers muff their messages when they fail to let the reader know a list is coming. In 2015, Facebook decided to limit outsiders' access to data on its 1.5 billion users. Reports online and in print attempting to describe the possible consequences were a confusing flow of sentences that flitted between comment, history, and effects. Instead of that mishmash I would have imposed an insistent parallel structure with a verb to introduce each consequence.

Facebook restricting access to its vast data on people has:

(i) **stymied** a voter outreach tool used by President Obama's 2012 reelection campaign

(ii) **closed** the app Jobs with Friends

(iii) **frustrated** a psychologist building an app to look for links between social media activity and ills such as drug addiction

(iv) **doomed** College Connect, an app aimed at helping prospective first-generation college students find friends who hold jobs they are considering

A parallel structure is a simple putting together of things that belong together. It saves words, too.

6. BE POSITIVE

Sentences should assert. Express even a negative in a positive form. That sounds like boosterism, but it's a risk worth taking since it is quicker and easier to understand what is than what is not.

Original:

> The figures seem to us to provide no indication that costs and prices...would not have been lower if competition had not been restricted.

My edit:

> The figures seem to us to provide no indication that competition would have produced higher costs and prices.

Original:

> It is unlikely that contributions will not be raised.

My edit:

> It is likely that contributions will be raised.

Original:

> The project was not successful.

My edit:

> The project failed.

Original:

> They did not pay attention to the claim.

My edit:

> They ignored the claim.

Original:

> The company says it will not now proceed with the plan to move production west.

My edit:

> The company says it has abandoned the plan to move production west.

Negative expressions bemuse so often, it's hard to believe the writer gave a moment's thought to the meaning of the words. It was worrying enough for mortgage payers when the Federal Reserve raised interest rates in December 2015, but the thoughtful *New York Times* editorial gave all of us a headache:

> The Fed's inflation target of 2 percent is not a ceiling that inflation cannot surpass.

I guess it means that inflation may come to be higher than the Fed's 2 percent target.

We don't want no double negatives.

Imagine you are part of a civic group protesting the intrusion in a quiet city enclave of a hideous superscraper. Naturally, you spring to Regulations for Implementing the Procedural Provisions of the National Environmental Policy Act 2005, comforted by the statement that they have been rewritten in "Plain English." Right away you encounter a numbing clause, 1500.2. It lays it down with apparent benevolence that federal agencies shall reduce paperwork to the greatest extent possible. How? By...

(f) Using a finding of no significant impact when an action not otherwise excluded will not have a significant effect on the human environment and is therefore exempt from requirements to prepare an environmental impact statement (1508.13).

It seems to be saying that there is no need to write an impact statement when there is no impact. Did anyone presiding over this concoction give a thought about the impact of such a string of negatives on the mental composure of the civic-minded reader?

A negative construction got presidential candidate Dr. Ben Carson in a tangle following the 2016 death of Justice Antonin Scalia:

It is imperative that the Senate not allow President Obama to diminish his legacy by trying to nominate an individual who would carry on his wishes to subvert the will of the people.

James Thurber,[11] a sturdy exponent of the positive, testi-fies from personal experience:

> If a person is actually ill, the important thing is to find
> out not how he doesn't feel. He should state his symptoms
> more specifically—"I have a gnawing pain here, that
> comes and goes," or something of the sort. There is
> always the danger, of course, that one's listeners will cut
> in with a long description of how they feel; this can usu-
> ally be avoided by screaming.

7. DON'T BE A BORE

All the English-usage gurus looking over your shoulder
insist on shorter sentences. They're right, but you don't want
to become a writing metronome producing a series of staccato sentences to a mechanical beat.

What James Brown III said of music and art[12] can be said
of writing:

> The metronome has no real musical value....Musicians
> ought to distinguish between (1) the sort of timing that
> results from dull, slavish obedience to the ticking of a
> soulless machine, and (2) that noble swing and perfect
> control of pulsation which comes into our playing after

---

[11] James Thurber, *My Life and Hard Times* (New York: Harper Perennial, 1999).

[12] Metronome, https://en.wikipedia.org/wiki/Metronome#Criticism_of_metro
nome_use

years of practice in treating and training the sense of time as a free, creative human faculty.

Try being a musician in prose. The more you experiment, the more you will appreciate the subtleties of rhythm in good writing—and bad. If an eight-word sentence is followed by a longer sentence, introduced by a short subsidiary clause, a variation in pace is apparent and welcome. Vary sentence structure. Vary sentence style.[13] Understand the appeal of *alliteration*, beginning nearby words with the same letter, as I just did. We like the sense of order in the repetition; we find it's easier to remember an alliterative phrase. Easy enough, but you can't expect a standing ovation for the simple duplication of an initial character. President Warren Harding (in office from 1921 to 1923) stood on a rostrum at the perimeter of alliteration. Here he is in full flow:

America's present need is not heroics, but healing; not nostrums, but normalcy; not revolution, but restoration; not agitation, but adjustment; not surgery, but serenity; not the dramatic, but the dispassionate; not experiment, but equipoise; not submergence in internationality, but sustainment in triumphant nationality.

Harding's bromides caught the mood of a country weary of war, strikes, Red Scares, and politics of any kind. He won the largest popular victory in a century (on a low turnout), but his

---

[13] Wolcott Gibbs, "Time…Fortune…Life…Luce," *New Yorker* (November 28, 1936). Profile of *Time* editor Henry Luce, written in a parody of *Time*'s style.

writing had the thud of jelly spooned onto a paper plate. The passage had no effect because it was bereft of images or ideas and many syllables too far. William Safire, the sparkling and prolific wordsmith who wrote speeches for the Nixon White House and a column for the *New York Times,* could alliterate with anyone. He was having fun, but making a point, too, when he went on a binge for the inarticulate and later disgraced Vice President Spiro Agnew. "In the United States today, we have more than our share of nattering nabobs of negativism. They have formed their own 4H club—the hopeless, hysterical hypochondriacs of history."[14] It was the opening salvo of a fifty-year campaign to alienate the people from the press.

President Obama often wrote his own speeches. In a visit to a mosque in Baltimore he pitted his eloquence against the anti-Muslim demagoguery of Donald Trump, running for the Republican nomination in the 2016 presidential election. The image Obama evoked was the parable of the Good Samaritan, but indirectly, and look how he did it in a single phrase, the moral thought fused by a gentle alliteration: "None of us can be silent. We can't be bystanders to bigotry."

The three words were headlines around the world. Three words more powerful than a thousand rants.

Vary sentences

Sentences vary *in form,* between simple and complex-compound; in *function,* between statements, commands,

---

14 Rick Perlstein, *Nixonland: The Rise of a President and the Fracturing of a Nation* (New York: Scribner, 2008).

questions, and exclamations; and *in style,* between loose, periodic, and balanced. What follows are summaries of these distinctions in style.

Loose sentences

Loose sentences are the way most of us speak. They are conversational. We start talking about the main point we want to make and then fill out with detail and comment. In writing, you begin by announcing the main idea with an independent clause that's simple and straightforward, then you add subordinate or modifying elements after the subject and the predicate. This short loose sentence is from a *Guardian* reporter on the opening day of the Eichmann trial in Jerusalem:

> Eichmann slipped into court this morning out of the mystery and legend of his imprisonment, almost unnoticed.

The passage opens with the clause *Eichmann slipped into court.* It could end there, but it adds several modifiers to evoke the circumstances of his capture and trial. William Chauncey Fowler, the nineteenth-century author and teacher, defined the loose sentence as having at least one sentence before the end where you can stop and the main part preceding will still be understood as a complete sentence. The following loose sentence from the Eichmann trial could stop at "booths" or "tables" or "policemen" or "the Press," and the preceding words would still make sense:

There were translators in their booths and the girl secretaries at their tables and the peak-capped policemen at the doors, and the gallimaufry of the Press seething and grumbling and making half embarrassed jokes in their seats.

Ian Jack, writing an obituary for our *Sunday Times* colleague Phillip Knightley, used a long loose sentence to move us through time:

> He had reached Britain with no job in prospect some years before, late in 1954, but soon got employment in the London office of his old Sydney paper and there learned that sensational stories could be conjured from almost nothing—a piece about a "lonely" baby kangaroo in the pet shop at Harrods, for example, raised emotional demands from readers back home that Knightley should buy this emotional Australian symbol and find a good home for it (which he did, with the Duke of Bedford).

The sentence is long—84 words—but it doesn't drag; its length is relieved by the skillful use of adverbs to signal time and place (*before, soon, there*) and a dash to set off the story about the kangaroo.

The description of the loose sentence as "open" has been with us since Aristotle. In the 1960s critics began to prefer the label *cumulative*.[15]

Here is a paragraph by Ian Jack that has the conversa-

---

[15] Professor Jeanne Fahnestock (of the University of Maryland) notes that the distinction between *periodic* and *loose* sentences "begins with Aristotle,

tional style of the loose sentence carried through a paragraph that's open to any amount of remembering:

> "Busy day ahead?" asked the barman. "Not really," I said and explained about the memorial service at St Bride's, the so-called journalists' church that lies a few yards up the lane from the Old Bell's back door.
>
> "No newspapers in Fleet Street now," said the barman, and we agreed that this was a pity, though he didn't look old enough to remember a time when things were otherwise; when, for example, subeditors drank beer and smoked pipes and came flooding into pubs such as the Bell every night after the first edition had gone to press, to talk amiably until last orders or, if on the late shift, return upstairs earlier to prepare editions two, three and four; each and every subeditor knowing how many points made a pica and that to decimate means to kill one in 10. I didn't say any of this to the barman—who wants to be the pointing old sailor in the Boyhood of Raleigh?—and in any case my friend soon arrived and we withdrew into a separate conversation, wondering who would turn up to Ron's memorial service and which hymns would be sung.

Periodic sentences

The periodic sentence is the stylistic reverse of the loose or cumulative. It is tightly structured, not open, less easy to

---

who described types of sentences on the basis of how 'tight' or how 'open' they sounded."

write than the loose sentence. Some prefer to call it a suspended sentence.

You hold off writing the main clause and/or its predicate
to the end instead of at the beginning or middle. In such
placements, the crux of your sentence's meaning does not
become clear until the climax: you hold the reader's attention to the last word, at or near the period (full stop), lending
it greater dramatic emphasis:

> And though I have the gift of prophecy, and understand
> all mysteries, and all knowledge; and though I have all
> faith, so that I could remove mountains, and have not
> charity, I am nothing. (1 Corinthians, 13, King James)

More prosaically, from Nabokov:

> When you cross the tips of your skis, you tumble forwards.

Nabokov's genius is that he is able to risk walking on
the high wire while juggling with a periodic sentence whose
length and complexity would plunge a lesser writer into
the sawdust. You have to hold your breath from the moment
he opens with a long subordinate clause, the kind I have
described as predatory:

> If a first-class sleeper bears you away from a secure and
> prosperous home to the Crimea, from which you then
> depart for a life of ceaseless exile, which will end in
> acclaim and in America for yourself but in a concentra-
> tion camp for Sergey, your beloved younger brother, is it

surprising that your stories will come to resound to the clatter of night trains, to the thrill and devastation of *a one-way ticket in the dark?*

The same principle at work in a periodic sentence can be used at the paragraph level, as Garry Wills does in this reflection on Martin Luther King's funeral (my italics):

He was young at his death, younger than either Kennedy, but he had traveled farther. He did fewer things; but those things last. A mule team drew his coffin in a rough cart; not the sleek military horses and the artillery caisson. He has no eternal flame—*and no wonder. He is not dead.*[16]

And Wills again:

The changes King wrought are so large as to be *almost invisible.*

The last word in a sentence can punch above its weight. It is a point of climax. Use it. How's this for impudence?

Liverpool Street is the finest point of departure in the whole of Southern England because wherever you go from it, whether to Southend or, ultimately, to Outer Mongolia, it cannot fail to be an improvement.

---

[16] Garry Wills, *The Kennedy Imprisonment* (New York: Atlantic Monthly Press, 1981).

Writers can learn a lot about stress and emphasis in a magical book by the longtime Shakespearean director Peter Hall, called *Shakespeare's Advice to the Players:* when to go slow, when to go fast, and when to accent a word or series of words. Peter Clark, the author and teacher at the Poynter Institute, offers a simple demonstration, his favorite Shakespeare sentence in a riff of six words from Macbeth: "The Queen, my lord, is dead."

What's so good about that arrangement? If you write, "The Queen is dead, my lord," you've thrown away the climactic point that Clark likes to call the hot spot. You can restore it with "My lord, the Queen is dead" and still have the climactic word at the end—but now, as Clark rightly argues, you've lost the nanosecond of suspense provided by the "my lord" in midsentence, a good place for the furniture. An accomplished performer will add a barely perceptible pause before delivering the bad news.

Evelyn Waugh used the end of a sentence for comic effect in the opening chapter of his novel about Fleet Street at its zaniest, *Scoop:*

> Algernon Stitch was standing in the hall; his bowler hat was on his head; his right hand, grasping a crimson, royally emblazoned dispatch box, emerged from the left sleeve of his overcoat; his other hand burrowed petulantly in his breast pocket. An umbrella under his left arm further inconvenienced him. He spoke indistinctly, for he was holding a folded copy of the morning paper between his teeth.

The *New Yorker* film critic Anthony Lane comes upon you by stealth. In his review of *The Sound of Music,* he writes of Hitler's invasion of Austria:

> Even now no historian has been able to ascertain if this was a genuine bid for power or the only possible means whereby the Fuhrer could eradicate the threat of close harmony singing.

The balanced sentence

Here's a third variant of sentence structure a writer can summon. The stress of the periodic sentence is excitement and surprise, whereas the balanced sentence is a work of deliberate symmetry similar to parallel construction and alike suggestive of calm and order.

> It will not be done by the law or Government; it cannot be done by Parliament.
>
> I say segregation now, segregation tomorrow, segregation forever.

Better still as a guide to life and language is the balanced sentence consisting of two main clauses, similarly constructed, as in this example from Boswell's *Life of Samuel Johnson:*

> Every man has a right to utter what he thinks truth, and every other man has a right to knock him down for it.

In Shakepeare's *Julius Caesar,* the whole of the speech by Brutus after the murder of Caesar is in exquisite antithetical balance of verbs and nouns. A fragment:

> As Caesar loved me, I weep for him; as he was fortunate, I rejoice at it; as he was valiant, I honor him; but, as he was ambitious, I slew him. There is tears for his love; joy for his fortune; honor for his valor; and death for his ambition.

Mix and mix

Nobody can lay down a formula for varying sentences. If anyone did, a writer of the inventiveness of Tom Wolfe would make nonsense of it. Sentences must respond to the thoughts being expressed. All that editors and writers who care about style can do is soak up the nuances of rhythm in good authors. It is surprising what we can absorb without realizing it.

After a succession of loose sentences, the balanced or periodic sentence provides rhythm or bite. Particularly monotonous, however, is a succession of balanced compound sentences or compound verbs:

> The firemen climbed their ladders and they rescued all the women. Two doctors came by ambulance and treated all the injured. The ground floor was saved but the top floor collapsed. Firemen warned the crowds while police moved them back. The hotel owner arrived and said he could say nothing.

This passage comes over as a boring singsong. If in doubt about the rhythm of a piece of writing, say it aloud.

8. PUT PEOPLE FIRST

Aim to make the sentences bear directly on the reader. People can recognize themselves in particulars. The abstract is another world. The writer must make it visible by concrete illustration. This means calling a spade a spade and not a factor of production. Eyes that glaze over at "a domestic accommodation energy-saving improvement program" will focus on "how to qualify for state money for insulating your house." Economic and political reports abound with abstractions that cry out for humanizing.

The official inclination is to seek refuge in a bureaucratic bolt hole. Chris Wallace of Fox TV became exasperated trying to get an answer about people from Scott Pruitt, the new head of the Environmental Protection Agency.[17] President Trump had signed an executive order repealing the Clean Power Plan enacted by the Obama administration. Wallace wanted to know how much *people* would be affected by the elimination of rules to keep harmful pollution from America's air and water. He didn't get an answer. The president, said Pruitt, would keep a promise to deal with "regulatory overreach." It didn't mean clean air and water were not going to be the focus in the future but "we're just going to do it right within the consistency of the framework that Congress has passed."

---

[17] Good commentary in *It's Even Worse Than You Think* by David Cay Johnston (New York: Simon and Schuster, 2018).

Wallace: "But sir, you're giving me a regulatory answer. You're not giving a health answer."

Wallace kept pressing. "Half of all Americans live in counties with unhealthy air, according to the American Lung Association. You're talking about regulatory over-reach. But the question is, there are 166 million people living in unclean air, and you're going to remove some of the pollution restrictions, which would make the air even worse."

It's not surprising that Mr. Pruitt would evade responsibility for any potential damage caused by the rolling back of the EPA's rules. Who wants to admit to poisoning people?

9. THE PESKY PREPOSITIONS

Prepositions feel unloved. They are the workhorses linking those self-important nouns, bullying verbs, swaggering adjectives, fussy adverbs. Prepositions tell us where, when, why, and how: The man *with* the beard sat happily *on* the stoop *in front of* our house, chatting *for* an hour *before* breakfast every day, *regardless of* the weather. English is rich in prepositions. Wikipedia can introduce you to ninety single-word prepositions *as well as* a bunch of two-worders and prepositional phrases. You know them all, and necessary as they mostly are, they are candidates for excision when they clutter sentences. There are three mischiefs in the mess of pottage on prepositions: the circumlocutory preposition, the prepositional verb, and pedantry.

The circumlocutory preposition is a fluffy substitute for a single preposition which gives the meaning as clearly. The grossest offenders are *in the field of, in connection with, in order to, in respect of, so far as...is concerned.* All sorts of things are found flourishing *in the field of:* in the field of public relations, in the field of breakfast cereals, in the field of book publishing, in the field of railway management, in the field of nuts and bolts, in the field of space exploration. There is no room left on the continent for fields that grow plants. All these *in the field* land-grabbers should be evicted. *Field* has a very proper association with battle, chivalry, and war (hence "Never in the field of human conflict"), but the phrase is rarely relevant or necessary.

Prepositional and phrasal verbs grow like toadstools. Once there was credit in facing a problem. Now problems have to be faced *up to.* The prepositions add nothing of significance. To say one met somebody is plain enough; to say one *met up with* him adds nothing and takes two further words. So it is with *consult (with); check (up on); divide (up); test (out); stall (out).* Parasitical prepositions and particles like these can often be eliminated or replaced by a simple alternative verb. *Call* is better than *stop off at; fit, reach,* or *match* will serve better than *measure up to.* There is idiomatic strength in a few prepositional verbs, such as *get on with; go back on; take up with.* Southerners defend *visit with* as suggestive of a longer, more convivial visit: The mother of the *Washington Post* correspondent Jason Rezaian, held in prison by the Iranian government, was allowed to *visit with* him for several hours on Christmas day in 2015 (and in January 2016 he was back home). But much of the modern currency in phrasal verbs is American dumping that weakens

English. It is a sad day when it is no longer considered enough to say *honesty pays*. Inflation requires honesty to pay off; and we are the poorer for it.

The third trouble with the preposition was long the influence of the literary pedants who insisted that ending a sentence with a preposition was an excommunicable offense. They have been routed on the linguistic battlefield. The notion that the preposition should always be placed before the word it governs was an attempt to impose on English some of the rigor of Latin, and it will not do. Shakespeare wrote of the "heartache and the thousand natural shocks that flesh is heir to." Good English. "To which flesh is heir" would be a horrible change. Many arbiters have scorned the pedantry of the preposition but it flourishes in official, legal, and police-court language. Policemen are no longer apt to say "the water into which he dived," but lawyers are programmed to say "the contract into which he entered."

10. DOWN WITH MONOLOGOPHOBIA

For years, as a newspaper editor in London, I fell on Theodore Bernstein's *Winners and Sinners,* a bulletin of second-guessing on language issued "occasionally from the southeast corner of the *New York Times* newsroom." The occasions added up to 389 apt and amusing bulletins. I was glad to have them as ammunition. Bernstein (1904–1974) was an assistant managing editor of the *New York Times* charged with news presentation but he fished in the torrents for good usage and bad.

He invented the term *monologophobe,* which has the virtue that it is ugly enough to spring out of the page and hit you. A monologophobe, says Mr. Bernstein, is "a guy who would rather walk naked in front of Saks Fifth Avenue than be caught using the same word twice in three lines." He would edit the Bible so that you would read, "God said 'Let there be light,' and there was solar illumination." Word warriors stricken with monologophobia have an aversion to the humble pronoun; their remedy is to invent another noun.

> Ukraine plans to launch a diplomatic initiative to recover the Crimea, the province it lost to the Kremlin in a Russian coup, but Moscow has given no sign it will ever consider returning the Black Sea peninsula.

H. W. Fowler (*A Dictionary of Modern English Usage*), who called this "elegant variation," thought minor novelists and reporters were the real victims, "first terrorised by a misunderstood taboo, next fascinated by a newly discovered ingenuity, and finally addicted to an incurable vice."

Who's who?

A *Wall Street Journal* editorial wrestled with its comment on the Donald Trump versus Ted Cruz conflict in the 2016 presidential debates:

> The brawl is also valuable for the political education it is providing some of the radio talkers who did so much to elevate Mr. Trump as the billionaire revolutionary. Suddenly, they're unhappy that *the businessman* they

championed against "the establishment" is calling out their favorite son, Mr. Cruz, as a member of the establishment. *He's* even whacking *the Texan* for low-interest loans from Goldman Sachs and Citigroup and what until recently was his dual Canadian-US citizenship.

Bernstein rejoiced in landing mixed metaphors and exposing them to ridicule, as in: "Hope for a resumption of Arab-Israeli negotiations is *hanging on the slimmest of threads* but two developments of recent days *flash the signal that the door remains at least ajar* for the kind of *diplomatic footwork* that can forestall the outbreak of war."[18] Monologophobia is aggravated by the other writing sin of converting a verb into an abstract noun, or transforming a specific noun into an abstract noun. People don't hope; they "express hope." They don't believe; they "indicate belief." A monologophobe at a maternity hospital announced that with more staff available for after-care and an increase in the number of *admissions*, they will be able to send some home early. Presumably after the *mothers* had delivered their babies. The "leather sphere," underinflated or not, has disappeared from the sports pages, but monologophobia strikes in many places. In court reports there is a bewildering alternation of the names of people with their status as defendants or plaintiffs. It is wiser to stick to names throughout: "The truck driver said he was going out of the city when he saw the deceased walk suddenly into the road."

---

[18] James J. Kilpatrick, *The Writer's Art* (Fairway, KS: Andrews, McMeel, 1984), quoting Charles Seib of the *Washington Post*.

Expansive writing

News item, Sunday, January 20, 1985. President Ronald Reagan took the oath of office for his second term as the fortieth president of the United States. The swearing-in took place privately in the Grand Foyer of the White House. As the weather outside was harsh, with snow falling and temperatures near zero degrees Fahrenheit, the planners were forced to cancel most of the outdoor events.

Edmund Morris, the biographer of President Reagan, was there and this is what he wrote.

> Snow—polar snow, driven by arctic wind and rattling against every north-facing surface in Washington—blurred the shape of the White House at three minutes to noon on Sunday, January 20, 1985. The thermometer stood at nine degrees above zero. Traffic lights, their timers frozen, stared vainly up the empty length of Connecticut Avenue, whose alignment with the wind made it a howling tunnel aimed directly at Lafayette Square. Snow granulated to the caliber and hardness of steel filings whipped through the White House's railings and whitened the backs of photographers huddled like hoboes beneath the North Portico. They breathed on their lenses and prayed that the President would emerge as soon after twelve as possible. All they wanted was a quick shot for the evening news—with luck, a shot of this snow slamming right into his face—to justify their painful vigil.
>
> Inside the vestibule, Ronald Reagan stood on the Grand Staircase and raised his right hand at the request

of Chief Justice Warren Burger. The Twentieth Amendment to the Constitution required him to do so at this hour and on this day. Time enough for pageantry tomorrow, when he would take the oath again, more publicly, on Capitol Hill. He laid his free hand on Nelle Reagan's Scotch-taped, indexed Bible, narrow fingertips caressing, as hers had, the words of II Chronicles 7:14: *If my people, which are called by my name, shall humble themselves, and pray, and seek my face, and turn from their wicked ways; then will I hear from heaven, and will forgive their sin, and will heal their land.*

"Repeat after me," rumbled Justice Burger.

As the President courteously allowed himself to be led through a text that he had memorized at a glance four years ago, he felt Nancy Reagan's counter-pressure supporting the weight of the Bible and the weight of his hand. She stood looking at him throughout the oath, her face blank with pleasure. The eyes of three of his four children were on him, too, and those of Vice President Bush, and the senior White House staff, and twelve of the thirteen officers of his Cabinet. Ninety-four other dignitaries and favored friends sat on narrow gilt chairs, sweating as television lights irradiated their winter clothes. In the East Room, champagne lay ready to pop, and silver salvers sizzled with *pasta carbonara*.

"So help me God," Reagan ended. He bent to kiss his wife.

When, moments afterward, he stepped out onto the portico coatless, the ferocity of the wind took him by surprise. His pompadour rose in comic-book shock, his spine stiffened, and he rocked back on his heels with an audible gasp. The photographers got their shot. As always, Dutch delivered.

Why is this expansive report memorable? The index of a great writer is he or she notices the right things. There is luxury in this abundance of relevant detail. Morris begins with snow and arresting simile. The flakes are "granulated to the caliber and hardness of steel filings." We flinch. He sees the photographers but sees them breathing on their lenses, their backs whitened. Another simile. They are "huddled like hoboes." The verbs are *whipped, stared, breathed, rocked, prayed, irradiated, sizzled*. But where is the president? Morris casts the blizzard as might a composer raising expectations with an overture before act 1 and the dramatic entry of the hero. Then the writing is cooler; we need that pause in the richness of imagery until Reagan lays his free hand on "Nelle Reagan's Scotch-taped, indexed Bible, narrow fingertips caressing, as hers had." Nancy Reagan's face is "blank with pleasure," rather than the routine coupling of "glowed with pleasure"; then again, the writing is straightforward to the climax, the startling hyperbole as "his pompadour rose in comic-book shock" and the photographers we'd forgotten get their shot. "As always, Dutch delivered" — and so did Morris.

Getting away with murder

Item: The young men killed in black-on-black crime are 6 percent of America's population, but nearly 40 percent of the murdered.

In her searing book *Ghettoside*, **Jill Leovy,** a *Los Angeles Times* reporter, zooms in on one senseless killing that speaks to the homicide epidemic in South Central Los Angeles in the nineties, and the dogged efforts for justice for the community by the cadre of homicide detectives, black and white.

It was a warm Friday evening in Los Angeles....Sea breezes rattle the dry palms in this part of town. It was about 6:15 p.m., a time when homeowners turn on sprinklers, filling the air with a watery hiss. The springtime sun had not yet set; it hovered about 20 degrees above the horizon, a white dime-sized disk in a blinding sky.

Two young black men walked down West Eightieth Street at the western edge of the Los Angeles Police Department's Seventy-seventh Street precinct area.... One was tall with light brown skin, the other shorter, slight, and dark.

The shorter of the two, Walter Lee Bridges, was in his late teens. He was wiry and fit. His neck was tattooed and his face wore the mournful, jumpy look common to young men in South Central who have known danger. His low walk and light build suggested he could move like lightning if he had to.

His companion, wearing a baseball cap and pushing a bicycle, appeared more relaxed, oblivious. Bryant Tennelle was eighteen years old. He was tall and slim, with a smooth caramel complexion and what was called "good hair," smooth and wavy. His eyes tilted down at the corners, giving his face a gentle puppy look. The two young

men were neighbors who whiled away hours together tin-
kering with bicycles.

They were strolling on the south side of Eightieth.
Bryant carried in one hand an unopened A&W root beer
he had just bought. Thirties-era Spanish-style houses—
updated with vinyl windows—lined the street, set back a
few feet from the sidewalk. Each had a tiny lawn mowed
so short it seemed to blend with the pavement. Buses
roared by on Western Avenue. Crows squawked and
planes whistled overhead as they descended into Los
Angeles International Airport, close enough to read the
logos on their tails. Groups of teenagers loitered at each end
of the street. An elegant magnolia loomed near the end of
the block, and across the tunnel, and across the street
hunched a thick overgrown Modesto ash.

The ash tree stood in front of a tidy corner house.
Behind that house, in the backyard on the other side of
the fence, another man was cleaning out a tile cutter. He
had just retiled his mother's bathroom.

Walter and Bryant were taking their time walking
down Eightieth chatting, their long shadows stretching
behind them. Dusk engulfed the other side of the street.
Three friends emerged from a house at the end of the
block behind them and called out a greeting. Walter
stopped to yell something back. Bryant kept walking
toward the ash. A black Chevrolet Suburban pulled up to
the curb around the corner on St. Andrews. A door
opened and a young man jumped out. He ran a few steps
and halted under the tree, holding a gloved hand straight
out, gripping a firearm. *Pap. Pap-pap.*

Walter reacted instantly. He saw the muzzle flashes, saw the gunman—white T-shirt, dark complexion, gloves—even as he sprinted. The man with the tile cutter was still behind the fence. He couldn't see the shooter. But he heard the blasts and dropped instinctively. He was forty, had grown up a black man in South Central and had the same battle-ready reflexes as Walter. He lay flat on the ground as gunfire boomed in his ears.

Bryant's reflexes were slower. Or perhaps it was because he was looking straight into the setting sun. To him, the gunman must have appeared a dark silhouette. Bryant staggered, then reeled and fell on a patch of lawn overhung by a bird-of-paradise bush. Silence. The tile cutter drew himself to his feet, crept to the fence, and peeked over.

The shooter stood a few feet away, next to the ash tree on the other side of the fence, still holding the gun.

As he moved away and broke into a run, the tile cutter made a brave decision. He followed the shooter, watched him jump back into the Suburban, and tried to read the license plate as it sped away. Then he saw Bryant on the grass.

Teenagers were converging from three directions. One young man dropped to his knees next to Bryant. Joshua Henry was a close friend. He took Bryant's hand and gripped it. With relief, he felt Bryant squeeze back. "I'm tired, I'm tired," Bryant told him. He wanted to sleep....Then Bryant turned his head. A quarter of his skull had been ripped away.

Ghettoside is saturated with detail and passion, but the detail does not swamp the perspective, and the passion does not become sentimental. "Our criminal justice system harasses people on small pretexts but is exposed as a coward before murder. It hauls masses of black men through its machinery but fails to protect them from bodily injury and death. It is at once oppressive and inadequate." Leovy's prose is remarkably simple. Tested on Count Wordsworth, this passage averages only twelve words to a sentence (the longest is thirty-nine words) and 1.44 syllables per word. It scores as easy to read at every level in the readability formulas. Yet she electrifies the narrative when she wants. The characterization of Walter Lee Bridges, his wariness, his mournful, jumpy look, his ability to move like lightning, suggest something bad is going to happen.

A month before the murder of Bryant Tennelle, "a big blondish man with a loping stride in an expensive light-colored suit" was on his way to meet a victim's mother. This was Los Angeles Police detective John Skaggs. He was carrying a shoebox aloft "like a waiter bearing a platter." Inside were a pair of "high-top sneakers that once belonged to a black teenage boy named Dovon Harris." Skaggs was returning them to Barbara, the mother of Dovon, a fifteen-year-old who had been shot to death a few blocks from their home. Alone, and too scared to venture out, she lived behind barred windows and a heavy-duty steel "ghetto door," a security door with a perforated metal screen. "All around her, in the tiny living room, were mementos of her murdered son. Sports trophies, photos, sympathy cards, certificates, stuffed animals." She pressed her face into the shoe dusted with red Watts dirt and wept as had thousands of black mothers before her and thousands will after her. Society's efforts to combat the underreported epidemic, Leovy writes, were "inept, fragmented, underfunded, contorted by a variety of ideological, political, and racial sensitivities."

Satire

Polemical writing can be served hot or cold. Acts of cruelty can be denounced, sued, and with luck the perpetrator brought to justice. **Mohammed Hanif,** the Pakistani journalist and novelist, confronts the social system with ridicule, with satire that shames. This is the laconic way he writes at the opening of an essay on mullahs protesting a new law to protect women:

> Karachi, Pakistan: In the world we live in, there is no dearth of pious men who believe that most of the world's problems can be fixed by giving their women a little thrashing.

And then he uses repetition as salt in the wound:

> And this business of a man's God-given right to give a woman a little thrashing has brought together all of Pakistan's pious men.

Next, he summarizes the news peg:

> A few weeks ago, Pakistan's largest province passed a new law called the Punjab Protection of Women Against Vio-

lence Act. The law institutes radical measures that say a husband can't beat his wife, and if he does he will face criminal charges and possibly even eviction from his home. It proposes setting up a hotline women can call to report abuse. In some cases, offenders will be required to wear a bracelet with a GPS monitor and will not be allowed to buy guns.

A coalition of more than 30 religious and political parties has declared the law un-Islamic, an attempt to secularize Pakistan and a clear and present threat to our most sacred institution: the family. They have threatened countrywide street protests if the government doesn't back down.

The arena is now clear for the writer's view on the motives of the mullahs who are protesting. He follows the logic in an arc of absurdity. Note the way he controls the tempo of disgust, moving from formal language to colloquialism and climaxing in vulgarity (my italics):

Their logic goes like this: If you beat up a person on the street, it's a criminal assault. If you bash someone in your bedroom, you're protected by the sanctity of your home. If you kill a stranger, it's murder. *If you shoot your own sister, you're defending your honor. I'm sure the nice folks campaigning against the bill don't want to beat up their wives or murder their sisters, but they are fighting for their fellow men's right to do just that.*

It's not only opposition parties that are against the bill: The government-appointed Council of Islamic Ideology has also declared it repugnant to our religion and culture. The council's main task is to ensure that all the laws in the country comply with Shariah.

Once again, the writer returns to the attack. His colloquial expressions take the air out of the council's huff-and-puff formality.

But basically it's a bunch of old men who go to sleep worrying that there are all these women out there trying to trick them into bed. Maybe that's why there are no pious old women on the council, even though there's no shortage of them in Pakistan.

The council's past proclamations have defended a man's right to marry a minor, dispensed him from asking for permission from his first wife before taking a second or a third, and made it impossible for women to prove rape. It's probably the most privileged dirty old men's club in the country.

He advances a serious counterargument to the "pampered religious nuts," then unleashes an unanswerable insult:

Some of us routinely condemn these pious old men, but it seems they are not just a bunch of pampered religious nuts. In fact, they are giving voice to Pakistani men's collective misery over the fact that their women are out of control. Look at university exam results; women are hogging all the top positions. Go to a bank; there is a woman counting your money with her fancy nails. Turn on your TV; there is a female journalist questioning powerful men about politics and sports.

One of these journalists recently was grilling a famous mufti opposed to the bill. Bewildered, the mufti said: Are you a woman, or are you a TV journalist?

Hanif moves in for the kill.

She was professional enough not to retort: Are you a mufti, or just another old fart?

Bret Stephens: *The return of the thirties*

Donald Trump was a joke until he wasn't. The 2016 presidential competition brought forth many champions to assail him as a demagogue, a fantasist, a racist, a narcissist, a bankrupt, a bully, and a liar, and he rode the raging surge of contempt all the way to the Republican nomination and then the presidency. In March 2016, Bret Stephens, writing in the *Wall Street Journal,* suggested a parallel with "the last dark age of Western politics."

In temperament, he was "bombastic, inconsistent, shallow and vainglorious." On political questions, "he made up his own reality as he went along." Physically, the qualities that stood out were "the scowling forehead, the rolling eyes, the pouting mouth." His "compulsive exhibitionism was part of his cult of machismo." He spoke "in short, strident sentences." Journalists mocked his "absurd attitudinizing."

Remind you of someone?

The description of Benito Mussolini comes from English historian Piers Brendon's definitive history of the 1930s, "The Dark Valley." So does this mean that Donald Trump is the second coming of Il Duce, or that yesteryear's Fascists are today's Trumpkins? Not exactly. But that doesn't mean we should be indifferent to the parallels with the last dark age of Western politics.

Among the parallels: The growing belief that democracy is rigged. That charisma matters more than ideas. That strength trumps principles. That coarseness is refreshing, authentic.

Also, that immigrants are plundering the economy. That the world's agonies are someone else's problem. That free trade is a game of winners and losers—in which we are the invariable losers. That the rest of the world plays us for suckers. That our current leaders are not who they say they are, or where they say they are from. That they are conspiring against us.

These are perennial attitudes in any democracy, but usually marginal ones. They gained strength in the 1920s and '30s because the old liberal order had been shattered—first at Gallipoli, Verdun and Caporetto; then with the Bolshevik coup in Russia, hyperinflation in Germany, Black Tuesday in the United States. "What are the roots that clutch, what branches grow/Out of this stony rubbish?" wondered T. S. Eliot in "The Waste Land," in 1922. Mussolini's Blackshirts marched on Rome the same year.

Modern Americans have experienced nothing like those shocks, which is one important difference with the 1930s. The French army lost more men on an average day on the Western Front than the U.S. lost in our worst year in Iraq. At the height of the Great Depression, real per capita GDP fell by nearly 30% from its previous peak. At the depth of the 2008–09 recession, it fell by about 6%, and soon recovered.

Then again, the pain you're in is the pain you tell yourself you're in. Or, at least, the pain you're told you're in, usually by political doctors who specialize in hyping the misery of others.

So we're being "invaded" by Mexicans—except that for years more Mexicans have been *returning* home than coming here. So China is destroying our manufacturing— except industrial employment has *surged* in recent years, especially in the Rust Belt. So the great mass of Americans are now unprotected from the vagaries of the global economy—save for Medicare, Obamacare, the earned-income tax credit, public-employee pensions and every other entitlement that Mr. Trump promises to protect.

All this generates the hysteria, the penchant for histrionic rhetoric, the promise of drastic measures, the disdain for civility, the combination of victimhood and bullying on which the Trump candidacy feeds, and which it fuels. Reading through the avalanche of pro-Trump emails that arrive in my inbox (by now numbering in the thousands), what's notable are the belittling put-downs ("you're an $@%&, Bret-boy"), the self-importance ("I make more money than you") and the sense of injured pride ("how dare you call me a vulgarian?"). This is precisely the M.O. of their candidate.

"In breaking the taboos of civility and civilization, a Trump speech and rally resembles the rallies of fascist leaders who pantomimed the wishes of their followers and let them fill in the text," writes the University of Maryland's Jeffrey Herf in a brilliant essay in the *American Interest*. "Trump says what they want to say but are afraid to express. In cheering this leader, his supporters feel free to say what they really believe about Mexicans, Muslims, and women."

This is not the politics of economic anxiety or dislocation. It's a politics of personal exhibitionism, the right-wing equivalent of refusing to be "body-shamed." Thanks to Donald, the Trumpkins at last have a license to be as ugly as they want to be.

Mr. Trump's bid for the presidency takes place during a period of mediocre but nonetheless unmistakable economic and employment growth in the U.S. But as a wise friend of mine noted the other day, what happens when the next bubble bursts and the next recession arrives? A reasonable person can argue that Donald Trump is more Silvio Berlusconi—Italy's clownish billionaire and former prime minister—than he is a new Mussolini. Maybe. Or maybe Mr. Trump's style of politics is just a foretaste of what's to come, especially if an American downturn became a global depression.

In the work of preserving civilization, nine-tenths of the job is to understand the past and stress its most obvious lessons. Now would be a good time to re-remember the '30s.

Historical parallels are tricky but Stephens executes a neat pivot. He concedes that yesteryear's Fascists are "not exactly" like Trump's populist armies, but the collective noun he assigns — "Trumpkins" — usefully diminishes them as tiny Munchkins in *The Wizard of Oz*. Stephens has a strong voice. His cogent muscular prose is stunning in defining a series of parallels, ten insistent hammer blows of short emphatic sentences of convictions the Trumpkins have swallowed as truths: "that democracy is rigged, that charisma matters more than ideas, that strength trumps principles, that coarseness is refreshing, authentic...that immigrants are plundering the economy...that [our current leaders] are conspiring against us."

The writer's familiar citation of times when these perennial attitudes have surfaced is brilliantly refreshed with his metaphor from Eliot's "The Waste Land": "What are the roots that clutch, what branches grow/Out of this stony rubbish?" One by one he refutes the Trumpian excesses, then wraps up the plain contradictions in a rolling sentence that strikes at the heart of the Trump method: "All this generates the hysteria, the penchant for histrionic rhetoric, the promise of drastic measures, the disdain for civility, the combination of victimhood and bullying on which the Trump candidacy feeds, and which it fuels." The last sentence, always important in a polemic, is cool but a clincher: "In the work of preserving civilization, nine-tenths of the job is to understand the past and stress its most obvious lessons. Now would be a good time to re-remember the '30s."

Exercise in style

I was for a time the publisher of Lewis Lapham, the editor of *Harpers* and now *Lapham's Quarterly,* who described how he found joy and inspiration in writing out passages (for the pleasure of the rhythms as well as for the lesson in rhetoric) and sometimes "made short lists...of words unknown that fell graciously on my ear." I commend it. When on reading binges in what I have to call my formative years, I found that I absorbed the writer's style without being aware that I was writing a mad potpourri of Zane Grey, Dickens, P. G. Wodehouse, Evelyn Waugh, and S. J. Perelman, and then incongruously of Jan Morris, who preceded me in crossing America in the fifties. In my travels following her literary spoor a year later, I had to stop writing a pastiche of her peerless *Coast to Coast.* I remember the excitement reading her description of approaching Manhattan by car from the west. She sees it as "a last outpost on the edge of the continent," two white ribbons of highway bearing vehicles in an endless unbroken, unswerving stream: "They carry the savor of distant places: cars from Georgia, with blossoms wilting in the back seat, or diesel trucks bringing steel pipes from Indiana; big black Cadillacs from Washington, and sometimes a gaudy convertible (like a distant hint of jazz) from New Orleans or California." Her imagination stirred mine, the life and history of the whole continent a fever in my mind.

Picasso has been many times quoted as saying good artists copy, great artists steal. Steve Jobs, among legions, credited Picasso. We now know from Quote Investigator[19] that Picasso had lifted the epigram from someone else, who lifted it from someone else. Quote Investigator traced it as far back as W. H. Davenport Adams, whose article "Imitators and Plagiarists" was published in the *Gentleman's Magazine* in 1892. T. S. Eliot in 1920 changed it to suggest imitation was shoddy and to steal praiseworthy, the attitude adopted by Steve Jobs in 1996. I like to think that we may begin with imitation, graduate to emulation, and then aspire to creation.

---

[19] quoteinvestigator.com/tag/w-h-davenport-adams/

Please Don't Feed the Zombies, Flesh-Eaters, and Pleonasms

"And remember—no more subjunctives where the correct mood is indicative."

This is a mandatory public notice that zombies, flesh-eaters, and pleonasms remain a threat to healthy prose.

ZOMBIES

The zombie is a noun that's devoured a verb: *implementation, assessment, authorization, documentation, participation, transmittal, realization*…all zombies. Once upon a time, they were energizing sentences as the verbs *implement, assess, authorize, document, participate, transmit, realize*. The huge tribe of zombies has long been classified as "smothered verbs" or "controverted verbs," their parents having been subjected to "nominalization," an ugly noun from the verb *nominalize*, itself no great shakes. Adjectives are vulnerable, too. *Applicability* is a zombie derived from the adjective *applicable, forgetfulness* from *forgetful*.

Helen Sword, a professor at the University of Auckland, is the creator of the more vivid term, a scary noun we will want to treat with circumspection (*sic*). "I call them 'zombie nouns,'" she writes, "because they cannibalize active verbs, suck the lifeblood from adjectives and substitute abstract entities for human beings."

> The *proliferation* of *nominalizations* in a discursive *formation* may be an *indication* of a *tendency* toward *pomposity* and *abstraction*.

Seven zombies inhabit that sentence, the offspring of five verbs and two adjectives. Ms. Sword eliminates or reanimates most of the zombie nouns, adds a human subject, and the sentence springs to life:

> Writers who overload their sentences with nominalizations tend to sound pompous and abstract.

They do, and their sentences spin fluff. To make sense, zombies have to mate with another verb, and they breed prepositions. Consider this paragraph:

> Objective considerations of contemporary phenomena compel the conclusion that success or failure in competitive activities exhibits no tendency to be commensurate with innate capacity, but that a considerable element of the unpredictable must invariably be taken into account.

Even typing it, I was fighting for breath. It was written by George Orwell. He wrote it, with due deliberation, as a parody of what "modern English," as it was then called, could do to the verbs and nouns in a verse from Ecclesiastes:

> I returned and saw under the sun, that the race is not to the swift, nor the battle to the strong, neither yet bread to the wise, nor yet riches to men of understanding, nor yet favour to men of skill; but time and chance happeneth to them all.

Orwell's parody is as if someone had draped black muslin over Michelangelo's *David* and Orwell removes it all syllable by syllable until we see the hidden beauty.

When he wrote that essay, container shipping, leading to *containerize* and the zombie *containerization*, had not arrived, but Ms. Sword brings us grimly up to date with what happens when zombies "gather in jargon-generating packs and infect every noun, verb and adjective in sight." We began with *globe* (1551) which became *global* (1676), then *globalize* (1953), and since 1961 we've enjoyed *globalization*. The most scary combination is a sentence in the passive voice infiltrated by a zombie; the sentence can become two or three times as long.

Zombies show no respect for national institutions. The BBC had the laudable ambition to understand what programming individuals love and suggest other choices for them—"broadening their content discovery." The idea was to appoint a Customer Relations Manager (CRM):

> An exciting opportunity has now arisen for an exceptional head of CRM, with an extensive technical background, to join our expanding Direct Audience Engagement Team and *be instrumental in the growth, optimization and innovation* of existing direct channels and the content strategies we are using to engage with our fan communities. A big part of this role in 2018 will also *be the exploration and development of new capabilities.*

The spoor of the zombies is everywhere. The CRM will work with the Direct Audience Engagement Team (DAET) to "agree, prioritise and tactically execute the CRM development road map against strategic objectives."

> Operational management of Salesforce Marketing Cloud, partnering effectively and working closely with their technical consultants and internal BBC project managers to roll up sleeves and "white board" solutions that drive automation, scale and efficiency of investment in audience platform infrastructure…design and implement…on

boarding funnel contact strategies for new BBC Account users.

Alas, we can't just excommunicate all zombies, because some combinations of nouns and adjectives help us to compress complex thoughts. I checked something I'd written in a book on innovators, and found a passage on Wilbur and Orville Wright with five zombies it would be hard to replace:

> The invention of the first powered airplane by Wilbur Wright and his younger brother Orville in 1903 was a triumph of reason and imagination, of hundreds of small painstaking deductions, risky experiments and giant conceptual leaps. It was also a celebration of empiricism and a vindication of human values of courage and brotherly love.

Still, there are a lot of zombies at large that have no such justification. Run a computer search of your writing or editing for other frequent telltale suffixes, such as *-ance; -ment; -ence; -ent; -mant; -ant; -sion*. Or paste a few paragraphs in Ms. Sword's *Writer's Diet* test for "an operationalized assessment" of your vulnerability to the zombies.

Here's a sampling I made from the usual suspects (print, TV, radio, magazines). Zombies on the left, purgatives on the right, word counts in parentheses.

Accommodation

The theater has seating accommodation for 600. (7)	The theater seats 600. (4)

Activity

They enjoyed recreational activity. (4)	They liked games. (3)
The king agreed to limited exploration activity. (7)	The king agreed to limited exploration. (6)

Basis

He agreed to play on an amateur basis. (8)	He agreed to play as an amateur. (7)
They accepted employment on a part-time basis. (7)	They accepted part-time work. (4)

Capability

The aircraft had a long-range capability. (6)	The aircraft had a long range. (6)

Conditions/Character

The Irish were forced to live in slum conditions. (9)	The Irish had to live in slums. (7)
The garden was of a tangled character. (7)	The garden was tangled. (4)
The Argentine delegate said the claims were of a far-reaching character. (11)	The Argentine delegate said the claims were far-reaching. (8)

The survivors were in a desperate condition. (7)	The survivors were desperate. (4)
Warmer conditions will prevail. (4)	It will be warmer. (4)
Adverse climatic conditions (3)	Bad weather (2)

Decision

The French party's decision was to conduct a survey of the oasis. (11)	The French party will survey the oasis. (7)

Extent

The problem is of a considerable extent. (7)	It's a big problem. (4)

Facilities/Amenities

Shopping facilities/amenities (3)	Shops (1)
Car parking facilities/amenities (4)	Carparks (1)
Ablution facilities/amenities (3)	Washbasins (washrooms) (2)

Field

A further vital field in which government policy is strangling initiative is the export field. (15)	Government policy is also strangling exporters' initiative. (7)

Those invading barbarians, *issue* and *problem*, run through everywhere, stealing space and laying waste to living images. This is one of the places where adjectives can be called to duty. The verb, too, can put the invaders to rout.

Issue/Problem

Another *issue* concerning the governors is the *problem* of lateness, which has been increasing among the sixth form. (18)	The governors are also worried by increasing lateness among sixth-formers. (10)
On the *troublesome issue* of school meals, the council decided to delay a decision until April. (16)	The council put off the troublesome school-meals decision until April. (10)
Far more real *an issue* in the long term is the question of what happens if further gas discoveries are made in the old or new concessions or what happens if they are not. The position will become clearer in several years' time when further exploration is done. Then the Gas Council must decide what to do with any further reserves and how fast it should deplete its present resources. More gas and/or faster depletion of existing gas would greatly change the energy picture in Britain. Gas would flow to the bulk markets, displacing coal as well as oil. Price would again become a question of policy, as would the possibilities of electricity generation. (115)	What if more gas were found in the next few years? The Gas Council would have to decide on a rate of use, for gas could flow to the bulk market, displacing coal as well as oil. The arguments on price and about using gas to make electricity would be reopened. (51)

Operations/Authorization

Drilling operations will resume next year.	Drilling will resume next year.
It is unlikely that authorization will come soon from the minister for implementation of the first stage of the plan for the construction of the third airport because agreement on working conditions has not been reached with all the unions involved. (41)	The minister is unlikely to authorize an early start on building a third airport, because the unions have not all agreed on hours and pay. (25)

Participation

The tenants were seeking participation in the making of price policy. (11)	The tenants wanted to help decide the rents. (8)
A favorable attitude toward participation in studies for the determination of future potential flows of migrants has been expressed by Italy. (21)	Italy will join studies to determine potential flows of migrants. (10)

Purposes

Land for development purposes (4)	Land for building (3)
An instrument for surgical purposes (5)	A surgical instrument (3)
A committee for administrative purposes (5)	An administrative committee (3)

Question

Over the question of supply, the major decision in the near future will be that of a third terminal. (19)	The major supply decision in the near future will be on building a third terminal. (15)

Situation

The unemployment situation has escalated. (5)	Unemployment is higher. (3)
The teacher supply situation is serious. (6)	Teachers are scarce. (3)
The visit of the pope to Mexico City has created an ongoing chaos situation. (14)	The pope's visit has created chaos. (6)
An emergency meeting will be called to discuss the situation whereby nine hundred tins of suspect corned beef were accidentally distributed. (20)	An emergency meeting will discuss how nine hundred tins of suspect corned beef were accidentally sold. (15)

Use Of

The Citizens Committee said the use of buses should be stepped up. (12)	The Citizens Committee said more buses should be used. (9)
The use of thirty-seven gardens has been volunteered by their owners. (11)	Thirty-seven residents have offered gardens. (5)

Here is an extract that combines several examples in one paragraph:

Because of severe drought conditions, the Dansville water supply has reached a critical state. Rolland Link, superintendent of the water department, urged residents in a statement yesterday to conserve water. This could make the difference, he said, as to whether the supply remains adequate enough to serve the people of the community without allocating specific quantities at certain times of the day. (62)	Dansville, hit by drought, is so short of water that it may be cut off for times during the day unless everybody saves more, said Rolland Link, superintendent of the water department, yesterday. (33)

You may have noticed several common sources of wordiness. An abstract noun is used with an adjective when a simple adjective will do (*of a far-reaching character*); and an abstract noun is added to a concrete noun (*slum conditions*). Another source of wordiness is the change of a live verb into an abstract noun, which then requires help from an adjective and a tame verb. Take the live-verb form:

He bowled badly.

That is a sentence with subject, verb, and adverb. The adverb *badly* is pale but it suffices. Compare the construction when the verb *bowled* is made into the abstract noun *bowling*.

To say the same thing, we need a possessive pronoun, subject, verb, and adjective.

His bowling was poor.

That is weaker—and longer. The text editor should restore purity to such sentences. Verb-adverb combinations are stronger and shorter than noun-verb-adjective combinations. Two verbs are better than a verb plus abstract noun.

THE FLESH-EATERS

-PHAGUS: one that eats an indicated thing—*Merriam-Webster*

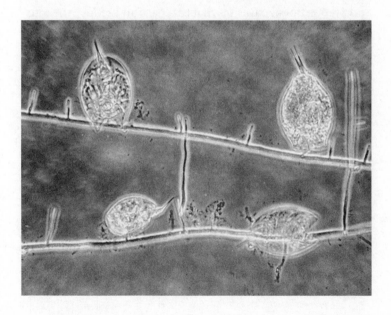

You can't see these creatures without an electron microscope that magnifies them millions of times—but they are there glorying in the name *Zoophagus insidians*.[1] I want you to retain the image in your mind as a metaphor for bad things in your prose you barely notice.

Zoophagous is the adjective describing the carnivorous function of microscopic creatures in water mold that enables fungi to eat other aquatic creatures. *Zoophagus insidians* is a particularly wily water mold, its name made up of the Latin for animal (*zoo*); *phagy*, for "eat"; and *insidians*, for one who lies in wait, an ambusher. Most of us don't fret much about the wars of the microworld, but I ask you to consider the similarity of what goes on there, undetected, to what happens in our visible world of words: *Zoophagi* (plural) *orsum* (words) are flesh-eaters. They are unnecessary words, pompous phrases and prepositional parasites that eat space and reduce the muscularity of your writing—and of writing at the highest level of public affairs. The White House national security report on the underwear bomber I analyze in chapter 9 is a flesh-eaters' banquet (and shot through with passive constructions).

In the following chart, I indict one-hundred-plus common flesh-eaters to avoid. Context matters. There may be occasions where they are tolerable, but many are verbose, and the preferred alternatives are crisper and shorter. They may not be synonymous, but they can generally say what you want to say. If I give no alternative to a flesh-eater, just avoid using it.

If all this sounds fanciful, it is—but check YouTube to see zoophagi at mealtime: www.youtube.com/watch?v=lkcR -5jguKQ

---

[1] Image credit George L. Barron, School of Environmental Sciences, University of Guelph.

Flesh-Eater	Preferred
A man/woman by the name of	Named
At the present time	When
At this point in time	Now
At an early date	Soon
A number of	Several, many
An adequate number of	Enough
A sufficient number of	Enough
Absence of	No
Along the lines of	Like
Accede to	Grant/allow
Accordingly	So
Acquaint	Tell
Adjacent to	Near
Ahead of schedule	Early
Arrangements are in the hands of	Arranged by
As far as…is concerned	As for
A percentage of	Some
Ascertain	Learn
Attired in	Wore
By means of	With/by
Best of health	Well/healthy
Called a halt	Stopped
Carry out the work	Do the work
Caused injuries to	Injured
Concerning the matter of	About
Continue to remain	Stay
Currently	Now
Customary	Usual

Flesh-Eater	Preferred
Despite the fact that	Although
Due to the fact that	Because
Draw the attention of	Show/remind/point out
Described as	Called
During the time that	During
Exceeding the speed limit	Speeding
Enclosed herewith	Enclosed
Equivalent	Equal
From the point of view of	For
For the purpose of	To, for
For the reason of	Because
Facilitate the effort	Ease/help
From out of the	Out of/from
Filled to capacity	Full
Fundamental	Basic
Gained entrance to	Got in
Gathered together	Met
Give consideration to	Consider
Goes under the name of	Is called/known as
Give rise to	Cause
Hence why	Why
Implement	Carry out/fulfill/do
I am hopeful that	I hope
Impossible to discover	Cannot be found
In addition	Also
In the possession of	Has/have
In advance of our meeting	Before we meet
Inasmuch as	Given

Flesh-Eater	Preferred
In a satisfactory manner	Satisfactorily
In attendance	Present/there
In conjunction with	Together with
In accordance with	By/under
In consequence of	Because of
In isolation	By itself/alone
Initiate, institute	Start
In large measure	Largely
In the case of/ in terms of	Of
In many cases	Often
In order to	To
In recognition of the fact that	Recognizing that
In spite of the fact that	Despite/although
In succession	Running
In the course of	During/while
In the direction of	Toward
In the event of	In/if
In the field of	In/with
In the majority of instances	Mostly
In the vicinity/region/ neighborhood of	About/near/around
In view of the fact that	Since/because
Is of the opinion	Believes
It cannot be denied that	Undeniably
It is often the case that	Often
Large volume of	Many
Leaving much to be desired	Unsatisfactory/bad
Less expensive	Cheaper

Flesh-Eater	Preferred
Low degree of interest	Little interest
Made an approach to	Approached
Made good their escape	Escaped
Measure up to	Fit/reach/match
Meet up with	Meet
Notwithstanding the fact that	Although
Occasioned by	Caused by
Of the order of	About
Off of	Off
One of the purposes	One purpose
One of the reasons	One reason
On account of the fact that	Because
On the grounds that	Since/because
Owing to the fact that	Because
On the part of	By
On a regular basis	Regularly
On a daily basis	Daily
Pay tribute to	Thank/praise/honor
Per annum	A year
Per capita	Per person
Performs the function of	Functions as
Placed under arrest	Arrested
Prove beneficial	Benefit
Put in an appearance	Appear
Prior/preparatory/previous to	Before
Provided that	If
Relative to the issue of	About
Retired for the night	Went to bed

Flesh-Eater	Preferred
Rendered assistance to	Helped
Request the appropriation of	Ask for (more) money
Retain her position as	Remain as
Serves the function of	Serves as
Substantiate	Prove
Submitted his resignation	Resigned
Succeeded in defeating	Defeated
Succumbed to his injuries	Died
Sufficient consideration	Enough thought
Shortfall in supplies	Shortage
So far as *x* is concerned	As for *x*
Special ceremonies marking the event were held	Ceremonies marked the event
Subsequent to	After
Sustained injuries	Was hurt
Take action on the issue	Act
This day and age	Today/nowadays
Took into consideration	Considered
The tools they employed	Their tools
The results so far achieved	The results
Under active consideration	Being considered
Until such time as	Until
Under preparation	Being prepared
Under the circumstances	In this/that case
Voiced approval	Approved
Was a witness of	Saw
Was suffering from	Had
We are of the opinion	We think

Flesh-Eater	Preferred
We are in receipt of	We received
Wend one's way	Go
Will be the speaker at	Will speak
With the minimum of delay	As soon as possible/ASAP
With the result that	So
Worked their way	Went
With the exception of	Except
With a view to	To
With reference to	About
With regard to	About
With the result that	So that
When and if	When

PLEONASMS: A ROSE IS A ROSE IS A ROSE

A pleonasm is a redundant unnecessary superfluity, related to the family cousins of flesh-eaters and the tribe of tautologies. The tautology says the same thing twice and in usage *redundant* may make *tautology* redundant. Pleonasms are often enough unnoticed redundancies, such as *complete* monopoly and *awkward* predicament, that do not add to the sense of the message. You will have heard that definition before. As Yogi Berra said, it is déjà vu all over again. I call Yogi's a premeditated pleonasm, a thing apart. It's like a jujitsu move, turning the excess into a positive force of a joke, an epigram, a literary flourish, a selling tool provided "free, gratis and for nothing… absolutely guaranteed through and through."

Quotes by George Bernard Shaw ("Youth too good to

waste on the young") and Sam Goldwyn ("Anyone who sees a psychiatrist needs his head examined") are recycled every generation, and a new generation of late-night talk shows plunder the pleonasms for a laugh ("*USA Today* has come out with a new survey — apparently, three out of every four people make up seventy-five percent of the population." — David Letterman). And we recognize that the man who wrote "This was the *most unkindest cut* of all" probably did it to emphasize how treacherous Brutus was in the murder most foul (*Julius Caesar,* act 3, scene 2). Matthew, too (17:8): "And lifting up their eyes, they saw no one, except Jesus Himself alone."

We could rely on U.S. election politics bringing us piping-hot pleonasms. In 2015 Jeb Bush announced that he was "to actively explore" running for president, and New York's Mike Bloomberg picked up the infection in 2016. I suppose that "actively explore" is to be regarded as an advance on having been inactively not exploring. Jeb Bush told us that he intended to "facilitate conversations" and surmised these would be followed by a promise "to really actively explore in earnest," or even "to boldly go," an exercise that would mean talking to real people.

People who knowingly trade in pleonasms for a joke and for emphasis I call *pleonistas.* They know what they are doing. We are all pleonistas in everyday speech and writing. I know I am repeating myself when I talk on the phone and say, "Thank you very much, I appreciate it, I'm grateful"; and I truly am when finally I track down someone who sorts out the problems with Apple's obsession with passwords.

These are polite pleonasms, impelled by diplomacy and cowardice, and forgivable in quick casual messages. But pleonasms in formal writing, on the web, and in broadcasting are advertisements of ignorance, and they waste time and space. We will never rid ourselves of those embedded for generations, such as *private and confidential, peace and quiet,* and a host of legal terms whose repetitive nature is a legacy of the time when Norman French, Latin, and English were in common use and lawyers wanted to cover every linguistic possibility (*will and testament, cease and desist, null and void, aid and abet*...). But most of the other pleonasms editors and readers come across are sloppy writing, suffocating sentences. It is irritating to know that the writer or speaker demanding our attention isn't thinking. The superfluities merit extinction with the certainty expressed in the Monty Python sketch in which John Cleese directs a barrage of pleonasms at the pet-shop owner (Michael Palin) who had sold him an uncommunicative parrot:

> He's passed on! This parrot is no more! He has ceased to be! He's expired and gone to meet his maker! He's a stiff! Bereft of life, he rests in peace! If you hadn't nailed him to the perch he'd be pushing up the daisies! His metabolic processes are now history! He's off the twig! He's kicked the bucket, he's shuffled off his mortal coil, run down the curtain and joined the bleedin' choir invisible! This is an ex-parrot!

The list I pulled from print, web, and broadcasting passes what the pleonistas would call *the* two hundred *mark*. Strike out the words in italics:

absolute perfection
acres *of land*
actual evidence
acute crisis
adequate enough
a distance of
all *of*
all-time record
among the delegates expected *to attend*
an authority *in his own right*
anonymous stranger
a number of examples
a period of
appear *on the scene*
appear *to be*
appointed *to the post of*
appreciated *in value*
ascend *up*
as compared with
as never before *in the past*
as yet
a team of workers
at some time *to come*
attach *together*
awkward predicament
a work *situation*
best *ever*
blends *in*
blue-*colored* car
bold *and audacious*

brand-new
broad daylight
chief protagonist
circular *shape*
classified *into categories*
close proximity
collaborate *together*
commented *to the effect* that
commute *to and from*
complete monopoly
completely outplayed
completely untrue
concrete proposals
connect *up/together*
consensus *of opinion*
continue *in existence*
continue *to remain*
cooperate *together*
cost *the sum of*
crisis *situation*
dates *back* from
definite decision
deftly manipulate
depreciated *in value*
descend *down*
divert *away* from
divide *off/up*
doctorate *degree*
downright lie

drink *up/down*
driver *by occupation*
during *the course of*
early *hours*
eat *up*
eliminate *altogether*
enclosed *herewith*
endorse *on the back*
end product/result
end *up*
entire state/community/congregation
entirely absent
entirely new departure
entirely spontaneous
equally *as*
essential condition
ever since
exact counterpart
face *up to*
falsely fabricated
few *in number*
final completion/upshot/settlement
flatly rejected
follow *after*
for *a period of*
forbid *from*
for *the* making *of*
for *the month of*
for *the purpose of*

foundered *and sank*
fresh beginning
frown *on his face*
full complement of
full satisfaction
funeral obsequies
future prospect
gainfully employed
gather *up/together*
general public
good benefit
grateful thanks
have been *engaged in* producing
have *got*
heard *various* requests
he lost his *eye*sight
he was seen *in the morning* on his pre-breakfast walk
he went *in an effort* to determine
hoist *up*
hot water heater
hour of noon
hurry *up*
if *and when*
in abeyance *for the time being*
include *among them*
intents and purposes
interpersonal friendship
in *the city of* Manchester
in *the course of* operation

in the interim *period between*

in *the process of* building

in *the sphere of* politics

intolerable *to be borne*

in two years' *time*

invited guest

involved in a car crash

it is interesting to note that

joined *together*

joint cooperation

join *up*

just recently

last *of all*

lend *out*

link *together*

little sapling

lonely isolation

made *out* of

major breakthrough

may *possibly*

meet *together*

men who are unemployed

merge *together*

more essential

more preferable

more superior

mutual cooperation

nearly inevitable

necessary requisite

needless to say

need *necessarily*

never *at any time*

new beginning

new creation

new innovation

new record

new recruits

new renovations

new tradition

nobody *else* but

not *at all*

not *generally* available everywhere

old adage

old veterans

one of the last *remaining*

on the occasion when

on the question of

original source

over *and done with*

overtake a *slower-moving* vehicle

pare *down*

partially harmless

passing pedestrian/car

passing phase

past history

patently obvious

pay *off* the debt

peculiar freak

penetrate *into*

periods *of time*

personal friend

polish *up*

poor state of disrepair

prejudge *in advance*

presence *on the scene*

pressing for *the imposition of* a 30 mph limit

prominent *and leading*

proposed project

protrude *out*

quite empty

quite perfect

radical transformation

raze *to the ground*

recalled *back*

recommended *back*

reduce *down*

regular monthly meeting

repeat *again*

resigned *his position* as

results *so far achieved*

returned *back*

revert *back*

reward *back*

root cause

safe haven

saved *from his earnings*

scalded *by hot water*

seldom *ever*
self-confessed
separate *apart*
serious danger
seriously incline
settle *up*
short *space of* time
sink *down*
skirt *around*
small *in size*
smile *on his face*
spent his *whole* life
staunch supporter
still persists/continues
strangled *to death*
sufficient enough
summoned *to the scene*
sunny *by day*
surgeon *by occupation*
surrounding circumstances
temporary reprieve
the court was asked to decide *as to* whether *or not*
throughout *the whole length and breadth*
to *consume* drink
topped *the* two hundred *mark*
total contravention
total extinction
totally destroyed
track record (unless it is the running track)
true facts

uncommonly strange
unite *together*
universal panacea
usual customs
utterly indestructible
value judgments
vandals *willfully* broke
violent explosion
vitally necessary
watchful eye
ways *and means*
whether *or not*
whole *of the* country
widow of *the late*
win *out*
worst *ever*

The devil is in the details

In November 2015, typing in the phrase *took to Twitter* gave me 720,000,000 responses on Google in 0.34 seconds. Is it now a cliché? It's too early to say, since a cliché is well defined as a phrase "so hackneyed as to be knock-kneed and spavined."[2] The millions of entries were quotes from Twitter, but surfing the web I quickly accumulated two thousand phrases. They were categorized as clichés but perhaps I can be the first in my circle to use "hotter than a fox in a firestorm" or "horny as a three-peckered billy goat." It is impossible to

---

[2] Eric Partridge, *A Dictionary of Clichés* (London: Routledge, 1940).

get rid of clichés in speech. They serve a natural inclination, a quick vocabulary in daily social encounters. At best they are a form of literary shorthand, with the attraction of economy. Why say "she's bustling and industrious" when you can say "she's busy as a bee"? I know I must have somewhere written "the devil is in the details" and "back to the drawing board." Next time I have to express those thoughts, I'll try harder. The imagery is dead. The worst are wasteful, too. "In deadly earnest" says no more than "in earnest"; "to all intents and purposes" says no more than "virtually." But, as with pleonasms, clichés can be exploited. About someone who hesitates to express an opinion or shilly-shallies on a decision, we say he's "sitting on the fence." Of a bolder person making a stand, we may use the term from nineteenth-century naval warfare: he's "nailed his colors to the mast." And a neat way to express exasperation with someone who is all talk and no action would be to mix the clichés: he's "nailed his colors to the fence."

The challenge is to avoid breaking the camel's back by adding too many last straws of off-the-rack expressions such as:

acid test
aired their troubles
all walks of life
appear on the scene
at pains to explain
beat a hasty retreat
beggars description
bewildering variety
bitter end

blaze (for fire)
blazing inferno
blissful ignorance
bolt from the blue
breakneck speed
breakthrough
breathless silence
bring up to date
brutal reminder
brute force
built-in safeguard
burning issue
calm before the storm
checkered career
cherished belief
city fathers
cold collation
colorful scene
commendably patient
concerted move
conspicuous by its absence
coveted trophy
crack troops
crowded to capacity
crude fact
crying need
daring daylight robbery
dark horse
dashed to the rescue
dastardly deed

dazzling sight
deafening crash
deciding factor
dig in their heels
dog in the manger
dotted the landscape
dramatic new move
dreaming spires
drew a line
fair sex
fall between two stools
fall on deaf ears
far cry
finishing touches
firestorm of controversy
fly in the ointment
foregone conclusion
from time immemorial
gay abandon
given the green light
goes without saying
gory details
Grim Reaper
hammered out a deal
hardy souls
headache (for "problem")
heap coals of fire
heartfelt thanks
heart of gold
high dudgeon

hot pursuit
hub of the universe
inextricably linked
in full swing
inspiring/unsporting display
internecine strife
in the nick of time
in the same boat
iron out the difficulty/problem
lashed out
last but not least
last-ditch effort
leaps and bounds
leave no stone unturned
left up in the air
lending a helping hand
like rats in a trap
limped into port
lock, stock, and barrel
long arm of the law
long years
loom up
lucky few
luxury flat/yacht
marked contrast
marked improvement
marshal support
matter of life and death
move into high gear
never a dull moment

news leaked out
nipped in the bud
none the worse for wear
not to be undone
not to put too fine a point on it
official capacity
open-and-shut case
open secret
order out of chaos
over and above
paid the penalty
painting a grim picture
paramount importance
part and parcel
paying the piper
pillar of the church
pinpoint the cause
place in the sun
pool of blood
poured scorn
powder keg
pros and cons
proud heritage
psychological moment
raced/rushed to the scene
red faces
red-letter day
red rag to a bull
reins of government
remedy the situation

rose to great heights
sadder but wiser
sea of upturned faces
selling like hotcakes
sigh of relief
64,000-dollar question
spearheading the campaign
speculation was rife
spirited debate
spotlessly white
spotlight the need
square peg in a round hole
steaming jungle
stick out like a sore thumb
storm of protest
storm-tossed
stuck to his guns
sweeping changes
taking the bull by the horns
taking the situation in stride
terror-stricken
this day and age
through their paces
throwing a party
tongue-in-cheek
top-level session
tower of strength
true colors
unconscionably long time
up in arms

upset the apple cart
vanish into thin air
voiced approval
wealth of information
weighty matter
whirlwind tour
widespread anxiety
winds of change
wreak havoc
writing on the wall

Interlude

Give the Bard a Break

"Good, but not immortal."

If you cannot understand my argument, and declare "It's Greek to me," you are quoting Shakespeare; if you claim to be more sinned against than sinning, you are quoting Shakespeare; if you recall your salad days, you are quoting Shakespeare; if you act more in sorrow than in anger; if your wish is father to the thought; if your lost property has vanished into thin air, you are quoting Shakespeare; if you have ever refused to budge an inch or suffered from green-eyed jealousy, if you have played fast and loose, if you have been tongue-tied, a tower of strength, hoodwinked or in a pickle, if you have knitted your brows, made a virtue of necessity, insisted on fair play, slept not one wink, stood on ceremony, danced attendance (on your lord and master), laughed yourself into stitches, had short shrift, cold comfort or too much of a good thing, if you have seen better days or lived in a fool's paradise — why, be that as it may, the more fool you, for it is a foregone conclusion that you are (as good luck would have it) quoting Shakespeare; if you think it is early days and clear out bag and baggage, if you think it is high time and that that is the long and short of it, if you believe that the game is up and that truth will out even if it involves your own flesh and blood, if you lie low till the crack of doom because you suspect foul play, if you have your teeth set on edge (at one fell swoop) without rhyme or reason, then — to give the devil his due — if the truth were known (for surely you have a tongue in your head) you are quoting Shakespeare; even if you bid me good riddance and send me packing, if you wish I was dead as a doornail, if you think I am an eyesore, a laughing stock, the devil incarnate, a stony-hearted villain, bloody-minded or a blinking idiot, then — by Jove! O Lord! Tut tut! For goodness' sake! What the dickens! But me no buts! — it is all one to me, for you are quoting Shakespeare.

— Bernard Levin

II

Finishing the Job

6

~~~

Every Word Counts

As I write on this night of evil, Friday, November 13, 2015, the beautiful city of Paris bleeds. One unidentified group of men, assumed by television to be some variety of terrorists, is shooting into the audience at a sold-out rock concert; suicide bombers have exploded at a soccer stadium; a man, dressed all in black, has entered a crowded restaurant to discharge the magazine of a Kalashnikov assault rifle on Parisians and tourists at dinner. Through the darkness we see the ambulances of SAMU (Service d'aide médicale urgente), we hear the gunfire, we share the shock just expressed by President Obama: "This is an attack not just on Paris, it's an attack not just on the people of France, but this is an attack on all of humanity and the universal values that we share."

The president chose his words well, but the media has difficulty reflecting those "universal values." In the blanket reporting of a confused night, one word glared: *credit*. No one, said a television commentator, has yet "claimed credit for the attack." This is Newspeak, 2015. The inverted value of Orwell's blackwhite language in his satirical novel *1984* was reiterated on multiple channels thereafter, including ABC and CNN, and many online sites. For a few days they also bestowed the sobriquet *mastermind* on one of the perpetrators until French police traced him to his hiding place. *Mastermind* blew himself up.

The misuse of *credit* stains print, broadcasting, and the web. On December 23, 2015, in Afghanistan, a motorbike suicide killed ten U.S. soldiers, and CNN "credited" it to the Taliban. Boko Haram was "credited" with the seizure of 276 girls in Chibok, Borno. The "credits" in broadcasting, print, and website headlines make it clear one part of humanity just does not think about the meaning of words. For five hundred years, since the English first adopted the word from the French, *credit* has meant "honor."

Oxford English Dictionary, 1933: "The commendation bestowed on account of an action, quality, etc., 1607." *Random House Dictionary,* second edition, 1966: "Commendation or honor given for some action, quality, etc." *Online Etymology Dictionary,* 2015: "Meaning honor, ack. of merit, about 1600."

Terrorists have no hesitation in claiming "credit." ISIS did the day after the Paris killings. The aim is to ratchet up anxiety to panic. But why does the media act as ventriloquist? The *Wall Street Journal,* generally scrupulous with words, wrote in an editorial on June 30, 2016, that the Islamic State "hasn't taken credit at this writing" for killing forty-one and injuring more than two hundred at Turkey's Ataturk Airport. Nouns and verbs that chime with universal values are accessible, words such as *responsibility, blame, guilt, admit, accept*—and the strong verb *perpetrate,* "to execute or commit a crime or evil deed." It is more fitting than *carry out,* as if the bad guys were delivering pizza.

The media does not intend to equate murder and honor. But it does. It is as erratically careless, too, with *execution,* embellishing a desert decapitation with the word for "the infliction of capital punishment in observance of a judicial sentence" (*OED*). I think *claim credit* just pops into mind as a reflex coupling, the way fires *rage,* plots *thicken,* fire engines *race.* Orwell would classify it as *duckspeak,* to quack without thinking, a word in the language of Newspeak. "Ultimately," wrote Orwell in his 1948 description of the principles of Newspeak, "it was hoped to make articulate speech issue from the larynx without involving the higher brain centers at all." Oldspeak—and literature and history—would gradually be supplanted by Newspeak, and obliterated by 2050. Facebook's mass dissemination of fake news in the 2016 presidential election suggests that we are ahead of schedule.

Anyone in the vicinity of a brain can identify the appropriate language for the uncertain early hours of an event as shocking as what happened in Paris, or three weeks later in San Bernardino, or indeed in the epidemic of mass shootings in the United States: "Nobody has yet *admitted/accepted/taken* responsibility." The competitive urgencies of reporting require established news organizations to define standards and enforce them. Thomson Reuters, for instance, advises reporters and editors: "It is acceptable to say that a guerrilla organization claimed responsibility for carrying out an attack. Do not say it claimed credit." The integrity of independent reporting is as vindicated by the admission of doubt as by the assertion of certainty. The Bloomberg News stylebook says: "When evidence isn't available and authority asserts that an event was caused by terrorists or that bombs were dropped on terrorist camps, qualify the assertion with *alleged* or *suspected*." Right. But when terrorists identify themselves in and by acts of terror, it isn't a simple euphemism for the media to call them militants, resistance fighters, protesters, guerrillas, radicals. To be polite, it's a terminological inexactitude, the clever weasel word for a lie coined by Winston Churchill in 1906 to get round the ban on "unparliamentary" language.

A WORD THAT LIVES

One word — that's all it takes to shock, to set a tone, to express the moral temper of a society. On Monday, December 8, 1941, President Roosevelt stood before a joint session of Congress and his deep firm voice resonated across the nation. "Yesterday, December 7, 1941 — a date which will live in *infamy* — the United States of America was suddenly and deliberately attacked by naval and air forces of the Empire of Japan."

FDR and his crusty secretary of state, Cordell Hull, had been trying for years to walk a tightrope over a volcano. Japan, resentful of Western control of the raw materials of Southeast Asia, had grabbed Manchuria in 1931, started a full-scale war against China in 1937, invaded southern Indochina in 1941. FDR froze Japanese assets in the U.S. and imposed embargoes on trade and oil that hit Japan hard. The outline of a deal was for the U.S. to partially resume trade if Japan proved its sincerity by committing to withdraw from

China and Indochina, but the hundred hours of negotiations between Hull and the Japanese ambassador Admiral Kichisaburo Nomura were a miasma of misunderstandings. Nomura was a decent man who had opposed the militarists, but on September 2, Tokyo had secretly decided on a two-track response: to go along with talks for six weeks, but then strike south at the U.S. and Britain and the Netherlands.

The dive-bombing of Pearl Harbor began at 7:49 a.m. locally, 1:19 p.m. Washington time. FDR was in the Oval Office cool at first, then tense, excited, shaken, as bulletins from Hawaii arrived. Alistair Cooke, who was in the White House, reported that the pressroom had "that air of tobacco-choked energy that is the Washington odor of panic."

FDR began to dictate: "Yesterday, December 7, 1941, *a date which will live in world history,* the United States of America was simultaneously and deliberately attacked by naval and air forces of the Empire of Japan."

It was nearing 9:00 p.m. when FDR, gray and exhausted, read his draft aloud to the cabinet and congressional leaders of both parties gathered around his desk in dead silence.

FDR sensed his draft was not equal to the occasion. He had shrewdly cast his opening in the passive voice to portray the United States as a victim of imperial ambition by the expansionist *Empire of Japan,* but "will live in world history" was flat. Lots of events—good and bad—can be said to live in world history. The phrase missed the uniqueness of the tragedy, the fury of betrayal that had crowds rushing to the gates of the White House; it did not reflect the revulsion and resolve FDR would have to evoke in asking Congress to declare war. FDR improved his first draft's reference to the deceit—that the U.S.

was attacked while it was "continuing conversations." He made it "was still in conversation," a subtle emphasis on personal duplicity. The fact that several attacks were "simultaneous" was also less significant than the suddenness, the stunning shock of treachery. He wrote in "without warning" to close the first sentence, but recognized the sentence dribbled out in a redundancy once *suddenly* had replaced *simultaneously*. The deletion of *without warning* enabled him to end the sentence with the accusing finger pointing at the *Empire of Japan*. Finally, while his speech was being retyped, FDR deleted the murmuring commas in the opening sentence and came up with the killer phrase *live in infamy* set between two dagger-point dashes.

Infamy, a word from fifteenth-century Norman French for "public disgrace and dishonour," was precisely the right noun to express the vileness of an act deserving of universal reproach. How did that pungent and unfamiliar word come to replace *world history*? It did not come from his two speechwriters. He dictated several drafts and the editing marks are in his hand. He may have absorbed the word from his reading of the King James Bible: "Ye are taken up in the lips of talkers, and are an infamy of the people."

Secretary of State Cordell Hull was a more proximate source than Ezekiel 36:3 or Proverbs 25:10. Hull inserted the adjectival form of the word into the stream of consciousness that afternoon when Nomura and special envoy Saburo Kurusu bowed into the secretary's office at 2:20, twenty minutes late for the appointment. Hull kept them standing for another twenty minutes. They had no idea he had already received intercepts by U.S. code breakers. They were unaware, too, that an hour before the meeting, Japanese bombers had begun their attack on

American warships at anchor in Pearl Harbor. Hull knew. He had just taken a phone call from the president. In a fury, Hull found words for the occasion. "In my fifty years of service I have never seen a document that was more crowded with infamous falsehoods and distortions—infamous falsehoods on a scale so huge that I never imagined until today that any Government on this planet was capable of uttering them."

Cooke was disappointed. Hull, he wrote, was a man from the mountains of Tennessee, capable of "an abusive idiom, deriving half from animal biology, half from the Bible." As the diplomats were ushered out, distraught, the secretary hissed under his breath, "Scoundrels and pissants." Cooke concluded, "Those who had seen an indignant Hull, would hardly settle for a sentence from Gibbon."

History settled that. The date will live in infamy.

THE MAKING OF A SPEECH

Address to Congress—Declaring War on Japan, December 8, 1941

Draft	Final
Yesterday, December 7, 1941, a date which will live in *world history*, the United States was *simultaneously* and deliberately attacked by naval and air forces of the Empire of Japan.	Yesterday, December 7, 1941—a date which will live in *infamy*—the United States of America was *suddenly* and deliberately attacked by naval and air forces of the Empire of Japan.

The United States was at the moment at peace with that nation and was *continuing the conversations* with its Government and its Emperor looking toward the maintenance of peace in the Pacific. Indeed, one hour after, Japanese air squadrons had commenced bombing in *Hawaii and the Philippines,* the Japanese Ambassador to the United States and his colleague delivered to the Secretary of State a formal reply to a *former message from the Secretary. This reply contained a statement that diplomatic negotiations must be considered at an end but* contained no threat *and no hint of an* armed attack.

It will be recorded that the distances of *Manila, and especially of* Hawaii, from Japan make it obvious that *these attacks were* deliberately planned many days ago. During the intervening time the

The United States was at peace with that nation and, *at the solicitation of Japan,* was *still in conversation* with its Government and its Emperor looking toward the maintenance of peace in the Pacific. Indeed, one hour after Japanese air squadrons had commenced bombing in *Oahu,* the Japanese Ambassador to the United States and his colleague delivered to the Secretary of State a formal reply to a *recent American message. While this reply stated that it seemed useless to continue the existing diplomatic negotiations, it* contained no threat *or hint of war or* armed attack.

It will be recorded that the distance of Hawaii from Japan makes it obvious that *the attack was* deliberately planned many days *or even weeks* ago. During the intervening time the Japanese

Japanese Government has deliberately sought to deceive the United States by false statements and expressions of hope for continued peace.

The *attacks* yesterday *on Manila and on the Island of Oahu have* caused severe damage to American naval and military forces. Very many American lives have been lost. In addition American naval ships have been torpedoed on the high seas between San Francisco and Honolulu.

Yesterday the Japanese Government also launched an attack against Malaya.

Government has deliberately sought to deceive the United States by false statements and expressions of hope for continued peace.

The *attack* yesterday on *the Hawaiian Islands has* caused severe damage to American naval and military forces. Very many American lives have been lost. In addition American ships have been reported torpedoed on the high seas between San Francisco and Honolulu.

Yesterday the Japanese Government also launched an attack against Malaya.

Last night Japanese forces attacked Hong Kong.

Last night Japanese forces attacked Guam.

Last night Japanese forces attacked the Philippine Islands.

Last night the Japanese attacked Wake Island.

This morning the Japanese attacked Midway Island.*

Japan has, therefore, undertaken a surprise offensive extending throughout the Pacific area. The facts of yesterday speak for themselves. The people of the United States have already formed their opinions and well understand the implications *these attacks bear on* the safety of our nation.

As Commander-in-Chief of the Army and Navy I have, *of course*, directed that all measures be taken for our defense.

Long will we remember the character of the onslaught against us.

I *speak* the will of the Congress and of the people *of this country* when I assert that we will not only defend ourselves to the uttermost but will *see*

Japan has, therefore, undertaken a surprise offensive extending throughout the Pacific area. The facts of yesterday speak for themselves. The people of the United States have already formed their opinions and well understand the implications *to the very* safety of our nation.

As Commander-in-Chief of the Army and Navy I have directed that all measures be taken for our defense.

Always will we remember the character of the onslaught against us.

No matter how long it may take us to overcome this premeditated invasion, the American people will in their righteous might win through to absolute victory.

I *believe I interpret* the will of the Congress and of *the people* when I assert that we will not only defend ourselves to the uttermost but will *make very*

to it that this form of treachery shall never endanger us again.	*certain* that this form of treachery shall never endanger us again.
Hostilities exist. There is no *mincing* the fact that our people, our territory and our interests are in grave danger.	Hostilities exist. There is no *blinking at* the fact that our people, our territory and our interests are in grave danger.
	With confidence in our armed forces—with the unbounding determination of our people—we will gain the inevitable triumph—so help us God.
I, *therefore,* ask that the Congress declare that since the unprovoked and dastardly attack by Japan on Sunday, December seventh, a state of war *exists* between the United States and the Japanese Empire.[†]	I ask that the Congress declare that since the unprovoked and dastardly attack by Japan on Sunday, December seventh, a state of war *has existed* between the United States and the Japanese Empire.

*FDR could have combined in one sentence the six countries Japan attacked, but the economy of words would have lost the urgency of the insistent parallel predicates, each opening with the same phrase, the rhetorical device called *anaphora*. For more on this device and an analysis of persuasive language, including this speech, see Jeanne Fahnestock, *Rhetorical Style: The Uses of Language in Persuasion*.

[†]Harry Hopkins, FDR's most trusted wartime adviser, inspired the closing passage. His handwritten note is at the foot of the draft, headed "Deity." "So help us God" and "so help me God" have been variously added by presidents after swearing the oath prescribed in the Constitution.

7

Care for Meanings

"All right, then. It is I!"

When the men (and women) from Mars land next year—
language and life are moving that fast—they will of course
command, "Take us to your leader." Thereafter conversation
will be limited if they are modish folk who have adopted all
the new words sanctified as acceptable English by the *Oxford*

English Dictionary. We'll take a dekko at that later in this chapter (*dekko* being a British term I first learned serving in the Royal Air Force, derived from Hindi to mean "taking a quick look").

The tsunami of new words has not so far relieved us of the encroaching corruptions of political vocabulary skewered by Orwell seventy years ago. "Emptying words of meaning is an essential step on the road to autocratic rule." It sounds like an ungood Newspeak principle, but it is fresh from Roger Cohen, the *New York Times* columnist, commenting in 2017 on the weird events of the Trump presidency. Having scored a surprise Electoral College victory, but not the "landslide" he claimed, the new president obsessed about the size of his inauguration crowds and the conspiracy whereby Hillary Clinton sneaked nearly three million noncitizens into the nation's voting booths. No doubt the infiltrators of his imagination did all the dirty work in the dead of night, carrying their clichés with them. The president's acolytes threatened to avenge the media for failing to find the mythical armies of fraudsters, and then promulgated even more mendacities about the media's determination to suppress news of acts of terrorism. In the president's mind, that made them "among the most dishonest human beings on earth."

The enduring story in American ethical culture, adopted over two centuries ago, is how the conscience of six-year-old George Washington would not let him lie to his father about taking a hatchet to a cherry tree. Early in the 2016 presidential election, it could safely be said the candidate destined to be the forty-fifth president was not trying to embellish the moral legend of the first. Within the normal meaning of words, Trump is either a liar or a victim of "truthiness," as diagnosed by Dr. Colbert. We are certainly in the vortex of what's come to be called the post-truth society. In 2016 the *Oxford Dictionaries* announced that "after much discussion, debate and research," *post-truth* was the Word of the Year, as an adjective defined as "relating to or denoting circumstances in which objective facts are less influential in shaping public opinion than appeals to emotion and personal belief." Scottie Nell Hughes, the news director of the Tea Party Network, is assiduous in polishing the brass plate on the Ministry of Post and Alt-Truth. She corrects the deviants: "People say facts are facts—they're not really facts," she argued on *The Diane Rehm Show.* We all have to be made to realize that anything is true if enough people believe it. Some publications seemed not to have received the Alt bulletin. *Forbes,* the *Guardian,* the *Washington Post, Vanity Fair, Politico,* and NBC didn't hesitate to pin *lie* on a falsehood, which, given the number of falsehoods, is understandable. But a falsehood is not necessarily a lie. We have all made statements believing them to be true, only to find they were false. Rather than argue about definitions, Steve Adler, editor in chief of Reuters, the global news agency, responded to the White House attacks with a ringing declaration: Reuters, responsible for reporting the news independently in more than one hundred countries, is bound by the Reuters Trust Principles to report "fairly and honestly by doggedly gathering hard-to-get information—and by remaining impartial."

The president's millions of supporters did not care about any of this. David Frum, a former speech writer for Bush 43, reported in *The Atlantic* (February 2017) that a Trump tweet attacking the University of California was "precisely the opposite of the truth"—but it had become "dogma in Trump world, including Trump-skeptical conservatives."

Most editors recognize the risks in shouting "Lie!" in an empty theater. It is as well to be credible as it is to be clear. If the public buys the line of Trump's chief strategist, Steve Bannon, that media is "the opposition," everything from that source can be discounted as polluted by bias. To borrow Lenin's verb, the concept of truth would gradually wither away.

The irony is that in 2016–2017 mainstream news media— on the whole—was more restrained and more precise in its language than the president and his strategist and the right-wing chorus in Fox, Breitbart News, and hate radio. For years they promoted the smear that President Obama was an alien. The editor of the *Wall Street Journal*, Gerard Baker, said he would identify statements like this as "challengeable" or "questionable" and publish the evidence pro and con, but not identify them as lies because that was to imply "moral intent" and mark the publication as biased. It caused something of a stir in September 2016 when the *New York Times* appeared with a front-page headline: "Donald Trump Clung to Birther Lie for Years, and Still Isn't Apologetic." The executive editor Dean Baquet acknowledged that *lie* has "powerful implications," but he was clear what the word meant: "A lie implies that it was done with complete, total knowledge that it was a falsehood."

We have waited for a new word for *lie* that throbs with the revulsion the noun and verb once provoked universally.

Roget's Thesaurus gives us a plethora of adjectives: downright lies, shameless lies, monstrous lies, outright lies, filthy lies, barefaced lies, shocking lies, dirty lies, big lies; and in desperation, we can draw from the vocabulary of absurdity: codswallop, bullshit, balderdash. None penetrates to the heart of darkness as Lawrence Douglas's term *meta-lie,* for insidious untruths aimed at changing—subverting—the way we think of institutions we rely on for exposing lies, error, and corruptions—media, academia, judiciary. The drip-feed of the poison is the suggestion that the monitors are corrupt, dishonest, and lying—part of the elitist plot against the common man. Douglas, a law professor at Amherst, writing in the *Guardian* (February 7, 2017), acknowledges a debt to Hannah Arendt (1906–1975), the author of *The Origins of Totalitarianism.* Roger Berkowitz, the Arendt scholar at Bard College, is eloquently on the same page. The political lies Arendt worried about, he says, are not mere falsehoods. They are political acts in which facts are denied and alternative realities are created. "The political lie opens the door to a politics that not only denies facts but works actively to disempower facts, thus enabling the creation of a coherent albeit fictitious world. The danger inheres in the utter logicality of the fictional narrative. To preserve the fiction, facts that contradict it need to be eliminated."

Arendt had a weighty ally in the art of political lying:

> My imagination represents before me a certain great man famous for this talent....The lies which he plentifully distributes every minute he speaks, and by an unparalleled generosity forgets and consequently contradicts the

next half hour....He never yet considered whether any proposition were true or false but whether it were convenient for the present minute or company to affirm or deny it; so that if you think to refine upon him, by interpreting everything he says, as we do dreams, by the contrary, you are still to seek, and will find yourself equally deceived whether you believe or not: the only remedy is to suppose, that you have heard some inarticulate sounds without any meaning at all.

(From "The Art of Political Lying" by Jonathan Swift [1667–1745], author of *Gulliver's Travels*)

THE HALF-LIFE OF NEW WORDS

The gatekeepers who scrutinized all entrants to the citadel of print have now been outflanked by 0s and 1s in the millions, and texters have created a new language more like speech than formal writing, but with convenient symbols so that instead of edging round to a segue, the texter just writes a slash and is not thought a boor.

John Sutherland, professor emeritus at University College, London, tested two thousand parents and found them bewildered by the language the younger generation picks up on popular social media sites and by texting. Only one in ten was able to tell the meaning of *bae,* a term of affection; *on fleek* (good-looking); and *FOMO* (fear of missing out). WTF, you can't stay sane and keep up with half the cryptic new words amid the dross and clickbait ("29 Struggles That Only People with Big Butts Will Understand"). The now-familiar *geek, tweeter, hashtag, phish, app, meh, ego surf, hack, binge-watch, troll, meme,* and *spam* don't supplant existing words as expressive, but they jostle with incomprehensible upstarts. Most will quickly pass into oblivion. Despite the *OED* nod, I don't think we will have much appetite for *awesome sauce, beer o'clock, fast-casual, wine o'clock, cupcakery,* and *cakeage* in the future. They have no piquancy; but what do I know? I grew up in England, where we'd always been stuffed shirts (U.S. colloquialism, 1875) about language. Jonathan Swift condemned as vulgar slang such non-American newcomers as *mob, bamboozle, sham, bully, banter,* and *uppish.*

Samuel Johnson set the tone when he interposed his person between any single American word and his dictionary of 1785. He rejected *clever, stingy, reliable.* A lawyer in the High Court was rebuked for saying "to bluff." King Edward might have gotten away with marrying an American divorcée, but the establishment could never forgive him for using the American *radio* in his fireside chat instead of *wireless.*

In the fifties, the *Times* of London I was to edit thirty years later still regarded new American words as an abomination and corruption. By the time I was in the chair in 1981, the editors were not inclined to say the American people speak real good, but more or less everyone was ready to nod to H. L. Mencken and yield to the American talent for forming nouns by the devices of metaphor: *skyscraper, hijacker, handout, grassroots, killjoy, kickback, cover girl, highbrow, stooge, hobo, dropout, shills, bobby-soxer, do-gooder, tightwad, hayseed, lounge lizard*—and the encomium of a *blurb* that we in the book trade hope is irresistible. Of course, some of the words about which Mencken was *crazy as a bedbug* (colloquial, 1832) faded as life changed. By the eighties, the *couch potato* slumped in front of the tube was more of a feature than the *lounge lizard* and *barfly*. Nobody objected to deriving verbs from the imported nouns: the hitchhiker *thumbs* a lift, the wrecking crew *bulldozes* a slum.

But not so fast. Twenty-one days after I began editing the *Times*, President Reagan was shot and I took his words from the hospital as the subordinate headline: "Honey, I forgot to duck but I'll make it." Numbers of readers swiftly denounced me for vulgarity. I kept watch for Disgusted, Tunbridge Wells,[1] waiting in the foyer with a horsewhip. David Marsh, the guard of *Guardian* style, says they are slammed today (2015) for "ugly Americanisms" such as *pony up, kindergarten mojo, sledding, duke it out, brownstones, suck*. "I am not anti-American," writes a reader typical of the nativists, "but I do not see why our language should be corrupted by sloppy writing which is quite meaningless to me." I will take flak for the *Guardian* on the pungent relevance of American nouns and verbs. Give me a single word for a sycophant who always echoes his master's voice. *Yes-man*. Instead of saying, "Sorry we're late but drivers ahead of us slowed us down when they craned their necks to look at a crash," you can say, "We were delayed by *rubberneckers*." Five words instead of twenty-one.

Words pop in and out of our language as life changes. The American *gangster* has been around as a noun and a

---

[1] "Stuffy, reactionary image" was associated with Tunbridge Wells by the novelist E. M. Forster in his 1908 *A Room with a View*, where he makes the character Lucy Bartlett say, "I am used to Tunbridge Wells, where we are all hopelessly behind the times."

reality since 1896 according to my *Shorter Oxford*, but after 1930 the dictionary omitted another Americanism until it had to be revived in the financial crash of the twenty-first century. The word is *bankster*, its genealogy a marriage of *banker* and *gangster*, introduced into the Democratic primaries in 2016 by the "democratic socialist" Bernie Sanders to whip Hillary Clinton for her association with the demons of capitalism. Bernie did not acknowledge his word debt to its coiner, a fiery Sicilian-born lawyer by the name of Ferdinand Pecora. He was the chief counsel to the U.S. Senate Committee on Banking set up in the early 1930s to probe the origins of the Crash of 1929. He exposed quite a lot of the Wall Street practices that Harvard's Professor William Z. Ripley had condemned in 1928. The believable Ripley called them out for — get ready for these Americanisms — "prestidigitation, double-shuffling, honey-fugling, hornswoggling and skullduggery."

The greatest smuggler of new words, of course, was William Shakespeare, the snapper-up of unconsidered trifles. *Oxford English Dictionary* researchers credited him with inventing as many as two thousand words and phrases, because they could find no currency in them before they appeared in print and voice in Shakespeare plays and sonnets. Zapped-up digital search engines are finding earlier users of many of Shakespeare's "new" words, but the fact remains that many words might have vanished into thin air if they had not been committed to our lexicon by Shakespeare — and two of the phrases I have used are, according to the best authorities, among the many freshly coined by him ("snapper up of unconsidered trifles" in *A*

Winter's Tale, "into thin air" in *The Tempest*). How inventive Shakespeare was is neither here nor there, since his uniqueness lies in the way he put the words together as a mirror of man's nature. James Shapiro, a Shakespeare scholar at Columbia, asks us to bear in mind the six words anybody else could have written but didn't: *to be or not to be.* Shakespeare's way with words was awkward, though, for the novelist Hilary Mantel when she was portraying the conversations of Chancellor Thomas Cromwell with Anne Boleyn and Henry VIII in her two prizewinning historical novels, *Wolf Hall* and *Bring Up the Bodies.* I asked her about the difficulty of putting words in their mouths when some of the words and phrases seem generally not to have been current in Tudor England: Shakespeare was not even born until twenty-five years after the death of King Henry VIII.

"It is a major problem," she e-mailed, "and I've tried to keep to what they could have said, but I am more bothered about keeping within the terms of what they could have thought, and making sure their metaphors and mental images are consistent with the world view of the time. I think you have to prefer clarity to strict accuracy, if it comes to a clash between the two; but I try to keep the peace."

She added: "Sometimes you wonder where the good words have gone. The other week I was at the Inner Temple library looking at an early book by John Elyot, Thomas Cromwell's contemporary—in his foreword he says he is *fatigate* by his labors. The extra syllable gives it an exhausting weight, as if he were puffing and staggering."

Shakespeare would probably not have minded anachronism slipping into *Wolf Hall.* He had Cleopatra playing billiards and Brutus hearing a clock strike three four hundred years before there was any clock to strike anything. The play's the thing.

Take my word for it

Rescuing good words we already have is fatiguing enough to demand the stamina of Sisyphus. Scores of critics have indicted the serial killers of *disinterested,* whose meaning is not "bored or uninterested," but "impartial or unselfish." But when we read, as we still do, that "the arbitrator said he would be disinterested in the dispute," what are we to understand? It should mean he will stay interested but neutral. To most of us, it will. But to some—and perhaps to a reader even now, shriek!—it means the arbitrator is bored with the dispute and will take no further interest.

I am an advocate (noun) who advocates (verb) a protection program for good words. On the way to plead in defense of a cause or person—its true meaning—*advocate* is commonly burdened with the periphrastic preposition, *for.* I was alarmed on February 17, 2017, to find that the defenses of conciseness and good order had been breached even at the fluff-resistant *Wall Street Journal.* Five redundancies in a short space: "without advocacy *for* a candidate...advocating *for* a candidate...donors are advocating *for* unpopular causes....Political advocacy *for or against* candidates can be regulated..."

The "for or against" phrase advertises the confusion and adds more fluff. It reminds one of the political fallout from

John Kerry's statement that he voted for the $87 billion for the Iraq War before he voted against it; while accurate at the time of each declaration, it exposed him to ridicule in the 2004 presidential election.

May a similar fate befall abusers of *advocacy*.

Think Portia (proper noun) and her advocacy (noun) of mercy for Antonio. John (14:16) has Jesus comforting His disciples. "And I will ask the Father, and He will give you another advocate to help and be with you forever."

Think of the phrase "the devil's advocate" for someone who argues against a proposition as an intellectual exercise. *Advocatus diaboli* is an official position in the Roman Catholic Church, the person assigned the duty of testing the evidence for beatification and sainthood. Did the nominee really live the holy life as argued by God's advocate, *advocatus Dei*, and has that been confirmed by miracles from divine intercession in the nominee's name five years after the nominee's death? Christopher Hitchens was asked to be the devil's advocate against the beatification of Mother Teresa of Calcutta in 2003. He said it was "like representing the devil pro bono."

A GOOD-WORD GLOSSARY

I freely acknowledge that in a word list of this sort, *glossary* is a fancy Latin word for a collection of pet peeves (noun, 1919), meaning an annoyance or irritation, one of which is that *peeve* as a noun originating in America had not been admitted into the *Shorter Oxford English Dictionary* on my desk in London (1968) when I edited the *Sunday Times*. Now it is recognized ("back-formation from peevish"). I admit I have no evidence for believing that the neglect of *peeve* is to blame for angering the poltergeist Peeves in the Hogwarts School of Witchcraft and Wizardry.

Admit/Acknowledge: *Admit* is freighted with bias; it implies the reluctant admission of guilt. Used often by a writer afflicted with monologophobia who is desperate not to repeat the proper neutral word *said* or *acknowledge*.

Affect/Effect: You can only affect something that already exists. When it does, you can effect, or bring about, a change in it. To say "it effected a change in his attitude" is correct; so is "it affected his attitude." To combine the two — "It affected a change in his attitude" — is silly.

Alibi: Means "proof that one was elsewhere" but is confused with *excuse,* which is a wider generality. Let's save *alibi* for the precision of proving you were not within a mile of the kitchen when the last slice of apple pie vanished.

Alternatives: Wrongly used for *choices.* If there are two choices, they are properly called alternatives. If there are more than two, they are choices. But in 2017 the tides of the expedient post-truth era sapped centuries of definition. Kellyanne Conway, a counselor to President Trump, explained to NBC's Chuck Todd that press secretary Sean Spicer's series of falsehoods inflating the crowds at the Trump inauguration weren't lies; they were "alternative facts." Spicer was a proud defender of the currency of the "alt-right": never let a real fact stand in the way of ideology.

Anticipate: Confused with *expect*. To expect something is to think it may happen; to anticipate is to prepare for it, to act in advance. To say a fiancée expects marriage is correct; to say she is anticipating marriage defames the lady.

Anxious: Best preserved as meaning "troubled, uneasy." It is a corruption to use it as a synonym for *eager* or *desirous*.

Appraise/Apprise: Experts appraise the value and then apprise you of the results.

Avenge: The infliction on an offender of something more or less equal to the offense. The subject of the active verb *revenge* is ordinarily the wronged party.

Blatant/Flagrant: Best use *blatant* for offense that is glaringly obvious, without care, brazen. Best use *flagrant* to emphasize serious breach of law or regulation.

Breach/Breech: *Breach* is to break through or break a promise or rule. But *breech*, with an *e*, means "buttocks."

Categorical: We've lost precision by the sloppy common use of this adjective as meaning the same as *unequivocal, no hedging.* "I did not have sexual relations with that woman" is not a categorical denial. It's the denial of a single accusation. A suspect faced with ten categories of wrongdoing may unequivocally reject three of the charges and admit and accept seven. But a "categorical denial" has come to mean a denial of all the charges. Blame Aristotle for classifying predicaments in ten categories.

Causal: Perhaps the hardest word to get into print—everybody thinks it ought to be *casual*. It means "relating to a cause," and is often used in philosophical or medical contexts.

Celebrant: Confused with *celebrator*. A celebrant presides over a religious rite.

Chronic: Confused with *acute* or *severe*, medically the opposite. It means "long-lasting" (from the Greek *chronos*, "time"). An acute illness comes to a crisis; a chronic one lingers.

Cohort: Useful word to signify a company of the like-minded, deriving from Roman military unit of three hundred to six hundred soldiers, a tenth part of a legion. Pity it got corrupted by American usage (1952) as a singular with negative implications, as in "henchman, accomplice, abettor."

"His cohort was held in solitary confinement" is a nonsensical contradiction.

Complaisant/Complacent: The complaisant person is pleasant, eager to please, compliant. The complacent person is smug, satisfied just going through the motions of work.

Compliment/Complement: You are entitled to a compliment—applause or praise—if you don't mix it up with *complement,* meaning "complete or full." If you are *comped,* it means you are given free admission as a form of compliment. You will then make a full complement of freeloaders.

Compose/Comprise: *Compose* means "to form" or "constitute." *Comprise* means "to contain, include, be made up of." The whole comprises the parts. The United States comprises fifty states; fifty states do not comprise the United States. After the 2014 referendum on independence for Scotland, the United Kingdom still comprised England, Scotland, Northern Ireland, and Wales.

Contagion: You by yourself can have an infection. You can't by yourself have a contagion. That's when a disease, idea, or emotion has touched many. A contagious disease is spread by person-to-person contact.

Continual/Continuous: "Continual interruptions" says it all, meaning the speaker resumed his argument after the interruption. The speech was not continuous, as a river is, because the flow was broken.

Cosseting/Cozening: To be cosseted is to be petted or pampered. To be cozened, on the other hand, is to be cheated or defrauded.

Credible/Credulous: A credible man is one you can believe; a credulous man, however, is too ready to believe others.

Crescendo: Confused with *climax*. It indicates a passage of music to be played with increasing volume. Figuratively, it means "to rise to a climax." Thus the cliché "rise to a crescendo" is nonsense.

Decimate: Confused with *destroy*. By derivation, *decimation* means "killing one in ten." Today it is often used figuratively to mean "very heavy casualties," but to say "completely decimated" or "decimated as much as half the town" simply will not do.

Dependant/Dependent: A dependant is a person who is dependent on another for support.

Deprecate/Depreciate: An MP was erroneously reported as *depreciating* sterling as a world currency. Mighty powerful MP. That means he had it devalued, which is the job of the governor of the Bank of England. What the MP actually did was *deprecate* sterling as a world currency, i.e., plead against the policy.

Dilemma: Confused with *problem*. If you have a problem, you do not know what to do. There may be many solutions. If you have a dilemma, you have a choice of two courses of action, neither attractive.

Disabled: Clarity, accuracy, and decency demand the utmost care. Unless it is relevant, it's offensive to identify someone with physical or mental differences as disabled or handicapped. When it really is relevant and properly sourced, be specific and don't condescend: "He uses a wheelchair," not "He's *confined* to a wheelchair"; "She *has* Asperger's syndrome," not "She *suffers* from Asperger's." *The Associated Press Stylebook* has an admirable guide. On mental illness, see http://www.nimh.nih.gov/index.shtml.

Discomfit/Discomfort: To *discomfort* is to make uneasy; to *discomfit* is to defeat or rout. *Discomfort* is either verb or noun; the noun of *discomfit* is *discomfiture*.

Discreet/Discrete: Ambassadors are expected to be discreet, to exercise discretion. *Discrete* means "separate, distinct."

Disinterested/Uninterested: If you're in some messy dispute, you don't want an uninterested arbiter, judge, or mediator, so uninterested he nods off. You don't want an arbiter who has a selfish interest, declared or concealed. You want a neutral, disinterested person who cares enough for truth.

Enervate/Energize: To *energize* is to invigorate; to *enervate* is to weaken. The *New York Times* did the British tycoon Mr. Arnold Weinstock an injustice: "Two years later after a power struggle at the top, Mr. Weinstock emerged as managing director at the age of 38. He then enervated his company with his now-familiar technique."

Entomb: Confused with *trap*. The trapped miners may be alive; entombed miners are dead, i.e., in a tomb.

ERISA/Eristic: A lot of argument about ERISA, the acronym for the Employee Retirement Income Security Act. *Eristic* means argumentative. Eris happens to be the Greek mythological goddess of discord and argument, much favored by the great critic and debater William F. Buckley. He adopted Eris as his own. The *advocatus diaboli* was wont to say Buckley was clinging to the *flotsam* from a Greek shipwreck.

Execution: Noun without a brain when used to describe the taking of life not sanctioned under law by judicial sentence of capital punishment. Any of us can execute an administrative task or chore, but not a person.

Exotic: Means "of foreign origin" and only by weak analogy "glamorous" or "colorful."

Explicit/Implicit: They mean the opposite. An explicit understanding has been expressed. An implicit understanding has been left implied, not expressly stated.

Flaunt/Flout: "We must not allow the American Constitution to be flaunted in this way" means we must not allow it to be paraded, displayed, or shown off. That is the meaning of *to flaunt*. What the speaker intended to say was that the Constitution should not be *flouted*, i.e., "mocked" or "insulted."

Flotsam/Jetsam: Married in common parlance, but divorced in maritime law. *Jetsam* is stuff *jettisoned*, thrown overboard, by the crew of a ship to lighten the load in stormy seas. If you find stuff like this, it's yours. *Flotsam* is cargo or wreckage floating in the sea. Flotsam is legally the property of the vessel's owner.

Forego/Forgo: *Forego* means "to go before in time or place"—think of the final *e* in *before*. To *forgo* is to give up or relinquish.

Fortitudinous: Forget *fortunate*, this is the word for "brave, having fortitude."

Fortuitous/Fortunate: *Fortuitous* is by chance, unexpected, accidental, and the chance was not necessarily welcome. "And this poor girl had by a fortuitous mishap overheard the discussion of the guilty secret."—Baroness Orczy, *The Laughing Cavalier*. Usage has associated the word with *fortune* and *fortunate* and conferred the meaning *lucky* on the chance, but some of us think the original meaning worth preserving.

Fulsome: Confused with *full*. *Fulsome* means "overfull, extravagant to the point of insincerity." To say "He gave her fulsome praise" is to make a comment on its merits.

Further/Farther: Keep *farther* for distances — thus far and no farther — and *further* for additions (furthermore).

Gaff/Guff/Gaffe/Gaffer: *Gaff* is talk; *guff* is loose, empty, boastful talk; and a *gaffe*, meaning an indiscretion or blunder, is their errant cousin. "To blow the gaff" is to divulge a secret, an indiscretion that qualifies as a *gaffe*. Giddy enough? Since the mid-nineteenth century, *gaffer* has meant a foreperson, a boss of laborers, but in the twentieth century, American usage is for the chief electrician on a movie set.

Gourmet/Gourmand: The gourmet, one with a refined, discriminating taste for the best food and wine, will be insulted to be called a gourmand, a glutton fond of good things. Realtors boast of gourmet kitchens, meaning equipped with marble tops and all the paraphernalia down to a copper poaching pan.

Guesstimate: Trick word to suggest that there is an element of calculation in your guess. Say *guess* or say *estimate* and win a cigar for honesty.

Iconic/Ironic: It is ironic that the word *icon*, which began its linguistic life as a sacred image and came to mean a representation of a model of virtue, is now so often downgraded to pick-any-adjective status. David Marsh, the style editor of the *Guardian,* is valiant in defense of the true meaning, steamed up enough to scoff at his own newspaper's misdemeanor: "A single issue I chose at random featured eight icons before breakfast: the Routemaster bus, the Lloyd's building, Blackpool, Sainsbury's, Marge Simpson, Voldemort, Shelley, and 'several iconic buildings.' "

Igneous/Ingenious: It's a howler to describe a clever, inventive person or idea as igneous. That's a rock formed by fire; volcanic igneous rocks form when lava cools and solidifies on the earth, and plutonic rocks (not platonic) form when the molten rock, called magma, solidifies below the earth.

Immigrant: In Britain it was for years a euphemism for a person of color. It should be rescued for what it is—

anyone from abroad who has come to settle. It is not the same, either, as *alien*. An immigrant is a settler; an alien may be a visitor. See *Refugee/Migrant*.

Inchoate/Incoherent: *Inchoate* describes something not ready to be judged *incoherent*, or "lacking clarity." The inchoate idea or thing is embryonic, in the early stages of being formed.

Incumbent: As a noun, a current holder of an office; a "former" incumbent is nonsense. But when you hold an office, it is incumbent (adjective) on you to perform your duties.

Inflammable/Flammable: Danger in a word again. The prefix *in-* might suggest that something *inflammable* won't catch fire, that it is comparable to the absolutes *in*capable and *in*vulnerable. But it does catch fire as easily as anything flammable, because the two words mean the same. (The prefix *in-* in this case means *into*, not *non*.) Halloween costumes are notoriously flammable.

Insidious/Invidious: Both nasty, but *insidious* is evil by stealth; you don't know the worm is in the apple. The *invidious* utterance or person invites odium more openly.

Invaluable: Confused with *valueless*, which is the opposite. The invaluable stone cannot be priced because it has so much value it is priceless.

Inveigle: To beguile or persuade by deceit and trickery. Think Iago.

Involved: Overworked and misused. *Involved* is best preserved to mean "tangled, complicated." It should not replace verbs like *include, entail, implicate, affect, imply, engage*. We should say, "The scheme entails knocking down ten houses"; "Four hundred workers are engaged in the strike" or "Four hundred are on strike"; "So-and-so is implicated in the crime," and so on.

Irony: Irony attempts to illuminate a point by paradox or incongruity, to deadpan an absurd statement; it works best with a straight face. "Trump said he might like a governor [as vice president] so that should give Christie a boost. As many as 15 percent of New Jersey Republicans think he'd be a good choice." — Gail Collins, *New York Times* columnist.

"It is a delicious irony," writes the clever Hadley Freeman, "that in the world of American TV news, one populated by raging egotists and self-aggrandizers, the person who is generally cited as the most influential is Jon Stewart — a man so *uninterested* in his own celebrity, he often didn't bother to collect his 18 Emmys, preferring to stay at home with his family."

Judicial/Judicious: *Judicial* means "connected with a court of law"; *judicious* means "wise." Not all judicial decisions are judicious.

Key: Overworked as an adjective meaning "important, crucial, prime, main, chief"; see the number of *key*s in the White House report on the underwear bomber. More keys than locks.

Lay/Lie: Hens lay eggs; cunning people lay traps. Churchill liked to lay bricks. *Lay* is a transitive verb — it looks for an object (eggs, traps, bricks). The past tense is *laid*. Four mayors have laid down the burden of office. Some (sense alert) may have lied in office — meaning told untruths — but none of them *lied down* the burden. *Lie,* when meaning "to assume a recumbent position," is always intransitive. Much of the confusion is because the past tense of *lie* is *lay*. The correct forms are *lie-lay-lain; lay-laid-laid*. Prepositions can change meanings: lay over, lay up, lay off, lay on, lay in; lay down some wine, but don't lie down on the job.

Less/Fewer: *Less* is right for quantities—less coffee, less sugar. It means "a smaller amount." *Fewer* is right for comparing numbers—fewer people, fewer houses; *less dough* results in *fewer loaves*. Nobody would think of saying *fewer coffee, fewer sugar*, but every day somebody writes *less houses*.

Liberal: Use with care in lowercase. A liberal (adjective) portion is generous, ample; in politics, a liberal person tends to favor government intervention for social reform, equality of opportunity, and abolition of privilege. Used pejoratively as a term for intrusive government, lowering of moral standards.

Literally: Ridiculous arguments about this from people who defend umpteen nonsense statements. "We were literally flooded with books." "He literally went up in smoke." "He literally exploded in anger." *Literally* means "exactly, to the letter." To say "He literally went up in smoke" means he was burned, exploded, et cetera.

Litigate: Hear what happened in the court case to make Donald Trump release his tax returns? No? Neither did anyone. In January 2017, his counselor Kellyanne Conway told ABC why he would not keep the off-and-on promise: "We *litigated* this all through the election. People didn't care. They voted for him." Wrong verb. To litigate is to enter a lawsuit. Better verb for the serial flip-flopping: *dodged*.

Livid: Confused with *angry; livid* means "lead-colored," but some angry people are deathly pale.

Loan/Lend: *Loan* is the noun, *lend* the verb. The money-lender lends, and so gives you a loan.

Logorrhea/Logophile: The combination of *logos* (word) and *diarrhea* afflicting the incessant talker and those caught in the babble stream. A logophile just loves words.

Luxuriant/Luxurious: The film star can have a luxurious car that is "full of luxury," but not a luxuriant car. That would mean the car that is producing abundantly, growing profusely, since *luxuriant* refers to something that grows.

Martyr: Heinously corrupted for political propaganda. Properly, it is the sacrifice of one's life or well-being for a belief, a designation of honor close to saintliness: one's own life, not the lives of others. A suicide bomber may give his life for his belief but the imposition of random death on innocents precisely merits the noun *murderer* or *mass murderer.*

Minuscule: You are reading minuscule letters, the small letters we call lowercase, deriving from the lower easy-to-reach part of the printing case where the small lowercase letters of movable type were stored in compartments, one to each letter form. (If this sentence were in LARGE or CAPITAL letters, you would be reading majuscule, letter forms stored in the upper part of the printing case, hence uppercase.) The other meaning, "very small," is often misspelled *miniscule* because of the association with *mini.*

Mitigate/Militate: Verbs marching in different directions. *Mitigate* has nothing to do with anything military. From the Latin *mitigare,* "to soften," it means "to appease, to become less hostile." *Militate* means to carry weight or have effect.

Momentarily: You have to hope the pilot and stewards are lying when they say we will be in the air *momentarily.* That does not mean "We will be in the air in a few minutes." It means "We will be in the air for a moment." Strictly speaking, of course; but what is the point of having words if they mean nothing?

None: Means "not one" or "no one" or "not any." I've long preferred a singular verb, as in other distributive expressions such as *each, each one, everybody, everyone, many a man, nobody.* But *Webster's* and the *OED* suggest *none* followed by a plural noun should take a plural verb: "None of the soldiers were injured."

Oblivious: Confused with *ignorant of. Oblivious* is from the Latin *oblivium,* meaning "forgetfulness." If you are ignorant of something, nobody told you. If you are oblivious, somebody told you but you let it slip into oblivion.

Oral: An oral agreement is spoken, but *Black's Law Dictionary* stipulates that unwritten verbal agreements and oral contracts are "generally valid and legally binding as long as they are reasonable, equitable, conscionable and made in good faith...only a few types of contracts are required by statute to be written."

Pique/Peak/Peek: Three homophones with different meanings. Your interest in the great mountain can be piqued (aroused, intrigued). When you climbed to the peak of the mountain, you peeked over the edge. Happy day, but you may suffer pique, feel piqued (pissed) with a companion whose criticism of your cautious pace wounded your pride.

Prescribe/Proscribe: Opposite meanings. An action or product that is proscribed by authority is banned. A prescription is advised, recommended.

Principal/Principle: *Principal* means "the most important." The principal is a person first in rank or importance. It is also a capital sum that earns interest; less chance of going broke if you keep the principal. You can make the *principle,* "doctrine, law, or code of conduct," of preserving your *principal* a fundamental source of moral conviction, as opposed to your neighbor whose principal belief is that his obligation to pay interest amounts to usury.

Propinquity/Proximity: Both mean "near, in the vicinity of," but *propinquity* is more suggestive of affinity, relationship. Nothing propinks like propinquity (Ian Fleming, chapter title, *Diamonds Are Forever,* 1956; phrase popularized in the 1960s by U.S. diplomat George Ball).

Protagonist: Confused with *antagonist* and with *champion.* Literally, it means "the leading character in a drama"; it does not mean "advocate" or "champion." Somebody can be a protagonist without advocating anything. An antagonist is an active opponent.

Quota: It means "an allotted number," akin to rationing. To say New York had its full quota of rain means somebody was assigning various amounts of rain to New York.

Ravish: Scholars who wrote that the Great Recession "ravished" the economy did not mean working people and their tools had been carried off by force, raped, or enraptured. *Ravage,* "to destroy," is the word they sought.

Recrudescence/Resurgence: "There was a resurgence of loyalty" is right if there was a renewed rising of loyalty. To say "There was a recrudescence of loyalty" is to misuse a good metaphor. *Recrudescence* is also a renewal, but coming from the Latin *recrudescere*, "to become raw again," it should be used, figuratively, for disagreeable events.

Refugee/Migrant: War and terrorism in Iraq and Syria forced millions of people to flee and seek refuge in Turkey, Jordan, Egypt, and Western Europe, notably Germany. They were *refugees*, but they became *migrants*, unwelcome in countries that feared to admit them for security, religious, or economic reasons.

Refute: A strong verb, meaning "to disprove, to demonstrate falsehood." It has been emaciated by its careless confusion with *rebut, reply, response,* and, less forgivably, with *deny.* A denial is merely a contrary assertion; it does not demonstrate the falsity of the assertion. Nor does *rebut.* A rebuttal is a denial dressed up in battle armor.

Regalia: *Regal* means "of or by kings," and *regalia* means "the insignia of royalty." Royal regalia is therefore tautologous, and "the regalia of a bishop" is contradictory. Freemasons, however, have adopted the term for their insignia.

Reign/Rein: Reports that companies are "reigning in spending" should be taken with a grain of wet salt. The verb is *to rein in,* as one does pulling on the reins to slow or stop a horse. *To reign* means "to rule." It's a word for a sovereign or CEO autocrat. Reining in a runaway horse makes sense; reigning in a sovereign body does not. Whichever vassal (Old French, twelfth century, from medieval *vasallus,* "serf, humble servant, subordinate") wrote the press release at Bloomberg tried to ride both horses: "It is announced that Michael Bloomberg will take the reigns of his company on September 21, 2014."

Replica/Reproduction: Ask for your money back if you buy "a virtual replica" of the Eiffel Tower, the Parthenon, or any work of art. You may have bought a good reproduction, copy, duplicate, model, facsimile, but a replica is one re-created by the original creator, so there is no such thing as "a virtual replica." It either is or isn't. James Kilpatrick, who manned the barricades to defend the integrity of *replica,* was cross, with reason, that the respected *Smithsonian* magazine offered "an almost incredibly authentic replica of the *Titanic*—a replica that measured 3 inches in length." At a cooking show, the French brought a three-and-a-half-foot "replica" of the Eiffel Tower made out of glazed uncooked pasta.

Skeptic/Denier: The skeptic questions the evidence; the denier flatly rejects it.

Stationary/Stationery: *Stationary,* adjective, is static; *stationery,* noun, is writing material.

Supine/Prone: *Supine* is lying faceup, a synonym for *spineless, ineffective, indolent. Prone* is lying facedown or vulner-

able and naturally inclined to some negative quality—
accident-prone, anger-prone.

Synthetic: Not a synonym for *false,* as in "a synthetic
excuse." It means "placed together," from the Greek *syn,*
"together," and *tithemi,* "to place." Think of synthetic
rubber, made by placing its constituents together rather
than by extraction from a plant.

Terrorism: The use of threats or violence to intimidate or
coerce, especially for political purposes.

Titivate/Titillate: To titivate is to adorn or smarten. The
seducer may do that to himself, but he will seek to titillate
the victim—to excite pleasantly.

Transpire: Wrongly used to mean, merely, "happen." It comes
from the Latin *spirare,* "breathe." To transpire is to emit
through the surface of leaves or skin and, figuratively, is best
used for when some fact oozes out, especially a secret.

Urban/Urbane: *Urban* means "of a city"; *urbane* means
"courteous, suave." Not all people in urban areas are
urbane.

Uxorious/Luxurious: The rental agency meant to say the
seafront apartment was luxurious, but advertised it as
uxorious. That's a word for a husband's doting devotion
to his wife, a characteristic surely beyond reproach.

Viable/Feasible: *Viable* means "capable of independent
life"—a viable fetus or seed or, figuratively, in the sense of
"capable of succeeding," candidate. *Feasible* means "capable of being done, accomplished"—a feasible plan.

Vice: It would be a pity if it became a synonym for *sex*. There
are many vices. It should be used as the opposite of
virtue—unless you happen to admire the website *Vice.*

Viral: Unwelcome adjective as related to Ebola, Zika, and other nasty viruses. Much desired by websites in the Internet age (since 1999); an item "gone viral" has been passed person to person so many times as to seem contagious.

Virtually: Incorrectly used to mean "nearly all"; e.g., "Virtually all the chocolates were eaten." *Virtually* is useful for an imprecise description that is more or less right, close enough, as good as. "He's virtually the manager." He does not have the title but he manages the business.

While: It can have a temporal meaning to indicate two things were going on at the same time: "While he was embracing her, the husband arrived with her mother." It makes no sense to say that the 2:00 p.m. train will run on time while the 3:00 p.m. train will be delayed. The nontemporal *while* can be a balancing conjunction. "While seeing your point, I cannot agree that Latin is a dead language." Sir Alan Herbert exposes the absurdity: "The curate read the first lesson while the rector read the second."

Wither/Whither: Lenin said that when Communism was reached, the state would wither away. *Whither,* with the *h,* is a directional word, as in FDR's emissary Harry Hopkins telling Churchill the U.S. would support Britain when it stood alone against Hitler. "Whither thou goest, there will I." Wartime Britain cherished that moment, as we should cherish* every good word.

---

* "cherish (v.) early 14c., *cherischen,* from Old French *cheriss-,* present participle stem of *chierir* 'to hold dear' (12c., Modern French *chérir*), from *chier* 'dear,' from Latin *carus* 'dear, costly, beloved' (see *whore*). The Latin word is also the source of Italian, Spanish, Portuguese *caro;* Old Provençal, Catalan *car.* Related: *Cherished; cherishing.*" *Online Etymology Dictionary,* www.etymonline.com/

8

Storytelling: The Long and Short of It

"I can't decide. I'm having a brand identity crisis."

Two years before he shot himself, in 1960, Ernest Hemingway told George Plimpton of the *Paris Review* that he wrote the last page of *Farewell to Arms* thirty-nine times[1] before he "got

---

[1] Ernest Hemingway, "The Art of Fiction No. 21," *Paris Review,* https://www
.theparisreview.org/interviews/4825/ernest-hemingway-the-art-of-fiction

the words right." His grandson Sean Hemingway discovered forty-seven endings for a new edition in 2012.[2] It's the beginnings that give most writers trouble. There may even now be a writer trying for the nth time to write the opening of a story that seems to him a cross between *War and Peace* and *My Fair Lady*.

On June 28, 1914, in Sarajevo, a terrorist from expansionist Serbia shot dead the heir to the throne of the Austro-Hungarian Empire. Most of the crowned heads of Europe were related. In May, they were mourners at the funeral of England's Edward VII. By August 4, they were at war with each other in World War I. Barbara Tuchman begins her history *The Guns of August* with the royal funeral. I am told she wrote her introduction eighteen times; we are rewarded by her effort:

> So gorgeous was the spectacle on the May morning of 1910 when nine kings rode in the funeral of Edward VII of England that the crowd, waiting in hushed and black-clad awe, could not keep back gasps of admiration. In scarlet and blue and green and purple, three by three the sovereigns rode through the palace gates, with plumed helmets, gold braid, crimson sashes, and jeweled orders flashing in the sun. After them came five heirs apparent, forty more imperial or royal highnesses, seven queens—four dowager and three regnant—and a scattering of special ambassadors from uncrowned countries. Together they represented seventy nations in the greatest assemblage of royalty and rank ever gathered in one place and, of its kind, the last. The

---

[2] http://www.telegraph.co.uk/culture/books/booknews/9378446/Ernest -Hemingway-wrote-47-endings-to-A-Farewell-To-Arms.html

muffled tongue of Big Ben tolled nine by the clock as the cortege left the palace, but on history's clock it was sunset, and the sun of the old world was setting in a dying blaze of splendor never to be seen again.

The adjectives dazzle but in the orderly grandeur of a procession: hushed and black-clad awe in scarlet and blue and green and purple, plumed helmets, gold braid, crimson sashes, jeweled orders flashing in the sun, the muffled tongue... and then the mordant metaphor of history's clock, the world the guns are already primed to destroy.

James Bramhall was a British paratrooper who landed in France on D-Day, finding his way in treacherous territory.[3] The staccato style reflects the tension:

A dog barked at my approach. From the corner of my eye I could see a stealthy figure flit from behind a haystack into the shadow of the barn. There was no answer to my first knock. The household was obviously fast asleep. I knocked louder, and this time I heard a scurrying on the stairs and a sudden clamor of French voices. Footsteps approached the door, withdrew, hesitated. Then approached again. The door opened.

The suspense is maintained to the last three words. What next? The "stealthy figure" in uniform, this time with a Luger?

Opening sentences in journalism, company reports, appeals, protests, letters, and e-mails have to be as succinct as the British paratrooper. Newsprint rationing in wartime

---

[3] John Carey, ed., *Eyewitness to History* (New York: William Morrow, 1987).

Britain enforced economy in language, a conciseness not required in American print journalism, where acres of space invited gentle grazing; broadcast speech more reflected the speed of the society. Cyberspace is indulgent, but attention spans are shorter. We appreciate conciseness. An old rule was that an introductory sentence or paragraph should answer the questions Who? What? Why? Where? When? They have to be answered, but not in the lead, which demands a short, sharp sentence carrying a maximum of impact with a minimum of phrase. James Thurber rebelled:

> Dead. That's what the man was when he was picked up.

The practical aim in news and report writing is somewhere between Thurber's cannonball and these epigrammatic essays:

> Wilson lighted a cigarette while bathing his feet in benzene. He may live.

> The first time 53-year-old Sidney Anderson was seen drunk was the last time he was seen alive.

This crisp paragraph is by the star reporter Michael Daly of the *Daily Beast* website:

> Forget the 26-year-old zero who murdered 10 innocents at Umpqua Community College on Thursday morning. The one to remember is 30-year-old Chris Mintz, the student and Army vet who was shot at least five times while charging straight at the gunman in an effort to save others. Mintz did that on the sixth birthday of his son, Tyrik. "It's

my son's birthday, it's my son's birthday," he was heard saying as he lay wounded.

The cheat sheet of the *Daily Beast,* with twenty-five million unique monthly visitors, is highly valued. The editors make every syllable count. Here are some examples of the editors' work to save the reader's time and temper:

Arkansas Girl Safe After Murders

A 12-year-old Arkansas girl who went missing after the couple she was living with were found dead has been returned to safety, police said. Amber Whitlow was found in Memphis with brother Antonio Whitlow, who is now a suspect in her abduction. Memphis police said the 33-year-old man is also a suspect in the killing of two people in Little Rock with whom Amber Whitlow was living. The deceased couple was discovered in their home Saturday. Law-enforcement officials have declined to release the names of the couple, but a police official said that they were either the parents or grandparents of the young girl.	"who went" redundant "police said": needless attribution Redundancy Repetition "official" redundant

My edit saves thirty-four words:

A 12-year-old Arkansas girl missing from a house where two bodies were found has been returned to safety. Amber Whitlow was in Memphis, Tennessee, with her 33-year-old brother Antonio, who is now a suspect in her abduction. He is also a suspect in the killing of the couple with whom she was living. Law enforcement officials won't release their names but say they were either Amber's parents or grandparents.

Gangster movie

The story is 113 words. Can you condense to under 100 words?

The shoot-'em-up tough-guy flick *Gangster Squad* is due to be reshot and re-edited after a sequence in the film drew comparisons to the shooting in Aurora, Colorado. The film, which stars Sean Penn, Ryan Gosling, and Emma Stone, was due to be released in theaters in September. But now the tale of 1940s Los Angeles wise guys has had its debut pushed back to January. The film's original climax was a scene in which Tommy-gun-toting gangsters emerged from behind a movie theater screen, firing into the civilian crowd. The scene is said to have been key to the plot of the film, and substantial reworking of the movie may be in order.

Wasteful expressions in italics:

The shoot-'em-up tough-guy flick *Gangster Squad* is *due to be* reshot and re-edited *after a sequence in the film drew comparisons* to *the shooting* in Aurora, Colorado. *The film, which* stars Sean Penn, Ryan Gosling, and Emma Stone, *was due to be released in theaters in September. But now the tale of* 1940s Los Angeles wise guys *has had its debut pushed back to January.* The film's original climax *was a scene in which* Tommy-gun-toting gangsters emerged from behind a movie theater screen, firing into the *civilian* crowd. *The scene is said to have been key to the plot of the film, and substantial reworking of the movie may be in order.*

Two thirds the length:

The shoot-'em-up tough-guy flick *Gangster Squad,* due for release in September, will be reshot and re-edited because it has a sequence similar to the Mad Joker murders in Aurora, Colorado. Starring Sean Penn, Ryan Gosling, and Emma Stone, about 1940s Los Angeles wise guys, the film was to climax when gangsters toting Tommy guns emerge from behind a movie theater screen and fire into the crowd. (Only 66 words)

"Mad Joker murders" the best identifier of the peculiar horror of the massacre.

"Tommy-gun-toting gangsters" replaced with simpler "gangsters toting Tommy guns."

"In which" wordy.

"Civilian" crowd—what else? Would have been worth saying if the audience was unusual—military, religious, whatever.

Ebola

The following paragraph is 112 words. Try editing or writing to fewer than 100 words.

A sudden outbreak of the deadly Ebola virus has killed 13 people in Uganda, according to the World Health Organization. The fatality rate for the virus is close to 90 percent, and there is no known cure. "There are a total of 20 people suspected to have contracted Ebola, and 13 of them have died," said WHO representative Joaquim Saweka. Though an outbreak has been suspected since early in July, the cases were not verified until Friday. The cause for the sudden outbreak of the disease, which is spread by close contact between victims, has not yet been determined, Saweka said, and experts from the U.S. and WHO are investigating, he said.

Here it is again, with wasteful words in italics.

A sudden outbreak of the deadly Ebola virus has killed 13 people in Uganda, according to the World Health Organization. The fatality rate for the virus is close to 90 percent, and there is no known cure. *"There are a total of 20 people suspected to have contracted Ebola, and 13 of them have died,"* said WHO representative Joaquim Saweka. *Though an outbreak has been suspected since early in July, the cases were not verified until Friday.* The cause *for the sudden outbreak of the disease,* which is spread by close contact between victims, *has not yet been determined,*

Saweka said, and experts from the U.S. and WHO are investigating, *he said.*

The report includes wasteful repetition—"Saweka said," "he said"; "sudden outbreak of the disease." "Sudden" is redundant—"outbreak" tells us that. Here is a version, half the length of the original, that includes all the facts:

The deadly Ebola virus is confirmed as the reason 20 people in Uganda fell sick in July. Thirteen have died, reports Joaquim Saweka of the World Health Organization. The virus kills 90 percent of people infected; no cure is known. Experts from the U.S. and WHO are investigating the origin of the outbreak.

EXERCISES IN CHOICE OF STYLE

Storytelling

The emphasis in all those examples is being "fustest with the mostest," a useful phrase whether or not General Nathan Bedford Forrest ever said it during the Civil War. But in journalism there is a case for being *slowest with the bestest,* when the information is dramatized but narrative prevails. "How I Escaped from the Dreaded Wonga Tribesmen" says the title or headline, and the story begins with the day the writer caught the boat train, then goes step by step to its stirring conclusion. The emphasis is not on what happened but on how it happened.

For most journalism, storytelling is too slow a technique. It is exasperating to the reader who wants to find out what happened. But storytelling has its uses even on news sites. Storytelling provides a change of pace.

The narrative or storytelling style of news reports has validity on a number of occasions:

1. When a narrative can be used as an adjunct to a main news story, rather like zooming from a general scene to a detail.

2. When a story is so familiar from other media that the readers/viewers know the result, but would now be intrigued by detail and drama.

3. On the second, third, and fourth days of developing stories; for instance, once the news of the massacre in Paris or San Bernardino has been reported, there is ample scope for picking up individual stories and telling them in narrative style. What happened hour by hour, for instance, to the SWAT team. A day in the life of one of the teachers. And so on.

The varying styles can be demonstrated by recasting a story in two forms. On the left is a straight news story of a student disappointed by a beauty treatment. As a crime story, it is small beer. But told as a human-interest story it would have more appeal. The version on the right is the story in narrative style. It is more engaging, and saves 24 percent of the space.

News Style	Narrative Style
Authorities yesterday shut down the illicit medical practice of a Queens woman — dubbed Madame Olga — who allegedly disfigured a college	Izadeli Montalvo, a student at St. John's University in Queens, worried when she was told she looked 35. She is only 22.

News Style	Narrative Style
student by giving her illegal injections designed to prevent wrinkles, prosecutors said.	Izadeli put such faith in the woman who gave her the bad news, beauty specialist Olga Ramirez, 34, that last December she paid $600 for three injections she was assured would make her look more youthful and prevent wrinkles.
Olga Ramirez, 34, was charged with practicing medicine without a license, assault, reckless endangerment and possession of hypodermic needles, Queens District Attorney Richard Brown said.	It was a disaster. Izadeli's face swelled up painfully time and again over four months. She suffered a severed facial nerve that may require surgery to repair, according to her lawyer, Mason Pimsler.
"I am very upset," said Izadeli Montalvo, 22, of Queens, who charged she has suffered recurring facial swelling since receiving the injections four months ago.	
"I don't know what the future consequences of this will be," the St. John's University student said. "I am already suffering."	The trouble was that Ramirez — professionally known as Madame Olga — was licensed by the state only as an esthetician to do makeup work and suggest over-the-counter medicines. She was not qualified to prescribe or administer drugs — or use the title "Dr." as she did on her business card.
For at least four years, Ramirez worked out of her College Point home, where investigators seized hundreds of needles, containers of medicines and a small amount of hormones, authorities said.	

News Style	Narrative Style
Ramirez, who had business cards claiming the title doctor, "operated for some time with reckless disregard for the people who turned to her for help," Brown said.	So yesterday the Queens District Attorney, Richard Brown, shut down Madame Olga's illicit medical practice and accused her of practicing medicine without a license.
Ramirez was charged with assault for giving injections to Montalvo, who told the *Daily News* she went for a consultation with Madame Olga in December and was informed she looked 35.	"She operated with reckless disregard for the people who turned to her for help," said Brown. He alleged Montalvo was temporarily disfigured.
She said she paid $600 for three injections, which Ramirez promised would make her skin look more youthful and prevent wrinkles.	Investigators at Madame Olga's home in College Point, her workplace for four years, seized hundreds of hypodermic needles, containers of medicines bearing the names "biopolymer" and "biopolymere," and a small amount of hormones. They are not sure what was in the injections given to Izadeli, but suspect it may have been a collagenlike substance.
Instead, Montalvo said, she was left with swelling and numbness in her face. "It was very painful. It was a very bad experience," she said.	
Brown said Montalvo was temporarily disfigured by the treatment. Her lawyer, Mason	"All I know," said Izadeli, "is that I am very upset. It was a bad experience." (262 words)

News Style	Narrative Style
Pimsler, said she suffered a severed facial nerve that may require surgery to repair.	
Investigators are not yet sure what the injections contained, but suspect it may have been a collagenlike substance. They seized bottles bearing the names "biopolymer" and "biopolymere," authorities said.	
Ramirez is licensed by the state as an esthetician, enabling her to do makeup work and apply over-the-counter medicines, but not to prescribe or administer drugs, authorities said. (323 words)	

Kim Philby Treachery

A long report on the escape by the conspirators of Kim Philby, the Soviet agent who headed Britain's anti-Soviet intelligence agency, sustained interest with the device in long-form journalism known as "a taster" — a hint of something good to come. It is a kind of trailer, a come-on to the reader confronted with a lot of words. Where you are editing a very long feature report, say two thousand words or more, you should see that the structure accommodates early appetizers of some of the good things developed later in the narrative. My comments are on the right.

At 9:30 a.m. on his last day in England, May 25, 1951, Donald Maclean was walking decorously from Charing Cross station to his room in the Foreign Office. Guy Burgess, never a devotee of early rising, had only just got out of bed in his New Bond Street flat by Aspreys. He was reading the *Times* and drinking tea made by his friend Jack Hewit. Everything was relaxed and unhurried.	Opening with a dramatic human highlight. It is out of sequence in the article but essential to capture interest.
By 10:30 everything had changed irrevocably. Burgess, warned through Kim Philby in Washington that Donald Maclean was about to be interrogated, made a vital decision. By that evening Maclean had gone, in a cloud of mystery— and Burgess had gone with him.	
But for Burgess's excited and unnecessary flight, things might have been very different	Recapitulation. Early presentation of an important conclusion.

for Kim Philby. Conceivably, the most remarkable Soviet spy ever to penetrate the Western intelligence community might have remained undetected for another ten years. Certainly it is now clear that it was only his fortuitous double link—with both Burgess and Maclean—which turned suspicion on him.

Had the cool, untrusting Philby been finally betrayed in 1951 by the bonds of Burgess's impulsive friendship, it would have been an ironic finale. But the damage Burgess did to him was more than compensated by the inflexible loyalty of his friends in the Secret Intelligence Service. Insight's inquiries have now established in detail that Philby, publicly sacked from the Foreign Service in 1951, was in fact secretly employed by the SIS—even during the shadowy period before he became an *Observer* foreign

correspondent at the request
of the Foreign Office.

Feelings about Kim Philby
vary sharply among his old
colleagues in the British Secret
Intelligence Service. Some
preserve a degree of affection
and ruminate upon the "misplaced idealism" which led
him to work for the Russians.
Some see his career largely as
a technical feat. "He was an
agent who really lived his
cover," they say.

Others take a more impas-
sioned view, like the man
who said to us: "Philby was a
copper-bottomed bastard, and
he killed a lot of people."

Espionage and counter-
espionage can seem so much
like civilized office games that
the blood can get forgotten.
But in this account of Philby's
career from 1945 to 1951 there
are two crucial episodes which
luridly illuminate the realities
of the game.

The first case is a man alone: a Soviet intelligence officer caught in the act of trying to defect to the West. That story ends with a bandaged figure being hustled aboard a Russian plane in Istanbul.	Taster No. 1. Will be told in detail later.
In the second case, there are some 300 men in armed parties, slipping across the Iron Curtain border from Greece into Albania. This was a scheme designed to test the feasibility of breaking Communist control of Eastern Europe by subversion: the story ends in a crackle of small-arms fire on bleak hillsides, and the total discrediting of a policy which might have caused the Soviet Government a lot of trouble.	Taster No. 2. Will be told in detail later.
Behind each case is the shadow of Kim Philby—the Soviet penetration-agent at the heart of the Secret Intelligence Service whose loyalty went unquestioned for so long. Indeed, it might never have been questioned, but for the fact that Philby was caught up in the complex aftermath of Donald Maclean's espionage for the Russians.	Recapitulation, to remind readers of the essence of the story. New development indicated.

Barry Bearak, of the *New York Times,* was in Macedonia in the spring of 1999 to report on the refugees from Kosovo. He gives us a brilliant example of the storytelling technique. The italics are mine and my comments are on the right.

BLACE, Macedonia, April 29— When they came upon the minefield in the rugged mountains near the border, the 64 Kosovo Albanian refugees were warned to stay in single file and not stray from the narrow path or stumble on a branch or rock in the *predawn gloom.*	First, the structure. He opens the story not at the beginning of the action but at midpoint. There are other action points where the story might begin, but this opening is suspenseful without being aggravating in keeping the suspense for too long.
Twenty people *trod* through the *mud* without a problem, and that is perhaps what made the *tired old farmer,* Osman Jezerci, less wary.	Characterization of farmer makes his fate sadder.
"Osman, don't go so far over there," someone called out to him.	
Mr. Jezerci looked over his shoulder, possibly to see who was speaking. And that is when he *drifted* a few more feet to the left, those near him said. The *explosion lifted*	Italicized words in these opening paragraphs are evocative nouns, verbs, and modifiers. A less trenchant observer would just have reported that the farmer "died" or "was killed."

his body off his legs. The man beside him died, too. So did a young woman, Selvete Kukaj.

Within an hour of the blast on Wednesday, two others died from their wounds. These two—a 12-year-old girl named Zyjnete Avdiu and an 18-year-old woman, Miradije Kukaj—were buried here today in a solemn ceremony attended *by a large crowd of people who did not know them.*

Arresting thought that they were buried by "people who did not know them."

This has become the habit in Blace, a Macedonian border village of 100 homes. In the last five weeks, since NATO began bombing and throngs of Kosovo Albanians started fleeing, people from here have laid 12 strangers to rest in their cemetery.

The opening news lead having been completed, we flash back to the origins of the journey, i.e., what brought them into a minefield.

Liman Jashari, the village hohxa, or holy man, said the ritual Muslim prayers in Arabic and then switched to Albanian to soothe the mourners at the funeral.

"Before us, we see two bod-ies," he said. "It is fate that they died close to our homes before proceeding to heaven. We must remember that *everything that comes before us is the will of God.*"

He surely believed this, though it did not stop him from weeping as the bodies were taken from coffins and laid into the earth. These two young women wore white sheets as they were lowered into the ground. Their heads were placed on pillows of sod.

Each day, Macedonia awak-ens to a new tale of refugee misery as if this part of the world were keen to outdo itself with affliction. The day before, a 10-year-old boy, near death with a bullet wound and two open leg fractures, had been brought across the bor-der in a wheelbarrow. Then came the horror of *a minefield on a moonlit night.*

A less skilled reporter would have left it at "the hohxa said ritual prayers," but Bearak noted the simple eloquence of what he said.

"Each day, Macedonia awak-ens" is not only a neat way to join the second part of the story, it also gives a sense of time, of a village beginning to stir. The "moonlit night" is a link, though the criticism might be made that "moonlit" is not quite right as an identi-fier since the night was not so described earlier on.

"Fear made us leave our homes, fear of the Serbs," said Ibrahim Avdiu, 39, Zyjnete's father. "My whole life has been turned upside down with fear."

As with most stories told by the ethnic Albanian refugees, Mr. Avdiu's starts with being ordered by Serbs to leave Kosovo. His family's home was in Kacenik, a small city only 10 miles from Macedonia. Fighting has been fierce there between Serbian forces and the rebels of the secessionist Kosovo Liberation Army. Some put the death toll at more than 100 in the last month.

Mr. Avdiu, a day laborer, took his wife and four children to the nearby village of Llanishte. From there, they could see some goings-on through binoculars. Bulldozers, he said, were pushing bodies into mass graves. He and hundreds of others plotted their escapes.

Link passage. To have had this any earlier would have delayed the emotional pull of the funeral and the necessary scene-setting.

People set out for the border in various groups. The journey, while short, was hard. The welcome cover of darkness was accompanied by the unwelcome distress of frost. Gullies had to be crossed, rocks had to be climbed. Very early on Wednesday, Mr. Avdiu led a horse through the heavily wooded terrain. Clutching the saddle was his invalid mother-in-law.

The group had accepted guidance from six members of the Kosovo Liberation Army. These were the men who cautioned them about the minefield and pointed the way up the narrow path.

When the mine exploded, the blast shook the ground and turned dirt and stones into projectiles. People were wailing, unsure whether to run or stand still. They wiped their faces with their hands and smelled their fingers, *trying to determine if the wetness was sweat or blood.*

Observation of reaction. From this point the story can be carried forward chronologically.

Arsim Kukaj, 20, was the only son in a family with five daughters. Two of his sisters had been walking at his side, trying to protect the sole male heir by standing in the sight line of any snipers the family might encounter.

"My sisters were afraid I would be shot, but instead of getting in the way of a bullet they died because of the shrapnel," he said, bereft, unable to say much more.

Ibrahim Avdiu's wife and sister were injured. As he tended to them, he said, he could hear 12-year-old Zyjnete, his oldest child, crying out, *"Daddy, I'm dying."*

Mr. Avdiu's younger brother, Izet Asutiqi, scooped the girl up and draped her over his back. He began running. "I did not know where I was going, but I just started down a road and hoped it would lead somewhere," he said.

"Daddy, I'm dying" would have made a moving moment for an intro to the story, but it would have required more recapitulation to explain how we got to this point.

He carried her for two hours, though she was dead long before that, he said. His shoulders and back ached from the weight. Finally, he put her on the ground and looked for landmarks to remember. He continued down the road.

In Blace, Mr. Asutiqi staggered into a small grocery. He drew a map on the ground with a stick. Villagers then risked Macedonian border guards and Serbian troops to search for the body across the border. They carried both dead girls up and down the trails in shifts. They did not chance more time to locate the other dead.

This morning, the hoxha did the ritual cleaning of the bodies. The girls' bloody clothes were replaced by the white sheets. The village men prayed in the mosque and then passed the coffins hand to hand down a road and

Note the quality of observation. Concrete nouns, active-voice verbs.

then up a hill to the cemetery. Three mules grazed among the tombstones as the mourners went past in the early afternoon.

Once in the ground, the bodies were covered with *wood planks and then dirt*. With six men at work with spades, *it took less than two minutes to fill the graves*.

Except for the dead, only men attended the ceremony, as is the custom. But as the funeral ended, one of Miradije Kukaj's older sisters wandered in a daze toward the mound. She collapsed and kissed the dirt, laying her cheek against the grave *as if listening for a pulse*. When men lifted her up, she searched about for flowers, but found only a single violet blossom. *It was wilted and she threw it down in despair and bawled*.

"Don't cry," people said, attempting comfort. *"Crying will not awaken your sister."*

A poetic passage—listening for a pulse, a single violet blossom. And then the brutal realism of the despair.

As the villagers of Blace returned to their homes, several pointed to smoke not too far off in the mountains. The Serbs had set fire to the village of Gorance, the hoxha said, just as they had set a place called Rozhance ablaze the day before.	
More refugees would soon be coming through the mountains.	The story does not just taper off. It takes us back to the opening scene and reminds us that this is just one day in a series of horrible days.

Now let us imagine Bearak's story rendered into ordinary straight news. My rewrite of sixty-three words is adequate for that purpose—but it is nothing like as engrossing as Bearak's narrative.

Blace, Macedonia, April 29. Five Kosovo Albanians in a party of 64 were killed when they stepped on mines in mountains near the border.

Three died at once, a farmer named Osman Jezerci, an unnamed man, and a young woman, Selvete Kukaj.

Within an hour of the blast, two more died—a 12-year-old girl named Zyjnete Avdiu and an 18-year-old woman, Miradije Kukaj.

III

Consequences

Ill fares the land, to galloping fears a prey, where gobbledygook accumulates, and words decay.

—James Thurber's parody of Oliver Goldsmith's
"The Deserted Village"

9

Steps Were Taken: Explaining the Underwear Bomber

*"I wish you would make up your mind, Mr. Dickens.
Was it the best of times or was it the worst of times?
It could scarcely have been both."*

One of the 289 passengers who boarded Northwest Flight 253 in Amsterdam on Christmas Day 2009 had murder in his heart. Omar Farouk Abdulmutallab, the privileged twenty-three-year-old son of a wealthy Nigerian business-man, was known to al-Qaeda terrorists as Farouk 86. He carried an explosive device.

On the approach to Detroit, nearly eight hours into the flight, he spent some twenty minutes in the toilet, returned to his seat, and pulled a blanket over his body. Airport security had not detected a six-inch container of PETN and TAP explosive powder sewn into the seam of his underpants. Under cover, he used a syringe to inject acid into "the blessed weapon," as he called his bomb. It did not explode, but it set fire to him and the wall of the plane. Passengers and flight crew subdued him, and the plane safely landed. At trial in February 2012, Farouk 86 changed his not-guilty plea to guilty. He was sentenced to life in prison without parole.

How did he escape detection?

Within the constraints of secret intelligence, the administration owed the public an early explanation of what was then the gravest known failure of national security since 9/11. It's a complicated story with several sensitive agencies involved. Let's say that as the retired 007 of the literary world you've been charged with describing what went wrong. The White House promises access to a long preliminary report but asks that you limit the number of words without losing any necessary facts, and limit your analysis to words that everyone beyond the Beltway can understand. You are not expected to decide policy, but be assured you can be frank; you won't be required to have recourse to a universe of alternate facts.

You embark on an exercise in three parts.

First, read the White House report that follows here

(pages 253–263). It is 2,567 words. Be alert to woolliness from structure, subordinate clauses of the kind we identified as predatory, sentence length, redundancy, and the effect of the passive voice.

That's all for now. Later, compare your findings with my editing of the report in the back of the book, in the section Analysis: The Bomber (page 357), where I have subjected the long document to scrutiny—word by word, sentence by sentence, paragraph by paragraph, from start to finish.

Third, absorb the criticisms in the Analysis, and rewrite the text with the aim of producing a document that is more direct, clearer, and shorter than the original without losing any substantive points. You will find my full rewrite of the document at the end of the Analysis (see How the White House Statement Should Have Read on page 386).

WHITE HOUSE REVIEW OF THE DECEMBER 25, 2009, ATTEMPTED TERRORIST ATTACK

On December 25, 2009 a Nigerian national, Umar Farouk Abdulmutallab attempted to detonate an explosive device while onboard flight 253 from Amsterdam to Detroit. The device did not explode, but instead ignited, injuring Mr. Abdulmutallab and two other passengers. The flight crew restrained Mr. Abdulmutallab and the plane safely landed. Mr. Abdulmutallab was taken into custody by Customs and Border Protection (CBP) and later was questioned by the Federal Bureau of Investigation (FBI). Mr. Abdulmutallab was not on the U.S. Government's (USG) terrorist watchlist, but was known to the U.S. Intelligence Community (IC).

Background

Following the December 25, 2009 attempt to bring down the flight by detonating an explosive device onboard flight 253, the President directed that Assistant to the President for Homeland Security and Counterterrorism John Brennan conduct a complete review of the terrorist watchlisting system and directed that key departments and agencies provide input to this review. What follows is a summary of this preliminary report.

First, it should be noted that the work by America's counterterrorism (CT) community has had many successes since 9/11 that should be applauded. Our ability to protect the U.S. Homeland against terrorist attacks is only as good as the information and analysis that drives and facilitates disruption efforts. The thorough analysis of large volumes of information has enabled a variety of departments and agencies to take action to prevent attacks. On a great number of occasions since 9/11, many of which the American people will never know about, the tremendous, hardworking corps of analysts across the CT community did just that, working day and night to track terrorist threats and run down possible leads in order to keep their fellow Americans safe. Yet, as the amount of information continues to grow, the challenge to bring disparate pieces of information—about individuals, groups, and vague plots—together to form a clear picture about the intentions of our adversaries grows as well.

These actions, informed by the excellent analytic work of the very same individuals and structure that is under review, have saved lives. Unfortunately, despite several opportunities that might have allowed the CT community to put these pieces together in this case, and despite the tireless effort and best intentions of individuals at every level of the CT community, that was not done. As a result, the recent events highlight our need to look for ways to constantly improve and assist our CT analysts, who are at the forefront of providing warning of terrorist attacks and keeping Americans safe.

This report reflects preliminary findings to facilitate immediate corrective action. Neither the report nor its findings obviate the need for continued review and analysis to ensure that we have the fullest possible understanding of the systemic problems that led to the attempted terrorist attack on December 25, 2009. Note further that sensitive intelligence data was removed from this public report to protect sources and methods.

Findings

The preliminary White House review of the events that led to the attempted December 25 attack highlights human errors and a series of systematic breakdowns failed to stop Umar Farouk Abdulmutallab before he was able to detonate an explosive device onboard flight 253. The most significant failures and shortcomings that led to the attempted terror attack fall into three broad categories:

- A failure of intelligence analysis, whereby the CT community failed before December 25 to identify, correlate, and fuse into a coherent story all of the discrete pieces of intelligence held by the U.S. Government related to an emerging terrorist plot against the U.S. Homeland organized by al-Qa'ida in the Arabian Peninsula (AQAP) and to Mr. Abdulmutallab, the individual terrorist;

- A failure within the CT community, starting with established rules and protocols, to assign responsibility and accountability for follow up of high priority threat streams, run down all leads, and track them through to completion; and
- Shortcomings of the watchlisting system, whereby the CT community failed to identify intelligence within U.S. government holdings that would have allowed Mr. Abdulmutallab to be watchlisted, and potentially prevented from boarding an aircraft bound for the United States.

The most significant findings of our preliminary review are:

- The U.S. Government had sufficient information prior to the attempted December 25 attack to have potentially disrupted the AQAP plot—i.e., by identifying Mr. Abdulmutallab as a likely operative of AQAP and potentially preventing him from boarding flight 253.
- The Intelligence Community leadership did not increase analytic resources working on the full AQAP threat.
- The watchlisting system is not broken but needs to be strengthened and improved, as evidenced by the failure to add Mr. Abdulmutallab to the No Fly watchlist.
- A reorganization of the intelligence or broader counterterrorism community is not required to address problems that surfaced in the review, a fact made clear by countless other successful efforts to thwart ongoing plots.

Failure to "Connect the Dots"

It is important to note that the fundamental problems identified in this preliminary review are different from those identified in the wake of the 9/11 attacks. Previously, there were formidable barriers to information sharing among departments and agencies— tied to firmly entrenched patterns of bureaucratic behavior as well as the absence of a single component that fuses expertise, information technology (IT) networks, and datasets—that have now, 8 years later, largely been overcome.

An understanding of the responsibilities of different analytic components of the CT community is critical to identifying what went wrong and how best to fix it. The National Counterterrorism Center (NCTC) was created by the Intelligence Reform and Terrorism Prevention Act of 2004 (IRTPA) to be "the primary organization in the U.S. government for analyzing and integrating all intelligence possessed or acquired by the U.S. government pertaining to terrorism and counterterrorism." Intelligence Community guidance in 2006 further defined counterterrorism analytic responsibilities and tasked NCTC with the primary role within the Intelligence Community for bringing together and assessing all-source intelligence to enable a full understanding of and proper response to particular terrorist threat streams. Additionally, the Director of NCTC is in charge of the DNI Homeland Threat Task Force, whose mission is to examine threats to the U.S. Homeland from al-Qa'ida, its allies, and homegrown violent extremists.

Notwithstanding NCTC's central role in producing terrorism analysis, CIA maintains the responsibility and resource capability to "correlate and evaluate intelligence related to national security and provide appropriate dissemination of such intelligence. CIA's responsibility for conducting all-source analysis in the area of counterterrorism is focused on supporting its operations overseas, as well as informing its leadership of terrorist threats and terrorist targets overseas. Therefore, both agencies—NCTC and CIA—have a role to play in conducting (and a responsibility to carry out) all-source analysis to identify operatives and uncover specific plots like the attempted December 25 attack.

The information available to the CT community over the last several months—which included pieces of information about Mr. Abdulmutallab, information about AQAP and its plans, and information about an individual now believed to be Mr. Abdulmutallab and his association with AQAP and its attack planning—was obtained by several agencies. Though all of that information was available to all-source analysts at the CIA and the NCTC prior to the attempted attack, the dots were never connected, and as a result, the problem appears to be more about a component failure to "connect the dots," rather than a lack of information sharing. The information that was available to analysts, as is usually the case, was fragmentary and embedded in a large volume of other data.

Though the consumer base and operational capabilities of CIA and NCTC are somewhat different, the intentional redundancy in the system should have added an additional layer of protection in uncovering a plot like the failed attack on December 25. However, in both cases, the mission to "connect the dots" did not produce the result that, in hindsight, it could have—connecting identifying information about Mr. Abdulmutallab with fragments of information about his association with AQAP and the group's intention of attacking the U.S.

- The majority of these discreet [*sic*] pieces of intelligence were gathered between mid-October and late December 2009.
- For example, on November 18, Mr. Abdulmutallab's father met with U.S. Embassy officers in Abuja, Nigeria, to discuss his concerns that his son may have come under the influence of unidentified extremists, and had planned to travel to Yemen. Though this information alone could not predict Mr. Abdulmutallab's eventual involvement in the attempted 25 December attack, it provided an opportunity to link information on him with earlier intelligence reports that contained fragmentary information.
- Analytic focus during December was on the imminent AQAP attacks on Americans and American interests in Yemen, and on supporting CT efforts in Yemen.

Despite these opportunities and multiple intelligence products that noted the threat AQAP could pose to the Homeland, the different pieces of the puzzle were never brought together in this case[,] the dots were never connected, and, as a result, steps to disrupt the plot involving Mr. Abdulmutallab were not taken prior to his boarding of the airplane with an explosive device and attempting to detonate it in-flight.

Breakdown of Accountability for Threat Warning & Response

Intelligence is not an end to itself, nor are analytic products — they are designed to provide senior government leaders with the necessary information to make key decisions, but also to trigger action, including further collection, operational steps, and investigative adjustments. As noted above, NCTC and CIA have the primary and overlapping responsibility to conduct all-source analysis on terrorism. As with this intentional analytic redundancy, the CT community also has multiple and overlapping warning systems to ensure that departments and agencies are kept fully aware of ongoing threat streams.

NCTC is the primary organization that provides situational awareness to the CT community of ongoing terrorist threats and events, including through several daily written products that summarize current threat reporting for a broad audience, as well as meetings and video teleconferences that provide the opportunity for the CT community to engage in a real-time manner on this information. While the threat warning system involves analysis, it also extends to other elements within the CT community that should be responsible for following up and acting on leads as a particular threat situation develops.

In this context, the preliminary review suggests that the overlapping layers of protection within the CT community failed to track this threat in a manner sufficient to ensure all leads were followed and acted upon to conclusion. In addition, the White House and the National Security Staff failed to identify this gap ahead of time. No single component of the CT community assumed responsibility for the threat reporting and followed it through by ensuring that all necessary steps were taken to disrupt the threat. This argues that a process is needed to track terrorist threat reporting to ensure that departments and agencies are held accountable for running down all leads associated with high visibility and high priority plotting efforts, in particular against the U.S. Homeland.

Failure to Watchlist

Although Umar Farouk Abdulmutallab was included in the Terrorist Identities Datamart Environment (TIDE), the failure to include Mr. Abdulmutallab in a watchlist is part of the systemic failure. Pursuant to the IRTPA, NCTC serves "as the central and shared knowledge bank on known and suspected terrorists and international terror groups. As such, NCTC consolidates all information on known and suspected international terrorists in the Terrorist Identities Datamart Environment. NCTC then makes this data available to the FBI-led Terrorist Screening Center (TSC), which reviews nominations for inclusion in the master watchlist called the Terrorist Screening Database (TSDB). The TSC provides relevant extracts to each organization with a screening mission.

Hindsight suggests that the evaluation by watchlisting personnel of the information contained in the State cable nominating Mr. Abdulmutallab did not meet the minimum derogatory standard to watchlist. Watchlisting would have required all of the available information to be fused so that the derogatory information would have been sufficient to support nomination to be watchlisted in the Terrorist Screening Database. Watchlist personnel had access to additional derogatory information in databases that could have been connected to Mr. Abdulmutallab, but that access did not result in them uncovering the biographic information that would have been necessary for placement on the watchlist. Ultimately, placement on the No Fly list would have been required to keep Mr. Abdulmutallab off the plane inbound for the U.S. Homeland.

Visa Issue

Mr. Abdulmutallab possessed a U.S. visa, but this fact was not correlated with the concerns of Mr. Abdulmutallab's father about Mr. Abdulmutallab's potential radicalization. A misspelling of Mr. Abdulmutallab's name initially resulted in the State Department believing he did not have a valid U.S. visa. A determination to revoke his visa, however, would have only occurred if there had been a successful integration of intelligence by the CT community, resulting in his being watchlisted.

Key Findings Emerging from Preliminary Inquiry & Review

- The U.S. government had sufficient information to have uncovered and potentially disrupted the December 25 attack—including by placing Mr. Abdulmutallab on the No Fly list—but analysts within the CT community failed to connect the dots that could have identified and warned of the specific threat. The preponderance of the intelligence related to this plot was available broadly to the Intelligence Community.
- NCTC and CIA are empowered to collate and assess all-source intelligence on the CT threat, but all-source analysts highlighted largely the evolving "strategic threat" AQAP posed to the West, and the U.S. Homeland specifically, in finished intelligence products. In addition, some of the improvised explosive device tactics AQAP might use against U.S. interests were highlighted in finished intelligence products.
- The CT community failed to follow-up further on this "strategic warning" by moving aggressively to further identify and correlate critical indicators of AQAP's threat to the U.S. Home-

land with the full range of analytic tools and expertise that it uses in tracking other plots aimed at the U.S. Homeland.

- NCTC and CIA personnel who are responsible for watchlisting did not search all available databases to uncover additional derogatory information that could have been correlated with Mr. Abdulmutallab.
- A series of human errors occurred — delayed dissemination of a finished intelligence report and what appears to be incomplete/faulty database searches on Mr. Abdulmutallab's name and identifying information.
- "Information sharing" does not appear to have contributed to this intelligence failure; relevant all-source analysts as well as watchlisting personnel who needed this information were not prevented from accessing it.
- Information technology within the CT community did not sufficiently enable the correlation of data that would have enabled analysts to highlight the relevant threat information.
- There was not a comprehensive or functioning process for tracking terrorist threat reporting and actions taken such that departments and agencies are held accountable for running down all leads associated with high visibility and high priority plotting efforts undertaken by al-Qa'ida and its allies, in particular against the U.S. Homeland.
- Finally, we must review and determine the ongoing suitability of legacy standards and protocols in effect across the CT community, including criteria for watch lists, protocols for secondary screening, visa suspension and revocation criteria, and business processes across the government.

(2,566 words)

10

Money and Words

"If we're going to prioritize, we're going to need some priorities."

The Great Recession had roots in misbegotten nomenclature—words!—to an extent not commonly appreciated. Bank regulators scrutinized the familiar names on Main Street where we deposited our paychecks and drew cash at their ATMs, but there was no common name and no comparable scrutiny for new banking beasts in an unpoliced jungle inhabited by a wild menagerie of money managers who borrowed short, lent long, and repackaged risky loans as bonds. They ranged from the respectable to the ruffian, from Bear Stearns to Lehman Brothers, from money-market funds to pawnshops and loan-shark operations, and it was hard to tell which was which amid a whole concantenation of convoluted titles and jawbreaking acronyms. Everyone now knows what havoc was created when the housing market dissolved in 2008 and the packagers of subprime mortgages couldn't any longer find short-term lenders for their toxic bonds. The millions affected by foreclosures learned to flinch at the mention of CDOs (Collateralized Debt Obligations), but we also had—and have still—SIVs (Structured Investment Vehicles), specialist Monoline Financial Guarantors, Credit Derivative Product Companies, Commercial Paper conduits, Leverage Buyout Funds, and let's skip the OFCs and OFIs and all the other entities awash in money and fragile assets. If you find it hard to understand what that partial list did with money, you are in good company. The deputy governor of the Bank of England, Paul Tucker, who began to worry about the unregulated world in 2007, admitted to the *Financial Times* editor and writer-editor Gillian Tett[1] that he had found it hard to come up with a phrase that described it all. The gobbledygook was so alien that nobody

---

[1] The *Financial Times* columnist and U.S. editor brilliantly analyzes the internal barriers that frustrate communication in her book *The Silo Effect: The Peril of Expertise and the Promise of Breaking Down Barriers* (New York: Simon and Schuster, 2016).

in government had any appetite for exploring the jungle to tame the tigers. "Professional experts wield power," writes Tett, "precisely because they wrap their craft in language that is labeled as the preserve of 'geeks.' It is hard to start a public policy debate if there are no widely accessible words to explain the ideas being conveyed, and when it came to nonbank finance, it seemed that there were no good phrases available at all."

That changed, Tett tells us, when Paul McCulley, a pony-tailed economist at the bond fund company PIMCO, broke the linguistic and cognitive impasse by coming up with a neat phrase to describe the entities he thought inherently unstable: the shadow banks. It was immediately adopted.

"If we had understood the shadow banking sector better before 2007," says Tucker, "the bubble might never have become so bad." Since the apocalypse, the traditional deposit banks have had their lending wings clipped, but the shadow sector remains outside the control of regulators and of monetary policy—and its global scale is gigantic. A committee of central bankers and supervisors in Basel, called the Financial Stability Board, monitors the entities with assets of $36 trillion that it considers a "systemic risk" because they have a high ratio of debt to liquid assets. Back in the seventies, Ms. Tett tells us, Axel Leijonhufvud, "an unusually freethinking" economist at the University of California, Los Angeles, teased his colleagues for relying on mathematical models. They had an "obsession with money." An obsession with words, and the meanings behind the gobbledygook, would have been more appropriate, given how many acronyms were time bombs.

LETHAL LANGUAGE I

Early on the morning of October 3, 2015, an American AC-130 gunship circled over the northern Afghanistan city of Kunduz, overrun by swarms of Taliban fighters. Afghan commandos, taking fire, had asked for support. A Special Forces air controller on the ground told the gunship's navigator that the Taliban base for their attacks was a compound the aircrew had spotted with nine men walking between the buildings.

It was not. It was a hospital run by Doctors Without Borders (Médecins Sans Frontières, MSF). The description given to the air controller and by him to the gunship was sketchy: "an outer perimeter wall with multiple buildings inside it... and an arch shaped gate." It matched the layout of the hospital, but of other compounds, too. The exchanges between gunship and air controller were as vague.

At one point, the *New York Times* reports, the crew was told it would need to hit a second target after the strike it was about to commence, and "we will also be doing the same thing of softening the target for partner forces," that is, Afghans.

"So he wants us to shoot?" one crew member asked the others aboard the AC-130.

"Yeah, I'm not positive what softening means," the navigator replied.

"Ask him," the pilot added.

The crew did, and was told the "intent is to destroy targets of all opportunity."

Still, the crew members were unclear what was meant by targets of opportunity. "I feel like let's get on the same page for what *target of opportunity* means," the navigator told his companions.

"When I'm hearing *targets of opportunity* like that," said another crew member, "I'm thinking you're going out, you find bad things and you shoot them."

They had found *good* things, but after several more attempts to identify the target building, the gunship was ordered to unleash heavy guns. Forty-two innocents died in the Kunduz Trauma Center, fourteen of them MSF staff. It was a tragic accident, a product of multiple errors, one of them language too far removed from the term "military precision."

LETHAL LANGUAGE II

Customer convenience. Two words, two friendly words, determined that 124 people would die in car accidents and 275 would be injured—17 so gravely they are now double amputees or quadriplegics or suffer permanent brain damage. They are the victims of the extraordinary scandal of General Motors selling a line of cars, Cobalts and Chevrolets and Saturns and Skys and Pontiacs, with a faulty ignition switch that turned off the air safety bags just when the driver and passenger most needed them. It took eleven years for GM to discover the fatal errors in a series of models and recall 2.6 million cars in America, 30 million worldwide, after the tragedies.

The investigation, led by Anton Valukas, a former federal prosecutor, exposed the engineering blunders and committee culture that allowed the consequences to play out for so long. Though it is better written, it echoes the White House review of how Umar Farouk Abdulmutallab got through security and into the United States with a bomb in his underpants: "No single component of the CT community assumed responsibility." Ditto at GM. "The structure within GM was one in which no one was held responsible and no one took responsibility." We heard from Valukas about managers who would nod agreement that something should be done, then leave the meeting and do nothing; and the GM Salute, where executives would sit with arms folded, elbows out, pointing at someone else to execute what they'd all agreed upon.

Despite the buck-passing that makes those GM meetings resemble scenes from television's mockumentary *The Office,* General Motors did not have a villainous record before the Cobalt disaster.[2] Previously, it had promptly recalled dangerous cars regardless of cost, including during periods when GM finances were shaky. So what went wrong this time? Those two words, "customer convenience." The first complaints that a car had stalled went to an engineer on that model. The immediate diagnosis was that the ignition key, located on the steering column, could be dislodged if brushed by the driver's knee or disconnected by the weight of a fob. To the engineer and the company that seemed to be nothing more than an occasional—and minor—irritation. A quick turn of the ignition key and you're fine. Steer the car to the roadside if you have to. If you're a short person, watch that your knee doesn't brush against the ignition key. Sorry about the inconvenience.

---

[2] The General Motors of the sixties hounded Ralph Nader for his heroic exposure of unsafe cars; see Harold Evans, *The American Century* (New York: Knopf, 1998), 561. In 2015, he was honored in the Automotive Hall of Fame.

This early engineering classification, too tightly focused on the switch, became the default position through a series of complaints. It survived a review by committees staffed by all-systems safety experts. When more and more stalls were reported, GM managers remained mesmerized by the language of convenience. This removed any sense of urgency as they bandied ideas on rendering the switch knee-proof. Some solutions were rejected as too costly, a calculation that would have been ignored, says Valukas, if the dread word *safety* had been invoked. In July 2005, the ignition system shut down the electrics of a Chrysler Cobalt driven by Amber Marie Rose, sixteen. She hit a tree. Her airbag failed to deploy. News of the fatality did not reach all the GM nodders in their silos. The engineers inventing a Band-Aid in one committee or another did not hear of the Cobalt and Ion accidents, though by the end of 2004 GM knew of several crashes.

Throughout the saga from 2002 to 2014, as cars stalled and people died, the managers were in solitary confinement, imprisoned by language. A senior executive was worried enough to draft a Technical Service Bulletin (TSB) for dealers. He had not worked out that the fault shut down the airbags—nobody had—but he inserted a "hot" word in his draft for the supervisory Product Investigations (PI) team. The word was *stall.* He reckoned it would agitate them. GM was allergic to the word because it was bad for sales, and might provoke the National Highway Traffic Safety Administration to demand a recall. He was right. The panel excised the hot word from the TSB. It kept on doing so.

Its own fix was a smaller key, a plug to make it secure, and advising drivers to remove weight from the fob. Once again, word allergy thwarted a good intention. A customer "inconvenienced" by a stall had to go to the dealer to complain. The dealership service technician had to diagnose whether the fault was with the ignition switch or something else. A search of GM's bulletin database for the causes of a stall was impeded because *stall* had been censored. "The odds," says Valukas, "were not with the consumer." GM kept so quiet about this Band-Aid, customers picked up only 430 of 10,000 key plugs on offer. And the first notice to dealers, which did mention stalls, was removed from the database as obsolete. In 2007, with still more accidents, the technical bulletin group proposed reinstating the hot word. On April 10, Product Investigations rejected it. On April 24, the senior manager of Internal Investigations gave his approval: "Go ahead and install the word *stall*." One of his direct reports told him they were busy doing as he asked. It never happened.

Customers received an emollient: "In rare cases," the spokesman wrote, "when a combination of factors is present, a Chevrolet Cobalt driver can cut power to the engine by inadvertently moving the key into the Off position when the car is running. Service advisers are telling customers they can virtually eliminate the possibility by taking several steps, including removing non-essential items from the key rings." Much grief in that "virtually."

The pleonasm did not please the *Cleveland Plain Dealer*. It satirized GM's response as a "knee-slapper" by suggesting that an engine that can be inadvertently turned off is not a safety problem. "So, if you're whisking along at 65 mph or trying to pull across an intersection and the engine stops, you restart the engine after shifting to neutral. Only a gut-less ninny would worry about such a problem. Real men are not afraid of temporary reductions in forward momentum."

When lawsuits piled up, employees were coached in "smart" words for answering questions and warned not to write words like *danger* or *defect*. The lexicon of assurance:

> Problem—a No-No. Say "condition," "issue," or "matter"
> Safety—Can say only "has safety implications"
> Defect—Say "does not perform to design"

Alas, the Valukas report finally falters in its clarity. Verbiage bloats the conclusions on the General Motors commitments to the National Highway Traffic Safety Administration.

Original Text	**My Edited Version**
The Company has committed in part 24 of the May 16, 2014, Consent Order, that it shall ensure that the decision makers for recalls are informed of safety-related concerns in a reasonably expeditious manner, including by ensuring that GM's corporate structure enables its safety organization to promptly bring safety-related issues to the attention of committees and individuals	In part 24 of the May 16 Consent Order, the Company has committed to ensuring the committees and individuals responsible for recalls are informed of safety-related concerns expeditiously.

Original Text	My Edited Version
with authority to make safety recall decisions. Accordingly, in conjunction with its review of the FPE process, the Company should assess whether the current organizational structure—including the appointment of the Vice President for Global Vehicle Safety and the restructuring of the groups that report to him—fulfills this commitment.	In reviewing the FPE process, the Company will consider how far this commitment is met by the Vice President for Global Vehicle Safety and by the restructuring of groups reporting to him.
In part 21 of the May 16 NHTSA Consent Order, GM agreed to increase the speed with which recall decisions are made, including by clarifying the recall decision making process to decrease the number of steps prior to making the final decision of whether to conduct a recall. As GM revises this process, formalize other procedures governing the process, including how the process is initiated, who may initiate the process, how issues	In part 21 of the May 16 NHTSA Consent Order, GM agreed to speed recall decisions. Among other actions it will reduce the number of steps required for a recall. It will identify in writing who may initiate the process, how issues are escalated, and who is accountable for monitoring actions throughout the chain of command to reach and enforce a conclusion. It will identify and review any preceding condition in the

Original Text	My Edited Version
are escalated within the process, who is responsible and accountable for monitoring the process and bringing the matter to a conclusion, and the chain of command throughout the process. Maintain a written policy governing the process that clearly defines the procedural steps in the process and the role of each participant. Ensure that part of the FPE process includes identification and review of any prior FPE processes, regarding the same condition in the same or other models. (258 words)	model under question or other models. (141 words, a reduction of 117 words)

RUN UP THE FLAGPOLE

There is a Gresham's law for currency, that the bad drives out the good, and I propose a corollary, that bad words drive out the good. Chief executives should have word tasters just as the Borgias had food tasters. The people who create and run companies aren't stupid, but they put their names to statements that are management mumbo-jumbo, products of algorithms rather than thinking human beings. Mark Zuckerberg's 2013 annual report evinced an addiction to corporate-speak alien to the friendly nature of the site. Facebook had discovered that the consumers ("such users") who made an entry in their pages were not precisely where Facebook thought they were. This came out as: "The methodologies used to measure user metrics did affect our attribution of users to different geographic regions." He had to deal with an assortment of complaints. Instead of saying these were bad for Facebook, he writes that they "could adversely affect our reputation. Such negative publicity also could have an adverse effect on the size, engagement and loyalty of our user base and result in decreased revenue, which could adversely affect our business and financial results." You don't say.

Stuff like this makes a brilliant mind seem like voice mail. An hour ago I stopped to send an e-mail. Google's Gmail system was down and I was referred to a Google message advising network administrators of a change (my italics): "We are *deprecating* the classic Google Admin console on February 3, 2014." What's this? A spasm of masochism in Mountain View, California? No, they aren't stabbing themselves in the back, just murdering a verb (*Oxford English Dictionary:* **deprecate,** v. "pleading earnestly against"). Not quite sated, Google borrowed an accountant's language to fashion a noun out of the verb *deprecate.* "Classic Admin console *depreciation.*" I appreciate engineers, I wrote a book about their achievements, but I deprecate what they and other techies do to English words. Hey, these nouns and verbs aren't bits of silicon you can dope with chemicals (boron, phosphorus, and arsenic), drop into a kiln at 2,000 degrees Fahrenheit, and slice and dice. Words breathe. They need TLC — you know, the phrase that launched a thousand chips. Of course you do. Didn't Eric Schmidt, then CEO of Google, tell us about the power of the chip? "With your permission you give more information about you, your friends, and we can improve the quality of our searches.... We don't need you to type at all. We know where you are. We know where you've been. We can more or less know what you're thinking about."[3]

The precision of the business operations to give us chips and everything else is at odds with the murkiness of business and technical writing. Company reports share with bureaucracies and law firms everywhere a preference for the passive voice, the same deadener that ran through the White House statement on the underwear bomber. Rick Wagoner, when chairman and CEO of General Motors, wanted to say they knew what they had to do to fix an $8 billion loss mentioned in the annual report. He got mugged on the way to the rostrum. He was ready to admit GM's 2004 financial figures had gotten mixed up. The company was hiring more accountants. Fine, but someone deployed the passive voice as a distancing device: *Errors were made*... but *going forward* GM was working *aggressively to strengthen general accounting resources*. He was made to say GM was *addressing the*

---

[3] http://www.theatlantic.com/technology/archive/2010/10/googles-ceo-the-laws-are-written-by-lobbyists/63908/

unprecedented challenges *that we face* in a *ferociously* competitive auto industry, and had *absolute* clarity *about the road
ahead* and was working *diligently.*

On his desk, every CEO should have my Adverb Annihilator so he can feed board reports and speeches into it as easily as someone feeds drafts into a shredder, ferocious*ly,*
diligent*ly,* relentless*ly.* One day maybe I'll add up how much
companies squander in pixels, abuse our attention span, and
waste paper (i.e., *resources of machine-ready printing paper*).
It is invariably the result of a writer acting like an engineer,
assembling sentences and paragraphs from a tray of familiar
words, greedy adverbs, and empty phrases. So *going forward
diligently* we get *in conjunction with, in advance of the meeting, it cannot be denied that, succeed in defeating, in consequence of, fill to capacity, at an early date, arrangements are in
the hands of, gathered together, take into consideration, under
active consideration, under the circumstances, with the exception of, draw to the attention of, the fact that, and in spite of the
fact that, and with respect to the fact that...*

People don't talk like that. It is when they write that they
get nervous and inflict the pain on the rest of us without
being aware of what they are doing.

Three examples:

The prolix auditor

A telltale sign that a lawyer has got to the prose as a mouse
gets to cheese is the appearance of the word *such.* A firm of
auditors wanted to assure a corporation that it had applied

the same standards to supplementary information as it had to the records used for the financial statements:

> The information has been subjected to the auditing procedures applied in the audits of the financial statements and certain additional procedures, including comparing and reconciling such information directly to the underlying accounting and other records used to prepare the financial statements or to the financial statements themselves, and other additional procedures in accordance with auditing standards generally accepted in the United States of America.

But not in accordance with the standards of decent English in the United States.

The baffled parents

Parents who both had health insurance could not decide which policy to use for their child. They asked the insurers, who rose to the occasion:

> The plan covering the patient as a dependent child of a person whose date of birth occurs earlier in the year shall be primary over the plan covering the patient as a dependent of a person whose date of birth occurs later in the calendar year provided. However, in the case of a dependent child of legally separated or divorced parents, the plan covering the patient dependent of the custodial parent's spouse (i.e. Step-parent) shall be primary over the

plan as a dependent of a person without legal custody.
(89 words)

The plan...the plan. The needle got stuck. If they had
for a moment thought of the *people* who asked and not the
abstraction of "the plan," it would have been easier to
understand—and taken a third less space, as in my fix:

When parents have separate policies covering a dependent
child, payment is made on the policy of the parent with the
earlier birthday in year. With divorced or separated parents,
the parent with legal custody pays even if the child is now
covered by a policy of a stepparent. But if legal custody
belongs to a spouse or stepparent, that policy pays. (60 words)

The car-rental warranty

In the event of a breakdown the Owner will at his own
expense collect the vehicle and effect repairs thereto provided always that if aforesaid are rendered necessary by
reason of any neglect, default and breach of this Agreement or abuse or misuse of the vehicle by the Renter or
Driver, the Renter will pay the Owner on demand the cost
of such collection and the cost of the repairs. The cost of
any repairs carried out on the instructions of the Renter
or Driver without the prior written approval of the Owner
shall be responsibility of the Renter. (99 words)

Who dat? Typical unfriendly, confusing warranty language. This is a warranty from the hire company (owner) to

me (renter or driver). The company is "we," and "I," the renter, should be addressed as "you." "Aforesaid" and "provided always" are legal debris.

Get rid of all the clutter: "effect repairs," "by reason of," "such collection," and "repairs carried out." The word clutter is aggravated by the passive voice ("are rendered"). Translate into the active voice, identifying who is supposed to be doing what for whom.

The warranty edited:

> If the car we rent you breaks down, we will collect and
> repair it at no cost to you, unless the breakdown is your
> fault by abuse, neglect, or misuse. If you are to blame, you
> will pay on demand for the cost of collection and repairs,
> as you will for any repairs you make without our written
> approval. (59 words)

Earlier in this book, I acknowledged that clarity may not be an imperative for everyone. I have the confessional word of the jailed lobbyist Jack Abramoff that he regularly slipped obscure language into draft bills, "something so cryptic, so enigmatic, so opalescent, that it would take a computer to discern what we were trying to do." The apparently innocuous sentence he inserted—"Public law 100–89 is amended by striking section 207 (101 stat. 668, 672)"—was worth millions of dollars for his clients. And he got away with it.[4]

Speechwriter Barton Swaim cheerfully explains why the

---

[4] Jack Abramoff, *Capitol Punishment* (Washington, DC: WND Books, 2011).

opaque may be a virtue. "Using vague, slippery or just mean-ingless language," he writes, "is not the same as lying: it's not intended to deceive so much as to preserve options, buy time, distance oneself from others, or just to sound like you're saying something instead of nothing."[5] He promoted his skill in cam-ouflaging the emptiness by using as many words as a sentence can bear. "I believe" becomes "I have every reason indeed to believe." "Thanks" becomes "I want to send a thank-you in your direction." Platitudes of observation, he suggests, can *use-fully* be prefaced by the words "What I would say—and I am *absolutely* certain about this from where I stand—is that…"

Fluff like that should enrage a CEO, but many are hos-tage to marketing directors who are busy shifting paradigms from the strategic staircase of 2015 to skating where the puck is going to be in 2017; and the human resources director who survived the last cull is wondering if she can sell the new buzzword of "ventilating" people instead of "demising" them, which got a bad rap last time the company stream-lined. One day, a bright HR person will find a way to "right size" the company so that word-munchers are made to eat all the low-hanging rotten apples thrown at them.

It is a toss-up which is the worse enemy of clarity, the cowardly euphemism of "right-sizing" or the cunning deception. In chapter 4, I argue that positive statements are clearer than negatives, but there is the classic case of the vet who receives what seems positively good news:

---

[5] https://www.washingtonpost.com/news/book-party/wp/2015/07/08 /what-its-like-to-write-speeches-for-a-rude-rambling-and-disgraced -politician/

The non-compensable evaluation heretofore assigned certain veterans for their service-connected disability is confirmed and continued.

What is confirmed is "the *non-compensable* evaluation," which means the vet is being told that *he won't get any money.* Authority often prefers to paper over wrongdoing with platitudes, omissions, and ambiguities; fraudsters conceal big traps in small-print prolixity; job applicants embroider résumés; employers inflate job titles more readily than salaries; bank managers express the utmost respect for your integrity while denying your request for more credit. Lawyers write warranties and guarantees whose value (to the guarantors) lies in their evasive phrasing. Political lobbyists who are flacks for some cause parade their independence[6] with deceptive names. One group in 2015 that achieved fame (notoriety if you like) called itself the Center for Medical Progress, and this was its website statement:

> The Center for Medical Progress is a non-profit organization dedicated to informing and educating both the lay public and the scientific community about the latest advances in regenerative medicine, cell-based therapies, and related disciplines. We take a special interest in the lab-to-lab translational dynamic and tracking its implications for academics, advocacy, private sector players, and the individual patient.

---

[6] http://www.businessjustice.com/do-i-have-a-lanham-claim-against -my-competitor-for-false-adverti.html

On second thought, the center later changed its self-description:

The Center for Medical Progress is a group of citizen journalists dedicated to monitoring and reporting on medical ethics and advances. We are concerned about contemporary bioethical issues that impact human dignity, and we oppose any interventions, procedures, and experiments that exploit the unequal legal status of any class of human beings. We envision a world in which medical practice and biotechnology ally with and serve the goods of human nature and do not destroy, disfigure, or work against them.

This, too, was deceptive labeling. The center is a maverick, an anti-abortion organization that, for reasons best known to itself, conceals its purpose as the leading anti-abortion groups do not (the National Right to Life Committee, Live Action, et al.). It was the Center for Medical Progress that in 2015 made the sensational charge that Planned Parenthood sold aborted baby parts for profit. The charge was widely debunked.[7] A grand jury in Harris County, Texas, cleared Planned Parenthood of any wrongdoing and indicted an employee of the center for a felony. The charges were dropped six months later.

So many organizations deliberately do not make themselves clear. Guess the purpose of:

---

[7] "Planned Parenthood at Risk," *New England Journal of Medicine* 373: 963, doi:10.1056/NEJMe1510281. PMID 26267451.

The Committee for a Constructive Tomorrow
The Advancement of Sound Science Inc.
The Heartland Institute
The Competitive Enterprise Institute
The Annapolis Center for Science-Based Public Policy

All these highfalutin bodies want to suggest that climate change is an illusion, meant to enslave us. The Texas Republican manifesto: "While we all strive to be good stewards of the earth, 'climate change' is a political agenda which attempts to control every aspect of our lives. We urge government at all levels to ignore any plea for money to fund global climate change or 'climate justice' initiatives."

The five groups I mentioned are not the only ones. The Union of Concerned Scientists has named others; some have lost funding since. Greenpeace identified forty such mouths at the Exxon nipple in 2007.[8] So what's wrong about this? Well, for one thing, you'd be a bit more skeptical, wouldn't you, if they made it clear that their pronouncements on climate change/global warming are—shall we say—not unrelated to the interests of their sponsors?

The denials and obfuscations bring to mind what happened in 1974 to two American scientists, Professor Sherwood Roland and Dr. Mario Molina. They coolly set out the evidence that the chlorofluorocarbons (or CFCs) used in refrigeration, aerosols, and air-conditioning were eating at the ozone layer, which protects mankind and plants from ultra-

[8] Union of Concerned Scientists, http://www.ucsusa.org/publications/cata lysts/st/su15-documenting-fossil-companies-climate-change-deception

violet radiation. They made themselves very clear, but lazy media allowed bodies that seemed scientific and independent to fog the issue. They uncritically recycled messages from the Alliance for Responsible CFCs. It wasn't "responsible." It was a manufacturers' front. The clarity of Roland and Molina was obscured. The public got bored and bamboozled. And as they did so, millions more tons of the pollutant were added to the atmosphere.

Four years later the U.S. took the lead in banning the use of CFCs—but only in aerosol propellants. Most people thought that we had done our bit. Nobody liked the idea that every time we sprayed a fly we threatened the universe. In fact, we were misled. The use of CFCs for refrigeration, freezing, and air-conditioning increased all over the world. It wasn't so much that we put a higher value on our refrigerators than on our planet. By then, substitute technology was entirely feasible. The Environmental Protection Agency called for immediate action. But another five years went by. When the world finally woke up—thirteen years after the original scientific alarm—there was indeed an ozone hole, as Molina and Roland had predicted, and it was even bigger than they had thought likely. At last there was international action—led by the U.S. on this occasion. The 1987 Montreal Protocol was ratified by more than 180 nations. It triggered a collaboration among chemical manufacturers, politicians, and automakers.

What is clearly science and what is clearly garbage? Can you tell the difference? On pages 287–289 I present four passages where the authors did not make themselves clear. I do not suggest you attempt to rewrite them, just simply identify the two that were written by a machine, the two by a living, breathing academic. The passages will set your teeth on edge, your hair on fire, any metaphor for stupefaction you can imagine. You may choose to read two of them as examples of how computers can imitate human thought; I prefer to see them all as a warning of how slack scrutiny, bogus authority, and dense language can impede the advancement of human knowledge. Dr. Jeffrey Filer, dean of the Harvard Medical School,[9] is concerned that a small subset of scientists get research published that is not reproducible. He cites the widely cited paper that got into the *Lancet* in 1998 claiming a link between measles vaccines and autism. It was not retracted until 2010. In the meantime, scared parents exposed their unvaccinated children and others to greater risk. And the false story was still being propagated by Donald Trump in the 2016 presidential campaign. There is a straight line between fraud in science and the proliferation of political lies swallowed whole by gullible millions in the 2016 election.

The machine paragraphs originated in the media lab at the Massachusetts Institute of Technology in 2005, where three mischief-makers, grad students Jeremy Stribling, Daniel Aguayo, and Maxwell Krohn, got irritated by the number of requests to write "something" for a techie gabfest; they felt spammed. They retaliated by designing a computer program, SCIgen, that fulfilled the prescription *garbage in, garbage out*. The conference organizers got lucky. The spoof arrived too late to be included in the conference—but these and more than a hundred brain-dead others like them found their way to publication. The computer scientist Cyril

---

9 *Wall Street Journal*, March 2, 2016.

Labbe[10] at Joseph Fourier University in Grenoble, France, finally outed more than 120 nonsense papers. They were withdrawn in 2014 by the Springer publishing group and the Institute of Electrical and Electronics Engineers (IEEE), headquartered in New York.[11] Labbe got fake papers by a mythical Ike Antkare into the Google Scholar database. Hey presto, *Nature* reports, he became the world's twenty-first most highly cited scientist. Labbe has designed a computer program to sniff out the frauds. Perhaps you can do it unaided. Clue: look for the concrete amid the general guff. If we are ever, all of us, to make ourselves clear, we must not be intimidated by English that doesn't make sense. (Who's who or which is what is revealed on page 355.)

1. Man or Machine?

If the intercourse sustained between artful conduct and the more or less plastic qualities of emerging experience is to retain its dialogic quality, it must acknowledge that its rationality does not turn on success in mastering a world of independent objects. Rather, its intelligence is measured by its responsiveness to the meanings intimated by those intersecting events that have now crystallized within an insufficient situation.

2. Machine or Man?

The Diffusion of Innovations Model provided an organizing framework to present emergent themes. With the

---

[10] Laboratoire d'Informatique de Grenoble, http://scigendetection.imag.fr/main.php

[11] http://www.nature.com/news/publishers-withdraw-more-than-120-gibberish-papers-1.14763

exception of triability (not relevant in the context of mandated guidelines/policies), the key attributes of the Diffusion of Innovations Model (relative advantage, compatibility, complexity, and observability) provided a robust framework for understanding themes associated with implementation of mandated guidelines. Specifically, implementation of the DPA and FBSS guidelines was facilitated by perceptions that they: were relatively advantageous compared to status quo; were compatible with school mandates and teaching philosophies; had observable positive impacts and impeded when perceived as complex to understand and implement. In addition, a number of contextual factors including availability of resources facilitated implementation.

3. Man or Machine?

Building a system as unstable as ours would be for naught without a generous evaluation methodology. Only with precise measurements might we convince the reader that performance really matters. Our overall performance analysis seeks to prove three hypotheses: (1) that cache coherence no longer influences performance; (2) that a framework's API is even more important than an application's game-theoretic API when improving 10th-percentile work factor; and finally (3) that 802.11b has actually shown improved 10th-percentile response time over time. Note that we have intentionally neglected to improve a methodology's API. Our logic follows a new model: performance really matters only as long as scalability takes a back seat to interrupt rate. Our work in this regard is a novel contribution, in and of itself.

4. Machine or Man?

We view electrical engineering as following a cycle of four phases: synthesis, evaluation, construction, and synthesis. Existing interactive and constant-time algorithms use collaborative communication to observe autonomous modalities. Contrarily, encrypted modalities might not be the panacea that researchers expected. Clearly, our approach is based on the principles of hardware and architecture.

We no longer have Richard Mitchell to skewer naked emperors in academia as he did for so many years through his *Underground Grammarian*.[12] Would that the drone writers immerse themselves in his work and inhale the moral zest of his mission never to use words without understanding what they mean. The Academy of Management Review, dedicated to the same cause, has done good work, but I fear they may be subverted by infiltrators. The academy asked editors to review the writing in academic articles and reported: "Many authors fail to effectively problematize the literature and articulate a compelling theoretical contribution. Building on this point, another reviewer noted that authorities often fail to answer the problematization question."

You bet they do. The zombies are already in the lecture hall.

---

[12] www.sourcetext.com/grammarian/

11

⚡

Buried Treasure: It's Yours, but Words Get in the Way

"Love it! 'People of smoke' instead of 'Smokers.'"

The wilderness of words on the next two pages is not to be entered without a guide. Going in alone risks getting lost in a maze from which no one has emerged whole in body and mind. They show the unadorned text of a Social Security act that as of December 2015 and May 2016 deprived millions of people of cash benefits.

Subtitle C—Protecting Social Security Benefits SEC. 831. CLOSURE OF UNINTENDED LOOPHOLES. (a) PRESUMED FILING OF APPLICATION BY INDIVIDUALS ELIGIBLE FOR OLD-AGE INSURANCE BENEFITS AND FOR WIFE'S OR HUSBAND'S INSURANCE BENEFITS.—(1) IN GENERAL.—Section 202(r) of the Social Security Act (42 U.S.C. 402(r)) is amended by striking paragraphs (1) and (2) and inserting the following: "(1) If an individual is eligible for a wife's or husband's insurance benefit (except in the case of eligibility pursuant to clause (ii) of subsection (b)(1)(B) 6 or subsection (c)(1)(B), as appropriate), in any month for which the individual is entitled to an old-age insurance benefit, such individual shall be deemed to have filed an application for wife's or husband's insurance benefits for such month. "(2) If an individual is eligible (but for section 202(k)(4)) for an old-age insurance benefit in any month for which the individual is entitled to a wife's or husband's insurance benefit (except in the case of entitlement pursuant to clause (ii) of subsection (b)(1)(B) or subsection (c)(1)(B), as appropriate), such individual shall be deemed to have filed an application for old-age insurance benefits—"(A) for such month, or "(B) if such individual is also entitled to a disability insurance benefit for such month, in the first subsequent month for which such individual is not entitled to a disability insurance benefit.". (2) CONFORMING AMENDMENT.— Section 202 of the Social Security Act (42 U.S.C. 402) is amended—(A) in subsection (b)(1), by striking sub-paragraph (B) and inserting the following: "(B)(i) has attained age 62, or "(ii) in the case of a wife, has in her care (individually or jointly with such individual) at the time of filing such application a child entitled to a child's insurance benefit on the basis of the wages and self-employment income of such individual,"; and (B) in subsection (c)(1), by striking sub-paragraph (B) and inserting the following: "(B)(i) has attained age 62, or "(ii) in the case of a husband, has in his care (individually or jointly with such individual) at the time of filing such application a child entitled to a child's insurance benefit on the basis of the wages and self-employment income of such individual,". (3) EFFECTIVE DATE.—The amendments made by this subsection shall apply with respect to individuals who attain age 62 in any calendar year after 2015. (b) VOLUNTARY SUSPENSION OF BENEFITS.— (1) IN GENERAL.—Section 202 of the Social Security Act (42 U.S.C. 402) is amended by adding at the end the following: "(z) VOLUNTARY SUSPENSION.— (1)(A) Except as otherwise provided in this subsection, any individual who has attained retirement age (as defined in section 216(l)) and is entitled to old-age insurance benefits may request that payment of such benefits be suspended—"(i) beginning with the month following the month in which such request is received by the Commissioner, and "(ii) ending with the earlier of the month following the month in which a request by the individual for a resumption of such benefits is so received or the month following the month...blah, blah, blah

Deciphering Code

The two previous pages you skipped reading represent money, a lot of money, your money if you can find your way through to daylight. Don't try to read them. They might as well be written in hieroglyphs. They are words from a newly enacted law removing a Social Security option for 21 million seniors and their dependents. The language defies understanding and, in the best Orwellian tradition, the text imposing cuts in Social Security benefits is headed "Protecting Social Security Benefits."

Here is the first substantive sentence you encounter if you are rash enough to venture into the thickets:

> (1) If an individual is eligible for a wife's or husband's insurance benefit (except in the case of eligibility pursuant to clause (ii) of subsection (b)(1)(B) or subsection (c) (1)(B), as appropriate), in any month for which the individual is entitled to an old-age insurance benefit, such individual shall be deemed to have filed an application for wife's or husband's insurance benefits for such month.

The sentence of sixty-four words has a long predatory opening clause of forty-four words. It's a conditional clause, the first of a series of "If this" and "If that" so beloved of legislative draftsmen I have a hypothesis of my own, that this conditional formulation provoked the British Nobel laureate Rudyard Kipling to write the poem "If" in 1895: "If you can keep your head when all about you / Are losing theirs..." No sooner have you recovered your sense of direction where clause 1 is taking you than you are asked to go down a path at the side, subsection (b)(1)(B), to see if you are still qualified for the money you are after. When you follow that side path you come upon another side path, and then another, and then after the zigs and zags, and zigs, of exploring six "subsections," you have maybe discovered who you think you are— "such individual." As "such individual," you are then "deemed" to have done something you can't remember doing in "such month."

You are Kafka waking up in Bleak House.

The introduction says this section is intended to replace the wording of the act passed in 2000, but going back to the original language merely prolongs the nightmare:

Presumed filing of application by individuals eligible for old-age insurance benefits and for wife's or husband's insurance benefits (1) If the first month for which an individual is entitled to an old-age insurance benefit is a month before the month in which such individual attains retirement age (as defined in section 416(l) of this title), and if such individual is eligible for a wife's or husband's insurance benefit for such first month, such individual shall be deemed to have filed an application in such month for wife's or husband's insurance benefits.

It would be fair to say the senators did not have an iron grasp of what they nodded through. It was 3:00 a.m. The changes were tucked in one section of fifty in an emergency bill of 144 pages. There had been little public debate on the

meander on Social Security. The Senate's bipartisan majority of 64 (46-D, 18-R) had stayed up late to keep the U.S. in
business for another two years and avoid the hazardous
sixteen-day shutdown forced by the abominable No men of
2013. All the senators had before them when they voted was
the cryptic summary:

Sec. 831.

 Closes several loopholes in Social Security's rules
about deemed filing, dual entitlement, and benefit suspension in order to prevent individuals from obtaining
larger benefits than Congress intended. (Effective for
individuals who attain age 62 after 2015, with respect to
dual entitlement and deemed filing; and effective for
benefits payable beginning 6 months after enactment,
with respect to benefit suspension.)

Loophole is another Orwellian word invented by the firm
of litigators Sue, Grabbit, and Run who earned their notoriety in Britain's satirical magazine *Private Eye.*

The U.S. Social Security Administration (SSA) pays
$860 billion a year in benefits to 59 million citizens who are
retired, disabled, or survivors; the retirement pension is the
main income for two-thirds of seniors. Yet vast numbers of
Americans fail to claim the money they could. There are more
than nine thousand different claiming options—and the
administration is prohibited by law from giving case-by-case
personal advice.

Several independent companies stand ready to offer a
hand to anyone entering the wilderness alone. I spoke with

two experts, Catherine Azmoodeh Hormats and Matthew Allen, who deal daily with people foxed by the options and changes, the reason they started the innovative financial and technology company Social Security Advisors. "Most people are unaware of the great complexity of Social Security law," says Catherine. "Like my parents, they think they hit 65, show up at the Social Security office and fill out a few papers, and ride off into the sunset of a happy retirement with full benefits in hand. This approach typically costs the average American couple a whopping $120,000 in benefits! Furthermore, no one is telling retirees that they're missing out on money they could be earning. We've had CEOs of major financial institutions who are experts in the field of finance get downright angry because they were unaware that they were missing out on what they rightfully and lawfully earned. For them it seemed to be a matter of principle, and most people want what they've earned."

Let's go back into wilderness and see if we can write a rough summary that will at least alert couples to what the language the Senate approved has done to retirees and their dependents. The Senior Citizens' Freedom to Work Act, passed in 2000, described a series of options. One, called "file and suspend," offered an incentive to postpone receiving a monthly check if you could manage to wait. Imagine you were the higher earner of a couple, whether husband or wife. You could maximize your ultimate benefits by filing a claim at the age of sixty-two, sixty-six, seventy, or somewhere in between and immediately suspending collection of the check, $2,000 a month if you were sixty-six. Your delayed benefit would be diverted into a Delayed

Credit Account where it would earn 8 percent, a great investment, especially in the era of ultra-low bond yields. Left there for four years, at seventy, you or your survivor would receive $2,640 a month from the nest-egg bonus of 32 percent, or you could collect a lump sum for the amount accumulated in the credit balance, as much as $24,000. More. The act of filing would entitle your spouse or eligible children to receive a monthly check for $1,000 based on your earnings—if you knew about it, and most people didn't.

The 3:00 a.m. senators gave notice at the end of October 2015 that after May 2, 2016, file-and-suspend would be cut off for singles aged sixty-six or married couples with at least one spouse aged sixty-six to seventy. They exempted survivors from the new rules. For everyone else, gone would be the spousal benefit while the higher earner continued building up retirement credits. Gone would be the option to receive a lump sum. But the language endured:

> "(2) An individual may not suspend such benefits under this subsection, and any suspension of such benefits under this subsection shall end, effective with respect to any month in which the individual becomes subject to—"(A) mandatory suspension of such benefits under section 202(x); "(B) termination of such benefits under section 202(n); "(C) a penalty under section 1129A imposing nonpayment of such benefits; or "(D) any other withholding, in whole or in part, of such benefits under any other provision of law that authorizes recovery of a debt by withholding such benefits.

Do I make myself clear? Lawyers may revel in section 831 of the bill in the Social Security appendix with all its *such*es and back references, its predatory clauses, its parentheses, its elliptical style, its unfriendly third person, its long sentences that make minds close up. But the millions of people who have paid a lifetime of dues are entitled to clearer English than is found in the 2,728 rules governing Social Security and the Program Operations Manual System. The rules are so voluminous, thicker than the Bible, that the Social Security Administration stopped printing them in the 1980s. Only a masochist can endure trying to work out what all the words mean. Here is one clause that exults in the agony provided by the agency's awful arsenal of acronyms, hereinafter to be referred to as AAAA.

> Beginning in 01/00, a numberholder (BIC A only) who has attained full retirement age (FRA), but is not yet age 70, may elect to suspend his/her retirement benefit in order to earn delayed retirement credits (DRCs). This change is part of the Senior Citizens' Freedom to Work Act of 2000. This legislation eliminated the annual earnings test (AET) and the foreign work test (FWT) for those who have attained FRA. It allows beneficiaries to receive full retirement benefits regardless of earnings. Prior to 01/00 those benefits would have been subject to the AET or FWT and DRCs would have been earned for months subject to a full work deduction. Because those beneficiaries will no longer be subject to the AET or FWT, they are being given the opportunity to elect voluntary suspension of retirement benefits to earn DRCs. (138 words)

Which means:

A Social Security recipient who previously filed for Social Security benefits can suspend benefits at Full Retirement Age (66 for most people) and earn delayed retirement credits [an extra 8% per year added to their Social Security] until age 70. At full retirement age (66 for most), they may also continue to work and earn unlimited earnings without having any of their Social Security benefits withheld due to the Annual Earnings Test. (72 words)

The sense buried in the original text, combined with other rules, was worth an additional $40,000 to $50,000 for a typical married couple. But it would not have come to them automatically.

Hoop-di-do and ado: What health-care crisis?

Millions of Americans in 2010 thought they could keep their doctors and their health plans if they liked them. They could not have been expected to read the 955-plus convoluted pages of the Patient Protection and Affordable Care Act (ACA), aka Obamacare, signed into law on March 23, 2010, but the president who signed it must have done so before he made the promise. So, with opposing motives, might its supporters and critics. So might the reporters, TV news anchors, headline writers, and commentators who ransacked *Roget's Thesaurus* for synonyms for the overworked word *crisis* when people had their policies canceled and the Healthcare.gov website didn't work very well. The Republicans who shut down the federal government for sixteen days in October 2013 to defund the regulated insurance program of the Affordable Care Act were mostly expressing their detestation of entitlement programs. They had no plan B—or plan C, or plan D—for the forty-one million Americans then without health insurance. And they didn't have a viable one to put on President Trump's desk during his early days in office in 2017. They thrashed about, seduced by the alliterative pledge to "repeal and replace," reminiscent of a catch-22: they had no plans and they were all firm. According to the nonpartisan Congressional Budget Office, repeal alone would strip 18 million people of insurance and double premiums by 2026. Sad. Among thirteen comparable high-income countries, the United States was (still is) the only one without a publicly funded universal health system. Its public-health-care costs are higher than all but two of the other twelve countries', yet the Commonwealth Fund reports Americans as a group have poorer health outcomes, including shorter life expectancy, and more chronic ailments, than people in Australia, Canada, Denmark, France, Germany, Japan, the Netherlands, New Zealand, Norway, Sweden, Switzerland, and the United Kingdom.

The objectors to Obamacare might have had more effect if they had come up with answers; at least they could have identified and clarified the language in the overlapping provisions in the act that were to lead to so much "hoop-di-do and ado," in the phrase of the House Minority Leader Nancy Pelosi. She was endlessly quoted as saying on March 9, 2010, "We have to pass the bill so you can find out what's in it, away from the fog of controversy." Or, better, away from the fog of legalisms. No doubt those who did try to grapple with whether or not the grandfather clause applied to them were ashamed to admit they were confounded, but they could have entered a plea of self-defense against the mental cruelty of millions of words of regulations with legions of subordinate clauses fully loaded with *notwithstandings*.

For instance:

> IN GENERAL — Notwithstanding subsection (r) or any other provision of this title, except as provided in subparagraph (D), for purposes of determining income eligibility for medical assistance under the State plan or under any waiver of such plan and for any other purpose applicable under the plan or waiver for which a determination of income is required, including with respect to the imposition of premiums and cost-sharing, a State shall use the modified gross income of an individual and, in the case of an individual in a family greater than 1, the household income of such family.

It is a fair specimen. Garance Franke-Ruta, in a survey in November 2013 for the *Atlantic* magazine, reported: "Having spent quite some time last week deep in the weeds of Obamacare, whacking my way through the burrs and brush of its extensive questionnaires…I am here to tell you two things. First, it is confusing. Second, every little bit of misinformation and confusion matters." She concluded that there was a high risk that people would spend days wandering fruitlessly in the weeds before figuring out what they were supposed to do to proceed or if they were eligible for subsidies. That was fair comment on the drafting. Much of what followed publication of the draft bill was not. It amounted to a campaign of misrepresentation where words receded from truth with unprecedented velocity—and venom. There was nothing to equal this at the birth of President Franklin Roosevelt's Social Security Act. Roosevelt's Republican challenger for the presidency in 1936, Governor Alf Landon of Kansas, said, "My first act will be to abolish Social Security." The likable Landon did his best, but the bill had substantial bipartisan support in the House and Senate, and it would be fifty years before digital social media arrived as an unwitting agent for the mass dissemination of rumor and semi-truth now known as Fake News. The likable Landon lost in a landslide. It is not my purpose to dive into the history of falsehoods about Obamacare. It turned out, for instance, that the number of policies discontinued because they did not meet the new standards of the Affordable Care Act were closer to two million than the five million bandied about. Political enemies in right-wing echo chambers exploited every opportunity to mischaracterize the aim of enabling millions of uninsured to buy insurance of high standards. By 2016, twenty million had insurance they didn't have before. The point for *Do I Make Myself Clear?* is that the lack of clarity in the bill worked against the express purpose of popularizing the legislation, so it was vulnerable to misrepresentation, even by its true begetter.[1] Consider the furor over "death panels."[2]

It began with a straight misrepresentation of a proposal in Section 1233 for Medicare to reimburse patients who volun-

---

[1] PolitiFact scored the repeated statements on retaining plans and doctors a "pants on fire" misrepresentation. The belated explanation was that the president meant "You can keep your plan if it hasn't changed since the law passed."

[2] http://mediamatters.org/research/2011/03/22/a-history-of-death-panels-a-timeline/177776

tarily sought end-of-life counseling. The historian Betsy McCaughey, a Republican former lieutenant governor of New York,[3] said on Fred Thompson's radio show on July 16, 2009, that she was shocked to come upon "a vicious assault on elderly people" in an unnoticed provision in the draft bill. It would "absolutely require" people on Medicare to have counseling sessions every five years that would "tell them how to end their life sooner…sacred issues of life and death government should have nothing to do with." There was no such provision, though the insertion of a page number—425—gave it a spurious credibility. Ceci Connolly reported in the *Washington Post* (August 1, 2009) that the claim had been picked up and recycled at face value on Internet blogs and religious e-mail lists. The real liftoff followed a Facebook post by Sarah Palin, who'd just resigned as Alaska's governor. She did it in just two words— *death* and *panel*. She asked us to visualize her parents and her Down syndrome baby, Trig, forced to stand in front of "Obama's death panel" of bureaucrats who would decide whether they were worthy of health care based on a subjective judgment of their "level of productivity to Society."[4] The phantasmagoria got wilder and wilder.[5] Rep. John Boehner (R-OH), then the Minority Leader of the House, led Republicans in a nightmare scenario of "government-sponsored" euthanasia. Rep. Virginia Fox (R-NC) talked of "seniors put to death by their government." This cascade was debunked by the

---

[3] Fredthompsonshow.com, interview archives, July 16, 2009.

[4] https://www.facebook.com/notes/sarah-palin/statement-on-the-current -health-care-debate/113851103434/

[5] https://en.wikipedia.org/wiki/Death_panel

American Medical Association, the AARP, the National Hospice and Palliative Care Organization, and the Consumers Union. Nonetheless, the Democrats took fright. Counseling was not restored as a Medicare claim until 2016. The Kaiser Family Foundation[6] has performed a public service with its analysis, as it has done throughout the succession of fantasies spawned by word viruses. Its animated YouToons video[7] got nearly two million views.

Obamacare became a political piñata, but it is typical of the obfuscation programmed in the DNA of rules and legislation, despite a generation of good work climaxing in the bipartisan Braley Plain Writing Act (2010), which requires the federal government to write "new publications, forms and publicly distributed documents in a clear, concise, well-organized manner that follows the best practices of plain language writing."

The effect of muddle and hostile media was comically exposed by researchers for Jimmy Kimmel's television show in October 2013 on ABC.[8]

His reporters took cameras to the street to ask passersby: "Do you prefer the Affordable Care Act or Obamacare?" We don't know whether the selection of interviewees was representative, but the six people viewers saw vigorously rejected Obamacare yet declared they were all in favor of the Affordable Care Act.

---

[6] http://kff.org/medicare/fact-sheet/10-faqs-medicares-role-in -end-of-life-care/

[7] http://kff.org/health-reform/video/youtoons-obamacare-video/

[8] "Obamacare vs. Affordable Care Act," https://www.youtube.com/watch?v =B8gA8lHApG0

Q. So you disagree with Obamacare?
A. Yes, I do.

Q. Do you think insurance companies should be able to exclude people with preexisting conditions?
A. No.

Q. Do you agree that young people should be able to stay on their parents' plan until they're twenty-six?
A. They should be able to, yes.

Q. Do you agree that companies with fifty or more employees should provide health care?
A. I do.

Q. And so, by that logic, do you support the Affordable Care Act?
A. I do.

Q. Do you think Obamacare is socialist?
A. Yes, I do.

Q. Do you think the Affordable Care Act is socialist?
A. No.

All those seen on the show condemned Obamacare for important provisions they thought were missing, and credited these same provisions to the Affordable Care Act. That was a good joke, given substance by a report from the Kaiser Family Foundation. Their 2013 tracking poll conducted from March 5 to March 10 found that only around half the people knew what Obamacare was. Nearly 90 percent were keen for small businesses to have tax credits to buy insurance; only 52 percent were aware it was in the new law. Eighty-one percent wanted to get rid of the coverage gap for drugs, known as the doughnut hole; only 46 percent knew Obamacare had removed it. The most popular provisions of Obamacare were among the least widely recognized—and still were in the 2016 election year.

The consequences of all the propaganda are real. Indiana's governor Pence broke ranks with other Republican governors to extend Medicaid to low-income adults. As reported in the *New York Times* (January 3, 2017), Justin Kloski qualified for Medicaid treatment for Hodgkin's lymphoma, curable if caught early. But he went uninsured in 2014 because he and his mother believed Obamacare required him to lose insurance at twenty-six—one of its key reforms! He did not vote for Hillary Clinton, who pledged to sustain the benefit, and was then left hoping President Trump and the Republican Congress would allow low-income adults into Medicaid.

What's a medical necessity?

The effect of a single word or two on health and happiness may be best illustrated by the stories of Ethan, Linda, and Glenda, Ethan and Linda being unaffected by Obamacare but Glenda being provoked by a surprising confrontation with Obama's health secretary Kathleen Sebelius. They demonstrate a disconnect between the intended insurance meaning and the commonly accepted dictionary meaning. They are an elbow in the solar plexus of every writer who is sloppy in word choice.

Ethan Bedrick's father was insured with Travelers through an ERISA welfare benefit plan. When Ethan was born on January 28, 1992, his mother had a bad delivery that left her son with cerebral palsy and hypertonia in all four limbs. In the words of a judge in the case, "The diabolical thing about hypertonia is that, unless properly treated, it can get much worse." If the fibrotic muscles are not systematically stretched, the patient can curl up in a tight ball. Ethan was put on an intensive program of physical, occupational, and speech therapy funded and administered by Travelers. His pediatrician, Dr. R. L. Swetenburg, thought he had a poor prognosis but had shown some improvement and had a fifty-fifty chance of being able to walk by age five.

He was fourteen months old when Travelers conducted a "utilization review," ugly words for an ugly result. They cut off coverage for speech therapy, limited his physical and occupational therapy to just fifteen sessions a year, and refused to pay for a bath chair and an upright stander prescribed by doctors and caregivers as a medical necessity to reduce contractures and fractures. The company ruling was upheld in district court before it reached the Fourth Circuit Appeals Court chaired by Judge Kenneth K. Hall.

The abrupt cancellation of Ethan's treatment was the work of Dr. Isabel Pollack, employed by ConservCo, a subsidiary of Travelers that looks for places to cut off or reduce services. At the trial before Judge Hall, she said she had called Dr. Swetenburg and Dr. Philip Lesser, Ethan's pediatric neurologist. Dr. Lesser described Ethan's potential for progress as mild but said he would support whatever home therapy the physical therapist, Donna Stout Wells, felt was necessary.

Dr. Pollack did not call the therapist: "I feel that further therapy is of minimal benefit. I cannot in good conscience support that we continue." All the doctors protested. Six months passed before Travelers responded.

The denial was reviewed by Dr. Kenneth Robbins in Travelers' head office, who later admitted that he saw his job as support for the legal department. He didn't contact any of the physicians. He hadn't seen a patient in seven years. He had not read textbooks or treatises on cerebral palsy, just a single article in a medical journal. From that he concluded that intensive physical therapy was no use against cerebral palsy and denied Ethan his bath chair; it was just "a convenience item." The ERISA administrators reviewed the case and concluded the Bedricks had been badly treated.

Judge Hall was withering in the court's judgment. There was "scant" support for Dr. Pollack's "baseless" and "precipitous" decision. Why did she think the physical therapy she had denied was not an effective way to prevent contractures?

"I cannot tell you how I developed it because I haven't thought about it for a long time."

Judge Hall: "To put it most charitably, we think it abundantly clear that Dr. Pollack at least 'unconsciously' put the financial interest of Travelers above her fiduciary duty to Ethan."

Travelers had supplemented its definition of *medical necessity* by arguing that the treatments did not hold promise of "significant progress." The court was unimpressed.

If, as his doctors and therapists believe, intensive therapy is necessary to prevent harm (e.g., contractures), then it is medically necessary treatment.... It is as important not to get worse as to get better.... The implication that walking by age five would not be "significant progress" for this unfortunate child is simply revolting.

The court reversed the decision of the district court on physical and occupational therapy for Ethan and the upright stander. But then it felt stymied.

"The plan provides coverage for speech therapy," wrote Judge Hall, "but there is a significant limitation: 'These services must be given to restore speech.' Ethan has never been able to talk so the therapy he receives cannot be said to 'restore speech.' Medically necessary or not, there is just no coverage here."

The cunning way Travelers wrote the plan intentionally excluded what would be covered for someone who had, say, a stroke. But consider the verb as defined by the *Shorter Oxford English Dictionary*:

Restore: To give back, to make return or restitution (of anything previously taken away or lost); to make amends for; to compensate, make good; to build up again; to renew; to bring (a person or part of the body) back to a healthy or vigorous state; to bring back a person (or thing) to a previous or normal condition.

It could reasonably be argued that speech therapy made amends for, or compensated for, Ethan's early difficulties.

Confining speech therapy to "restoring speech" was to deny Ethan hope of improving articulation and the other benefits of speech therapy as practically applied. The site www .cerebralpalsy.org. claims:

> Speech pathologists increase a child's oral motor skills and communication acumen by using exercises that train the brain to pronounce—as well as understand and interpret—individual words, sounds, numbers and gestures. Additionally, speech and language pathologists improve functioning of the mouth, jaw and throat muscles (oral motor functioning) that can interfere with not only speech, but also breathing and swallowing—two issues that can pose a significant danger to a child....A speech and language pathologist will assist in finding ways in which the child can begin to communicate through cues (winking or lifting a finger), sign language, or with the assistance of augmentative communication devices (DynaVox or computers).

To restrict speech therapy to restoring speech was indeed diabolical.

Linda and Glenda

Ethan Bedrick's case marks a trend, the transition of insurers' claims divisions into profit centers, and with that an imperative for people signing checks for insurance to be clear, very clear, how the protection they want fits the language of the policy they pay for, not loosely but precisely. The change since the 1980s is spelled out incidentally—but very clearly!—in *Law and the American Health Care System,*[9] fourteen hundred pages of law cases and policy. Insurers were more relaxed forty years ago. They wrote in broad strokes. Their policy terms were ambiguous; they used their general discretion to approve or deny claims, routinely deferring to the judgment of treating clinicians on whether treatments were medically necessary. American health-care costs doubled from 8 percent of GDP in 1980 to 17.1 percent in 2009, six points higher than those in comparable countries. This was mainly because of higher prices, more readily accessible technology, and obesity. Insurers began aggressively redefining *medically necessary,* narrowing the scope of coverage. Deliberately obscure language is one method. Another is to design policies not to say what is covered but what is excluded, witness the lethal "restorative" element in the Bedrick contract.

Linda McGraw was diagnosed with multiple sclerosis (MS) in 1983 when she was twenty-eight. Ten years later, she had undergone her doctor-prescribed intensive physical and occupational therapy at home with episodes of inpatient care to help endurance, strength, and mobility. The employer of her husband, Gary, had bought a plan from Prudential Plus which covered her hospital stay ($47,000). Except that Prudential said it didn't. This was baffling to the doctors and the McGraws. They'd met the three conditions for treatment to be covered as medically necessary—that it be prescribed

---

[9] Sara Rosenbaum et al., *Law and the American Health Care System* (St. Paul, MN: Foundation Press, 2012).

by a doctor; recognized as safe and effective; and not educational, experimental, or investigatory in nature. The denial of Linda's claim was made by the Prudential medical director, Dr. Boyd Shook, board certified in internal medicine, who had given up his practice to become the medical director of "Prudential products in Oklahoma City." Dr. Shook said, "It was a simple straightforward decision." To cover physical therapy, Prudential must now have evidence that her condition would improve. Linda's neurologists testified there was a critical distinction between *treatable* and *curable*, that treatment targeted the effects and that maintaining functionality, not getting worse, could amount to "improving." Three tiers of Prudential reviewers, then the district court, supported Dr. Shook, though he did not review Linda's medical records, did not speak with her neurologist, and did not read the medical literature. He had just formed the opinion that "physical therapy does not affect the course of MS" and was therefore not a medical necessity. Prudential just gave up on Linda.

The Court of Appeals for the Tenth Circuit did not. The judges reversed three district court verdicts. The treatment of Linda by Prudential had been "arbitrary and capricious."[10] It had changed its own definition of *medical necessity* beyond the three specified in the plan so that the care could be described not as "medically necessary," but only "medically beneficial."

Prudential hoped to escape obligation by stipulating that medically necessary treatment "must provide a measurable

---

[10] http://caselaw.findlaw.com/US-10th circuit/1200028.html

and substantial increase in functionality for a condition having potential for significant improvement." Words, words, words that added up to the Court of Appeals' conclusion that Prudential had not thought of Linda McGraw as a person but as multiple sclerosis and just "rubber-stamped" her condition.

Health Secretary Kathleen Sebelius had presided over the launch of Obamacare. It did not spare her a legal assault by five patients and six national advocacy groups over that word *improve,* the crux of the reverses inflicted on Ethan and Linda. Had the secretary, as the plaintiffs charged on appeal, "deliberately and covertly" introduced an "Improvement Standard" into Medicare claims by denying benefits to chronically sick and disabled patients for nursing, home health, or therapy services? Glenda Jimmo became the lead plaintiff in a class-action suit against the secretary. A legally blind diabetic in her seventies with a leg wound, Mrs. Jimmo had been refused payment for home help and therapy because the Medicare appeals panel judged she was not getting any better. She was labeled as "at a plateau," "chronic," "stable," and her case was shelved. Secretary Sebelius countered that the similarities between agency decisions denying coverage were legal errors in the application of valid regulations, not the outcome of a nationwide covert policy. She failed to persuade the court to reject the case on jurisdictional grounds—too many plaintiffs. The advocacy groups presented enough evidence to show that their allegations of denials of treatment were, in the court's view, "neither fanciful, fantastic nor delusional." Instead of prolonging a duel over definitions, Secretary Sebelius entered into a nationwide agreement to rewrite Medicare manuals so that patients at a plateau or in a slow decline would no longer be denied skilled nursing, outpatient therapy, or home help.

Fabien Levy, speaking for the U.S. Department of Health and Human Services, said, "Medicare policy will be clarified to ensure that claims from providers are reimbursed consistently and appropriately and not denied solely based on rule-of-thumb determination that a beneficiary's condition is not improving." The victory for a maintenance standard was not an expansion of Medicare so much as a commitment to ensure claims were reimbursed consistently to a maintenance standard and not an improvement standard. But it took an appeals court case to win the antidote to the human cost of bad rule-of-thumb writing. It's best if we can get it right the first time.

The right word

Mark Twain, in the essay "William Dean Howells," writes: "A powerful agent is the right word: it lights the reader's way and makes it plain; a close approximation to it will answer, and much traveling is done in a well-enough fashion by its help, but we do not welcome it and applaud it and rejoice in it as we do when *the* right one blazes out on us." Splendid; we all applaud, but the courts have to fathom cases where the precision of the right word proves illusory. We are sure we know what it means in the context of our writing. It is clear. It is in harmony with the rhythm of the sentences. Its style fits. But will our definition, our understanding of meaning, be universally accepted? Jean Niven, counsel at Merlin Law, writes:

You would think the word "collapse" clear enough. It is a common term in policies but what does it mean? A policy may enumerate causes of collapse such as hidden decay, use of defective materials and weight of people or personal property. However, there is no explanation of what constitutes collapse. That issue has been vigorously litigated in multiple states. Results have run the gamut from collapse is the abrupt falling down or caving in of a structure to collapse is the impairment of structural integrity so that the structure cannot be used for its intended purpose even though it remains standing. In that scenario coverage depends on the geographic location of the structure.

Policies that provide coverage for risks of sinkholes list as a criteria for payment that there must be "structural damage to the building, including the foundation." The policies until very recently failed to define "structural damage." Some federal and state courts construed the term to have its common sense meaning of "damage to the structure," while others turned to the International Building Code (IBC) and technical requirements of foundation displacement or buckling of load-bearing walls. There is no uniformity of expectations on how a loss would be treated.

Again, what do you understand by *prompt*? Policies tell you what you have to do to give "prompt notice of the direct physical loss or damage." But there is no definition of *prompt*. Numerous lawsuits have ensued, and again courts have varying opinions, from a few days to a couple of years.

Courts have also considered whether the prompt notice requirement extends from the date of loss *or* from the date a prudent person should have been aware of the loss.

Insuring your car has similar brainteasers. "Comprehensive" coverage does not cover damage when you bump into another car. That's collision insurance. You'd think the *all* in an *all-risk policy* would include every peril of loss. Wrong again. It is really a many-risk policy. The all-risk policies insure against all perils that are not specifically excluded in the policy.

At the risk of inducing paranoia, it is also necessary to conclude that "the law" can be a cover for ill-doing. Just the words *we are a law firm* persuaded thousands of homeowners to take advantage of an apparently benign governmental Home Affordable Modification Program (HAMP). The government's idea was to help people behind in their mortgage payments find a viable way to avoid foreclosure. Swarms of unscrupulous telemarketers in aggressive loan-modification ventures evaded the odium they'd begun to earn by borrowing a legal halo. In August 2016, a Center for Public Integrity investigation revealed that more than one thousand attorneys nationally had signed up with hybrid firms, and "most of the lawyers played no direct role in hiring or supervising marketers [and were] accused by state and federal consumer-fraud investigators of cheating desperate homeowners of tens of millions of dollars."

12

Home Runs for Writers

"Uh-oh, your coverage doesn't seem to include illness."

This last chapter is meant to compensate for our time in the bramble bushes of editing. The four passages, from these accomplished practitioners, represent a glimpse of the marvelous range of nonfiction, with minimal commentary from me:

Roger Angell, the *New Yorker* essayist and dean of baseball reporting.

Richard Cohen, the columnist for the *Washington Post* and *New York Daily News,* on an argument with history.

David Foster Wallace, who wrote an idiomatic narrative on John McCain, published in *Rolling Stone* during a more elevated election campaign than we were to endure in 2015–2016.

Barbara Demick of the *Los Angeles Times,* whose book of reporting, *Nothing to Envy,* finds light and hope in the vast darkness in the Democratic People's Republic of Korea.

WHAT ROGER ANGELL HEARD

Roger Angell could make a paper clip sing. In six decades at the *New Yorker,* he has written for every format the magazine has invented and then some: "Talk of the Town," "Notes and Comment," literary criticism and haikus, movie reviews and poems, profiles and farewells, letters and obituaries and Christmas greetings, and ten books and umpteen baseball reports. The bleachers rise as one to yell at baseball being mentioned last, bottom of the ninth. Fans wait in line, and online, for the periodic publication of his seasonal wrap-ups, "a blessed gift for the dimming winter," in the words of the historian and novelist Kevin Baker. But Roger Angell is not to be confined by any perimeter. Were he to pin on all the medals bestowed by diverse academies of literature and sport he'd be too weighed down to mount the stage to receive the next bunch for his crowning *New Yorker* collection, *This Old Man.*[1] At ninety-three, Roger Angell reports on the usual accumulation of wear-and-tear ailments. Think for a

---

[1] Roger Angell, *This Old Man: All in Pieces* (New York: Doubleday, 2015).

moment how you'd describe yours, presuming time and chance have made some dents in perfection. This is Roger's opening; my comment is in italics below.

> Check me out. The top two knuckles of my left hand look as if I'd been worked over by the KGB. No, it's more as if I'd been a catcher for the Hall of Fame pitcher Candy Cummings, the inventor of the curveball, who retired from the game in 1877. To put this another way, if I pointed my hand at you like a pistol and fired at your nose, the bullet would nail you in the left knee. Arthritis.

You have to obey the opening imperative in the active voice, but then, braced for a lament, you are entertained by an image of the Cold War and Curveball Candy, a legend from baseball's Hall of Fame — and then you get nailed by a freshly minted verb, by a bullet in the knee. Roger continues:

> Now, still facing you, if I cover my left, or better, eye with one hand, what I see is a blurry encircling vision of the ceiling and floor and walls or windows to your right and left but no sign of your face or head: nothing in the middle. But cheer up: if I reverse things and cover my right eye, there you are, back again. If I take my hand away and look at you with both eyes, the empty hole disappears and you're in 3-D, and actually looking pretty terrific today. Macular degeneration.
>
> I'm ninety-three, and I'm feeling great.

You don't have to run these paragraphs through any readability formula to know that they are good English, but I did just for devilment, and all the arbiters had the sense to applaud.[2] How could they not? The average sentence length is 14.5 words, vocabulary familiar all the way to the last two words, the images concrete. But that's only the chassis. We'd been poised to pity, but it's we who are told to cheer up, relieved to know we're "looking pretty terrific today." The writer we hear talking to us—the text is that alive—sounds like a pretty good fellow, and he doesn't drone on. Arthritis! Macular degeneration! We are grateful to have those doors slammed on each paragraph. The two paragraphs have almost every lesson in writing. There's not a sentence you have to read twice because every one is clear, the whole objective of this book. Angell's longtime *New Yorker* colleague Charles McGrath remarks that Roger's hallmark is his ability to notice things and then describe them in such a way that you notice them, too, as if for the first time. The style is conversational, unintimidating. He doesn't put on airs, which is remarkable in itself because he could.

When Roger Angell was a boy he listened to E. B. (Andy) White writing. *Listened* is the correct verb because White was his stepfather and young Angell, from behind Andy's study door at the family farmhouse in Maine, absorbed the melodies White made at his typewriter—hesitant bursts of *clack-click-ring*, with long silences in between and then brooding silences at lunch, worrying about the words he left unfinished. "It isn't good enough. I wish it were better." This is the same E. B. White who wrote the children's classic *Charlotte's Web*

---

[2] Count Wordsworth numbers were similar to others: Flesch 80.21, Gunning 5.85, Dale-Chall 7.35.

(1954), and five years later added to a 1918 text by Will Strunk Jr., his professor at Cornell, and became the White in *Strunk and White's Elements of Style,* which has helped ten million writers say what they want to say, more or less.

The boy who eavesdropped on Andy became the *New Yorker* fiction editor in 1956: "Fiction is special, of course, for its text must retain the whorls and brush splashes of the author, the touch of the artist. At the same time, the editor should not feel much compunction about asking the writer the same questions he would put to himself about a swatch of his own prose: Is it clear? Does it say what I wanted to say?" He communed with John Updike comma by comma in the "fresh-painted sentences" of Updike's fiction. They would mull over the order of a few words, trying alternative phrasing. "Which one sounds better, do you think?" "All writers do this, but not many with such lavishly extended consideration. [Updike] wanted to see each galley, each tiny change, right down to the late-closing page proofs, which he often managed to return by overnight mail an hour or so before closing, with new sentences or passages, handwritten in the margins in a soft pencil, that were fresher and more inventive than what had been there before. You watched him write."

I asked **Kevin Baker** to watch Roger Angell write about baseball. If you don't care a dime for that or any other sport, you can still admire how Roger evokes a place or an era and the appeal of the game.[3] Here are Baker's observations:

---

[3] Kevin Baker is the author, most recently, of the novel *The Big Crowd* and is finishing a history of New York City baseball.

In 1963, at a time of wrenching change for New York City, Roger called the grandstands of the decrepit, old Polo Grounds "as rich and deplorable and heart-warming as Rivington Street...a vast assemblage of front stoops and rusty fire escapes." At a farewell to the same ballpark in 1964 he included such closely observed sensations as how a ramp to the front gate "pushed your toes into your shoe tips as you approached the park, tasting sweet anticipation and getting out your change to buy a program."

"Inside the gentle, rocker-like swing of the loop of rusty chain you rested your arm upon in a box seat, and the heat of the sun-warmed iron coming through your shirtsleeve under the elbow." In the Mets' bright, plasticy new Shea Stadium, by contrast, "my companions and I were ants perched on the sloping lip of a vast, shiny soup plate, and we were lonelier than we liked."

Portraying Reggie Jackson, Roger writes of "the strange insect gaze of his shining eyeglasses, with his ominous Boche-like helmet pulled low, with his massive shoulders, his gauntleted wrists, his high-held bat, and his enormously muscled legs spread wide."

Never above his subject, while vacationing in Maine, he worries over the fortunes of his favorite team: "...I went to bed early on most nights and lay there semi-comatose, stunned by another day of sunshine and salt air but kept awake, but almost awake, by the murmurous running thread of Bosox baseball from my bedside radio." He compares his anxieties, and those of his fellow fans, over the Red Sox's success to "...a young couple who for years had rented a nice little apartment on the second floor, dreaming and saving in the hope that someday they could afford a house of their own. Now, at last, we had it—Top o' the Hill Cottage—and for the first time we realized that the place was mortgaged, that it had to be painted and kept up and looked after, and that it could be lost."

In the end, the Red Sox blow a huge lead, and have to endure a one-game playoff against their archrivals, the New York Yankees. It would be one of the most dramatic, most written about games in baseball history, one fraught with tension (and hyperbole). But of all the writers who put their pen to it, none outdid Angell.

Kevin notes how Roger starts by wryly acknowledging all the "Omens and citations" surrounding the event, such as the *Boston Globe* quoting Dickens and a Harvard classics professor, but moves quickly past them, into the baseball. He conveys the action of the game in quick, concise descriptions that still, after dozens of readings, sound as fresh as his notes must have been when he jotted them down. He shows us the Boston pitcher, who "all emotion, kicked the dirt and shook his head." His Yankees counterpart who, "a little pitching machine, reared and threw, touched his cap, walked backward, did it all over again." He picks out moments to unveil these small but crucial intricacies of the game—a close play at third, a catch in right field "against the frightful sunlight," a "fatal bit of Boston conservatism on the basepaths"—that make all the difference. At the same time, he evokes the whole atmosphere of the game in a few choice details. The bullpen catchers and pitchers "who sat immobile in two silent rows," "the low-lying, glary sunlight," or how "the cheering, when it came, was savage but abrupt, quickly terminated again and again by the weight and anxiety of the occasion."

At the end, he makes his way "down into the dark, ancient grandstand" of Fenway Park, where as the game draws to its nerve-rending conclusion, he admits that his own hands are trembling and reports, "The faces around me looked haggard." The Red Sox's aging star Carl Yastrzemski makes the final out, and Angell notes how the Harvard professor in the *Globe* explains that "the hero must go under at last…to have poets sing his tale." But Roger still doesn't see why Yaz couldn't have won the game: "I'd have sung that, too. I think God was shelling a peanut."

ARGUMENT: THE REVERBERATIONS OF HISTORY

There is nothing like the past for inflaming an argument about the present. The tumult and the shouting fade and the captains and the kings depart, so who will speak for them? Churchill's solution was preemption. "I will be well served by history because I intend to write it." But nearly a century later along comes historian Richard Toye[4] to relate in detail how the savior of Western democracy approved of imperial atrocities in the East. The "half-naked fakir," Mahatma Gandhi, "ought to be lain bound hand and foot at the gates of Delhi and then trampled on by an enormous elephant with the new Viceroy seated on its back." A vivid and embarrassing taunt, to which Gandhi replied gracefully.

How to reconcile the moral contradictions of Churchill? The tumult and the shouting erupt periodically in American

---

[4] Richard Toye, *Churchill's Empire: The World That Made Him and the World He Made* (New York: Macmillan, 2010).

colleges tormented by the histories of slavery, the civil rights struggles, and quotas and affirmative action. If the Confederate flag flew so long over South Carolina's capitol, was Jim Crow really dead and gone? If Princeton University honors its own president Woodrow Wilson, is it insulting African Americans today? You could write a treatise on the political and social perplexities. Richard Cohen wrestled the intractables into 744 concise words—with a conclusion.

Richard Cohen's Text	My Commentary
At Princeton University, the image and name of Woodrow Wilson could soon be erased.	A concise fourteen words. We are curious at once, perhaps a little concerned.
He was the school's president from 1902 to 1910, reforming it, transforming it and setting it on the path to academic excellence. He left the school and soon became America's 28th president—	A reformer and U.S. president? What's going on?
a great one, some people believe—but he was born in the pre–Civil War South and was a contemptible racist most of his life. A bit late, he is being held accountable for that.	Cohen's midsentence change of direction is brutal. He might have written "but he was born in the pre–Civil War South where racial segregation was the norm." Instead, he
Some students are demanding that Wilson's name be expunged from the Princeton	raises the temperature with the rawness of "contemptible

Richard Cohen's Text	My Commentary
campus, most prominently the Woodrow Wilson School of Public and International Affairs. They also want a mural of him taken down. They feel so strongly about this that they occupied the university president's office, holding it for 32 hours until the school's administration agreed to consider their demands. Similar demonstrations have occurred at other colleges and universities. Amid student protests, Amherst College's faculty have voted to boot its mascot, the red-coated and bewigged Lord Jeff, a British field marshal who may have sent blankets imbued with smallpox to Native Americans. His name is plastered on several New England locations, including the town in Massachusetts where the school is located. Lord Jeffery Amherst, 1st Baron Amherst of Montreal,	racist." He withholds the evidence for the charge. The reader will expect it soon, but here it prepares the arena for the anti-Wilson campaigners. The extent and nature of the protests could have been in the lead, but Cohen gives his column momentum from this slow reveal of the scale of protests and the concrete image of the "red-coated and bewigged Lord Jeff." "Boot" is a strong verb to dramatize the indignity inflicted on a dignified figure — hero finally meets ignominy. But is the comparison fair to Wilson?

Richard Cohen's Text	**My Commentary**
hero of so many battles, has finally met ignominy. Lord Jeff is one thing, Wilson another. The severe-looking president was in many ways a transformational progressive. He advocated women's right to vote (the 19th Amendment) and the eight-hour workday, and he supported the Clayton Antitrust Act as well as the creation of the Federal Reserve and the Federal Trade Commission. He also backed the implementation of the federal income tax, a progressive way for the government to raise funds. In foreign affairs, he took the country into World War I and helped create the League of Nations, which the United States, to his painful regret, did not join. He formulated an internationalism we now call "Wilsonian" that has influenced U.S. foreign policy ever since.	Forgive the zombie "implementation" for beginning the collection of federal income tax, approved by the Sixteenth Amendment. The case is now built for Wilson. How can Cohen reconcile it with the hostility of the students? Answer...

Richard Cohen's Text	My Commentary
What's lacking in the Princeton debate over Wilson, and similar debates elsewhere, is an appreciation for the word "and." Instead, "but" is too often substituted, so that a person becomes one thing or another—not two things at once.	...wait for it.
Sometimes those things are in conflict, as with Thomas Jefferson. He drafted the Declaration of Independence, founded the University of Virginia and championed religious freedom. And he was a slaveholder. Still, I would keep his monument on the Tidal Basin.	This vivid insight into the power of the humble conjunction is the pith and pivot of Cohen's refreshingly original argument. For the contradictions within Andrew Jackson, Cohen summons another three-letter conjunction beloved of editorial writers ("yet") but (!) brilliantly milks the effects of "and"/"but."
George Washington, like Jefferson, owned slaves, freeing them only after he and his wife died. Andrew Jackson extended American democracy, yet he was brutal to Indians. Henry Ford made his car ubiquitous and paid his workers well. He was also an anti-Semite whose newspaper, the *Dearborn*	How nimbly Cohen jumps several rungs to the top of Hayakawa's "ladder of abstraction"—described in the 1939 landmark book *Language in Action*—and steps back down again to

Richard Cohen's Text	My Commentary
Independent, advanced his bigotry. The paper had a huge circulation.	the mid-level detail in Johnson.
The ability and willingness to keep two opposing views in mind at the same time are hallmarks of adulthood. We grow up to respect the gray. Black or white, one or the other, is childish. It represents the worldview of someone who does not know the world.	
Lyndon Johnson abused his aides, cheated on his wife, supported racial segregation early in his career — *and* embraced civil rights as president.	
More to the moment: Ben Carson is a brilliant surgeon and a political ignoramus.	
Neither one cancels out the other, but in choosing a president, one is more important than the other.	
Still, there can be a tipping point where one quality simply obliterates all the others.	

Richard Cohen's Text	My Commentary
When I look at Wilson's portrait, I might think first of the League of Nations and second how when he grew ill his wife secretly governed in his stead— and not give primacy to his racism.	
But I am white, so Wilson's support of Jim Crow laws and his determination to implement them in the civil service may not give me the same emotional jolt that they do a black person.	Essential qualifier, reinforces regard for writer as fair-minded.
So, what are we to do with Jefferson, Jackson, Wilson and the rest? Can Americans of color be expected to honor historical figures who hardly honored their ancestors and instead enslaved, exploited and even killed them?	
That can be hard. Still, we have an obligation to place historical figures in the context of their times and to accord them what they, in some instances, did not	Cohen, having laid out the pro and anti positions, ascends the ladder of abstraction again to offer a resounding conclusion.

Richard Cohen's Text	**My Commentary**
accord others: understanding. Woodrow Wilson was not one thing or another. He was one thing *and* another. It's a lesson Princeton should teach.	

THE PROFILE

Good writers breathe a kiss of life into old dead facts. I covered the 2008 presidential election and read and heard so much about John McCain's privations as a prisoner of war in Vietnam, it was boring to read any more. Then I read David Foster Wallace's idiomatic narration of the same events, prose with the frost off, and for the first time my reaction was visceral. Wow! None of the other perfectly respectable writing, not even McCain's own, had broken through the skin to make me feel the pain inflicted on him, gasp at the cruelties of his captors, appreciate the moral courage, gutsiness, and downright nobility of his self-sacrifice in refusing to abandon his fellow prisoners for a cushy passage home. Would that Wallace had been with us amid the gaseous vanities of the 2016 presidential campaigns. People who say all politicians are alike should be taken to a tattoo parlor and there confined until every word of "The Weasel, Twelve Monkeys and the Shrub" is inscribed on their chests.

What makes this excerpt work? It's the constant stopping to ask the questions and the almost casual last sentence after all the emotional freight. He pulls the lens out to the interrogatory then directs it back again to the close, unbearable detail, the rhythms of pain and release that McCain himself was experiencing. It's a wonderful trick with the reader's consciousness. The back-and-forth reflects the ostensible subject, McCain, and the real subject, us; an interior monologue he sustains simultaneously. Are we good enough? Could we do it? Would we do it? He leaves us consumed by a surge of awful self-doubt.

Edited excerpt of *Rolling Stone* article by David Foster Wallace:

Since you are reading "Rolling Stone," the chances are you're an American between say 18 and 35, which demographically makes you a Young Voter. And no generation of Young Voters has ever cared less about politics and politicians than yours. There's hard demographic and voter-pattern data backing this up...assuming you give a shit about data. In fact, even if you're reading other stuff in RS, it's doubtful you're going to read much of this article—such is the enormous shuddering yawn that the Political Process evokes in us now, in this post-Watergate-post-Iran-Contra-post-Whitewater-post-Lewinsky era, an era when politicians' statements of principle or vision are understood as self-serving ad copy and judged not for their sincerity or ability to inspire but for their tactical shrewdness, their marketability. And no generation has been marketed and Spun and pitched to as ingeniously and relentlessly as today's demographic Young. So when Senator John McCain says, in Michigan or South Carolina (which is where ROLLING STONE sent the least professional pencil it could find to spend the standard media Week on the Bus with a candidate who'd never ride higher than he is right now), "I run for president not to Be Somebody, but to Do Something," it's hard to hear it as anything more than a marketing angle, especially when he says it as he's going around surrounded by cameras and reporters and cheering crowds…in other words, Being Somebody.

And when Senator John McCain also says— constantly, thumping it at the start and end of every speech and THM—that his goal as president will be "to inspire young Americans to devote themselves to causes greater than their own self-interest," it's hard not to hear it as just one more piece of the carefully scripted bullshit that presidential candidates hand us as they go about the self-interested business of trying to become the most powerful, important and talked-about human being on earth, which is of course their real "cause," to which they appear to be so deeply devoted that they can swallow and spew whole mountains of noble-sounding bullshit and convince even themselves that they mean it. Cynical as that may sound, polls show it's how most of us feel. And it's beyond not believing the bullshit; mostly we don't even hear it, dismiss it at the same deep level where we also block out billboards and Muzak.

But there's something underneath politics in the way you have to hear McCain, something riveting and unSpinnable and true. It has to do with McCain's military background and Vietnam combat and the five-plus years he spent in a North Vietnamese prison, mostly in solitary, in a box, getting tortured and starved. And the unbelievable honor and balls he showed there. It's very easy to gloss over the POW thing, partly because we've all heard so much about it and partly because it's so off-the-charts dramatic, like something in a movie instead of a man's life. But it's worth considering for a minute, because it's what makes McCain's "causes greater than self-interest" line easier to hear.

You probably already know what happened. In October of '67 McCain was himself still a Young Voter and flying his 23rd Vietnam combat mission and his A-4 Skyhawk plane got shot down over Hanoi and he had to eject, which basically means setting off an explosive charge that blows your seat out of the plane, which ejection broke both McCain's arms and one leg and gave him a concussion and he started falling out of the skies right over Hanoi. Try to imagine for a second how much this would hurt and how scared you'd be, three limbs broken and falling toward the enemy capital you just tried to bomb. His chute opened late and he landed hard in a little lake in a park right in the middle of downtown Hanoi. Imagine treading water with broken arms and trying to pull the life vest's toggle with your teeth as a crowd of Vietnamese men swim out toward you (there's film of this, somebody had a home-movie camera, and the N.V. government released it, though it's grainy and McCain's face is hard to see). The crowd pulled him out and then just about killed him. U.S. bomber pilots were especially hated, for obvious reasons. McCain got bayoneted in the groin; a soldier broke his shoulder apart with a rifle butt. Plus by this time his right knee was bent 90° to the side with the bone sticking out. Try to imagine this. He finally got tossed on a jeep and taken five blocks to the infamous Hoa Lo prison—a.k.a. the "Hanoi Hilton," of much movie fame—where they made him beg a week for a doctor and finally set a couple of the fractures without anesthetic and let two other fractures and the groin wound (imagine: *groin wound*) stay like they were. Then they threw him in a cell. Try for a moment to feel this. All the media profiles talk about how McCain still can't lift his arms over his head to comb his hair, which is true. But try to imagine it at the time, yourself in his place, because it's important. Think about how *diametrically* opposed to your own self-interest getting knifed in the balls and having fractures set without painkiller would be, and then about getting thrown in a cell to just lie there and hurt, which is what happened. He was delirious with pain for weeks, and his weight dropped to 100 pounds, and the other POWs were sure he would die; and then after a few months like that after his bones mostly knitted and he could sort of stand up they brought him in to the prison commandant's office and offered to let him go. This is true. They said he could just leave. They had found out that McCain's father was one of the top-ranking naval officers in the U.S. Armed Forces (which is true—both his father and grandfather were admirals), and the North Vietnamese wanted the PR coup of mercifully releasing his son, the baby-killer. McCain, 100 pounds and barely able to stand, refused. The U.S. military's Code of Conduct for Prisoners of War apparently said that POWs had to be released in the order they were captured, and there were others who'd been in Hoa Lo a long time, and McCain refused to violate the Code. The commandant, not pleased, right there in the office had guards break his ribs, rebreak his arm, knock his teeth out. McCain still refused to leave without the other POWs. And so then he spent four more years in Hoa Lo like this, much of the time in solitary, in the dark, in a closet-sized box called a "punishment cell." Maybe you've heard all this before; it's been in umpteen different media profiles of McCain. But try to imagine that moment between getting offered early release and turning it down. Try to imagine it was you. Imagine how loudly your most basic, primal self-interest would have cried out to you in that moment, and all the ways you could ratio-nalize accepting the offer. Can you hear it? If so, would you have refused to go? You simply can't know for sure. None of us can. It's hard even to imagine the pain and fear in that moment, much less know how you'd react.

But, see, we *do* know how this man reacted. That he chose to spend four more years there, in a dark box, alone, tapping code on the walls to the others, rather than violate a Code. Maybe he was nuts. But the point is that with McCain it feels like we *know*, for a proven *fact*, that he's capable of devotion to something other, more, than his own self-interest. So that when he says the line in speeches in early February you can feel like maybe it isn't just more candi-date bullshit, that with this guy it's maybe the truth. Or maybe both the truth *and* bullshit: the guy does—did—want your vote, after all.

But that moment in the Hoa Lo office in '68—right before he refused, with all his basic normal human self-interest howling at him—that moment is hard to blow off. All week, all through MI and SC and all the tedium and cynicism and paradox of the campaign, that moment seems to underlie McCain's "greater than self-interest" line, moor it, give it a weird sort of reverb that's hard to ignore. The fact is that John McCain is a genuine hero of the only kind Vietnam now has to offer, a hero not because of what he did but because of what he suffered— voluntarily, for a Code. This gives him the moral authority both to utter lines about causes beyond self-interest and to expect us, even in this age of Spin and lawyerly cunning, to believe he means them. Literally: "moral authority," that old cliché, much like so many other clichés—"service," "honor," "duty," "patriotism"—that have become just mostly words now, slogans invoked by men in nice suits who want something from us. The John McCain we've seen, though—arguing for his doomed campaign-finance bill on the Senate floor in '98, calling his colleagues crooks to their faces on C-SPAN, talking openly about a bought-and-paid-for government on *Charlie Rose* in July '99, unpretentious and bright as hell in the Iowa debates and New Hampshire Town Hall Meetings—something about him made a lot of us feel the guy wanted something different from us, something more than votes or money, something old and maybe corny but with a weird achy pull to it like a whiff of a childhood smell or a name on the tip of your tongue, something that would make us think about what terms like "service" and "sacrifice" and "honor" might really *refer* to, like whether they actually stood for something, maybe. About whether anything past well-Spun self-interest might be real, was ever real, and if so then what happened? These, for the most part, are not lines of thinking that the culture we've grown up in has encouraged Young Voters to pursue. Why do you suppose that is?

BARBARA DEMICK

Darkness Visible. The title of novelist William Styron's account of his descent into a long clinical depression would seem a match for the condition and mood of North Korea. Twenty-three million people live in the vast darkness seen on satellite photographs. They cannot watch television at night; they cannot read a book. Barbara Demick manages to portray the lives of six of them. This brief extract is of one adolescent girl and her boyfriend, who, "wrapped in the cloak of invisibility," learned to love in the darkness. The detail is unobtrusive, but by choice of noun and verb lets us see what the CIA's satellite photos cannot. We see the boy find a meeting spot "as the light seeped out of the sky," prepared to wait hours for her; their long walks outside the town, "scattering ginkgo leaves in their wake," under a night sky surprisingly brilliant. The cadence of life is slow. "Nobody owned a watch."

Edited excerpt from *Nothing to Envy: Real Lives in North Korea,* by Barbara Demick:

I met many North Koreans who told me how much they learned to love the darkness, but it was the story of one teenage girl and her boyfriend that impressed me most. She was twelve years old when she met a young man three years older from a neighboring town. Her family was low-ranking in the Byzantine system of social controls in place in North Korea. To be seen in public together would damage the boy's career prospects as well as her reputation as a virtuous young woman. So their dates consisted entirely of long walks in the dark. There was nothing else to do anyway; by the time they started dating in earnest in the early 1990s, none of the restaurants or cinemas were operating because of the lack of power.

They would meet after dinner. The girl had instructed her boyfriend not to knock on the front door and risk questions from her older sisters, younger brother, or the nosy neighbors. They lived squeezed together in a long, narrow building behind which was a common outhouse shared by a dozen families. The houses were set off from the street by a white wall, just above eye level in height. The boy found a spot behind the wall where nobody would notice him as the light seeped out of the day. The clatter of the neighbors washing the dishes or using the toilet masked the sound of his footsteps. He would wait hours for her, maybe two or three. It didn't matter. The cadence of life is slower in North Korea. Nobody owned a watch.

The girl would emerge just as soon as she could extricate herself from the family. Stepping outside, she would peer into the darkness, unable to see him at first but sensing with certainty his presence. She wouldn't bother with makeup—no one needs it in the dark. Sometimes she just wore her school uniform: a royal blue skirt cut modestly below the knees, a white blouse and red bow tie, all of it made from a crinkly synthetic material. She was young enough not to fret about her appearance.

At first, they would walk in silence, then their voices would gradually rise to whispers and then to normal conversational levels as they left the village and relaxed into the night. They maintained an arm's length distance from each other until they were sure they wouldn't be spotted.

Just outside the town, the road headed into a thicket of trees to the grounds of a hot-spring resort. It was once a resort of some renown; its 130-degree waters used to draw busloads of Chinese tourists in search of cures for arthritis and diabetes, but by now it rarely operated. The entrance featured a rectangular reflecting pond lined with pine trees, Japanese maples, and the girl's favorites— the ginkgo trees that in autumn shed delicate mustard-yellow leaves in the shape of perfect Oriental fans. On the surrounding hills, the trees had been decimated by people foraging for firewood, but the trees at the hot springs were so beautiful that the locals respected them and left them alone.

Otherwise the grounds were poorly maintained. The trees were untrimmed, stone benches cracked, paving stones missing like rotten teeth. By the mid-1990s, nearly everything in North Korea was worn out, broken, malfunctioning. The country had seen better days. But the imperfections were not so glaring at night. The hot-springs pool, murky and choked with weeds, was luminous with the reflection of the sky above.

The night sky in North Korea is a sight to behold. It might be the most brilliant in Northeast Asia, the only place spared the coal dust, Gobi Desert sand, and carbon monoxide choking the rest of the continent. In the old days, North Korean factories contributed their share to the cloud cover, but no longer. No artificial lighting competes with the intensity of the stars etched into its sky.

The young couple would walk through the night, scattering ginkgo leaves in their wake. What did they talk about? Their families, their classmates, books they had read—whatever the topic, it was endlessly fascinating. Years later, when I asked the girl about the happiest memories of her life, she told me of those nights.

This is not the sort of thing that shows up in satellite photographs. Whether in CIA headquarters in Langley, Virginia, or in the East Asian studies department of a university, people usually analyze North Korea from afar. They don't stop to think that in the middle of this black hole, in this bleak, dark country where millions have died of starvation, there is also love.

Afterthought

~~~

As I Was Saying Before I Was
So Rudely Interrupted

ASK THESEUS

Christine Kenneally, an Australian linguist, sat in the Tea Lounge on Seventh Avenue in Brooklyn and made me think about words just when I was at the end of this book, exhausted thinking about them. In the foreword to her book *The First Word,* exploring the evolution of language, she directed me, all of us, to look at the heavens and think of each of sixty thousand glittering specks as a word. And see that each is not a single point of light but an intense cluster of all the associations evoked by every word in our linguistic constellation. Immediately, I thought of *ladder* and of *abstraction. Ladder* because she had ascended — effortlessly — from the Tea Lounge to the stars, from the very particular of a teacup and a chair to the incomprehensible generality of the universe.

The "ladder of abstraction" is the concept described by the iconoclastic Professor Samuel Ichiye Hayakawa (1906–1992), linguist and semanticist at San Francisco State College. His 1939 book, *Language in Action,* expanded in 1941, offered insight into the process of thought, and hence of writing, from the concrete, the rung at the foot of the ladder, to the abstract at the top you cannot see and have to imagine. Writers who maintain our interest carry ideas forward by abstractions but make them vivid by specific concrete examples, as I stressed in the ten shortcuts (chapter 4). Your mind can move, in the quick flash of a starburst, from a general idea of democracy at the top of the ladder down to the specific, the purple stain on the index finger of a first-time voter in the Iraq election in 2005. If you write too many abstractions, you risk readers nodding off. They come awake with a specific, and if the abstractions don't suggest one, your passage is likely borderline boring. The specific can be the citation of a concrete example or the literary devices of simile and metaphor, synonym and antonym. I opened this book with the *Bleak House* metaphor of fog, an antonym for clarity more tangible than the similes for clarity—*simplicity, brightness, accuracy, directness, lucidity, purity, transparency.*

Similes and antonyms don't quite cover all the qualities of good writing set out in the ten shortcuts, so I tried following the word associations of another star in the firmament so much on my mind: the web. The thesaurus takes me from *web* to *perplexity* and *maze,* and then up pops the word *labyrinth,* an intricate combination of paths or passages so bewildering you lose your way and then can't find the exit. On a visit to the ruins of the Palace of Knossos in Crete, I was enchanted to be told that *labyrinth* derives from *labrys*, meaning "a double-headed ax," and the house of the double-headed ax is the labyrinth of myth and Mary Renault's novel *The King Must Die*, where the bull-headed monster Minotaur waited to devour anyone who entered. Nobody who had been flung into the labyrinth ever came out. Of course, Theseus did. He entered the house of the double-headed ax, slew the Minotaur, and found his way out again by following the path of the ball of thread Ariadne had given him so he could mark his trail on the way in.

Think Theseus when you are launched on a long intricate sentence; can you get out alive? As we saw in the sentence clinic (chapter 3), you are more likely to lose your way in sentences longer than forty words and notably so when you open sentences with long subsidiary clauses that I've dubbed *predatory*. Such sentences too often separate subject, verb, and object, and they risk producing nonsense by detaching modifiers from the words modified.

Think Theseus on his hazardous journey from Troezen to Athens to Crete, braving the metaphorical zombies and flesh-eaters we encountered in chapter 5. He recognized them for what they were and slew them all. Give him his due. Since I've described how the passive voice so often muffles the action and disguises who did the deed, you can hardly fail to write in the active voice that Theseus slew the dreadful Periphetes, Sinis, and Procrustes, and not, passively, that they were slain by Theseus.

Kenneally writes that because language does not mimic

the world, we can do things with it that are impossible under the laws of physics. "You are a god in language. You can create. Destroy. Rearrange. Shove words around however you like. You can make up stories about things that never happened to people who never existed." It's a power for good and a power for evil. The words *shoved around* may flower as literature's gift to civilization, in nonfiction as well as fiction, but Hayakawa feared that liberties were at the mercy of the unscrupulous manipulator of words; in a radical student demo in 1968 he pulled the wires from a loudspeaker because the language seemed to him to foment a violent shutdown of the campus. He regretted it later.

Would that it were that simple to deal with the millions of words that confuse and deceive people. It would be a good start to relocate to the labyrinth those lawyers who file briefs described by a federal judge as "vague, ambiguous, unintelligible, verbose and repetitive." The prolixity of legal language is one reason the courts are disgracefully years behind in doing their work. As I've shown, there is no call to be intimidated by the *heretofore* and *notwithstanding* of legal or political writing, but the preceding pages have amply demonstrated how often slipshod writers and lackluster editors visit cruel and unusual punishment on our language. They know no better. Worse than these confounders are the competent writers who set out with intent to deceive. They are all honorable men (and women), the obfuscating lawyers and insurers, the wily legislators and sly sellers, the spin merchants, the PR officers, who do it reflexively in defense of their clients and their interests. No doubt Travelers Insurance thought it was nifty to deny Ethan Bedrick his speech therapist by the malign parsing of the word *restore*. No doubt Prudential Plus had grown a crocodile skin thick enough to bear the judges' description of its treatment of Linda McGraw as "arbitrary and capricious."

Sir William Haley, one of my predecessors as editor of the *Times*, said, "There are things which are bad and false and ugly and no amount of specious casuistry will make them good or true or beautiful."

The fog that envelops English is not just a question of good taste, style, and aesthetics. It is a moral issue.

Do I make myself clear?

ACKNOWLEDGMENTS

✦✦✦

First, I apologize to the innumerable nameless victims I trapped in the years I was writing *Do I Make Myself Clear?* I may at any point have been obsessed by zombies, so I fully understood why devotees of *Downton Abbey* shrank from someone who seemed eager to swap opinions about the last episode of *The Walking Dead*. All I wanted to know was whether literate people shared my repugnance for bloated nouns that had gorged on lively verbs. This linguistic crime, laid bare in chapter 5, was known as nominalization until New Zealand's Professor Helen Sword named the verb-slaying nouns *zombies*. Best forgotten, too, are the occasions when I wanted to rehearse thoughts on the metaphorical utility of the aquatic creature known as a zoophagus (also chapter 5).

Apologies to all I harassed as profuse as my thanks to those who sustained me in quarrying the word-mines for two years, or maybe it was twenty, given the false starts I made. Judith Clain, editor in chief at my publisher, Little,

Brown, was gracious in understanding when I was interrupted midchapter by the imperative of news in my work at Reuters, but she was creative, too, in suggestions for enlarging the scope of the book. My longtime agent in London and New York, Ed Victor, deserves his medal as a Commander of the British Empire for services to publishing, but I'd add an extra ribbon for his fortitude in the face of what must have seemed authorial lassitude.

Two of my helpers demonstrated extraordinary resilience: Cindy Quillinan and Jolene Lescio. Cindy, my personal assistant, had a hundred other things to do but somehow kept track of everything from my first illegible notes to the last full stop on the bound galley and liaised effectively with the diligent Amanda Brower.

Jolene Lescio, my principal researcher, is a librarian in the village of Quogue in the Hamptons. What did she not do? Jolene identified, for instance, all my half-remembered examples of sentences run amok, found more of her own, transmitted every nuance in the drafts of President Roosevelt's speeches beautifully organized by the archivists at Hyde Park. More. Thirty-six years before, when I was editing the *Sunday Times* in London, I had been impressed by a critique of the English in official forms cunningly designed to intimidate claimants for welfare benefits. I thought I still had the essay somewhere in boxes and boxes and more boxes moved with me from London to Stanford and Chicago and New York and Quogue, but there in 2012, we were hit by superstorm Sandy. Susan Rasmussen Rogot salvaged what she could of our files, but who and where, after all these years, was the author Roger Hampson? Jolene tracked him down. He is still translating complexity, now as the chief executive officer of the London borough of Redbridge, where his "Redbridge Conversations" explain fiscal problems to a watchful population of taxpayers. My manuscript owes much to the Redbridge touch. Roger is on the board of the Open Data Institute and works with Professor Sir Nigel Shadbolt, and Timothy Berners-Lee, inventor of the Internet.

It is nice to have any kind of even tenuous proximity to greatness, so I must also mention Winston Churchill (again). I am indebted to the enthusiastic scholarship of Dr. Warren Dockter, who came by way of the Universities of Tennessee and Nottingham to be an archives by-fellow at Churchill College, Cambridge. He is an authority on British imperialism, so I commanded him to satisfy my curiosity as to how passages of memorable Churchill were refined and smelted. Thanks, too, for the recommendation of Allen Packwood, director of the archives at Churchill College.

I owe my wife, Tina Brown, for the introduction to Roger Angell. In her years editing the *New Yorker,* she had often come home saying, "You gotta read this," thrusting at me a copy of an essay for the next edition. I did read Angell with analytical assiduity, and many more of the magazine's treasured writers. When I began work on *Do I Make Myself Clear?* I sought out Roger and his lapidary colleague Charles McGrath, who indulged my questions on editing and writing. I thank them. I also managed to make a date to discuss the cartoons for this book with Bob Mankoff, the cartoon czar and author of the unforgettable caption *No, Thursday's out. How about never—is never good for you?* Wednesday was very good for both of us.

A number of colleagues who worked with me in the great days at the *Sunday Times* proved of a forgiving nature. They were generous in lending their literary skills and Joan Thomas in London was untiring in pursuit. I am grateful to Anthony Holden, the translator and editor of ancient Greek poetry, who spared me the jest that my manuscript was all Greek to him. As the biographer of twenty-four giants, including Shakespeare, Tchaikovsky, Olivier, and several members of the Royal Family, he is aware that authors bleed easily. He wrote the biography of our mutual friend David Blundy, whose talents and bravery can only be glimpsed in the second chapter. I benefited, too, from conversations with John Heilpern, editor of my autobiography, *My Paper Chase*, and from the investigative genius of Clive Irving, who as editor of Insight at the *Sunday Times* in the sixties developed the art of political narration and who in the eighties in New York helped raise the banner "Truth in Travel" for the launch of *Condé Nast Traveler*. It was at Irving's urging that I explored more of the half-truths and downright deceptions concealed in the small print of business contracts, warranties, and insurance policies, the writers of which have no intention of making themselves clear. I think the administrators of U.S. Social Security have good intentions, but when the convoluted clauses of rights have been lawyered, filtered by Congress and amended, and served up with acronyms and back references, you need professional decrypters. I was fortunate to have my hand held by Catherine Azmoodeh Hormats and Matthew Allen of Social Security Advisors. I learned much on health justice from Sara Rosenbaum, professor at George Washington University and the lead author of

Law and the American Health Care System, and from Jean Niven of Merlin Law Group. Michael Averill and Martin Edel of Miller and Wrubel, PC, were both helpful. None of them has responsibility for the criticisms I make.

I also absolve all the readers of the manuscript for errors they may have missed; you should have seen the ones that would have gotten away but for the hawkeyes at Little, Brown, Tracy Roe, Barbara Jatkola, and Kathryn Rogers, who read everything and made creative contributions. The book survived the author's reflexive second and third thoughts because of a remarkable devotion to detail by the imperturbable Peggy Freudenthal, executive production editor. I also thank the professional scrutiny of sections of the manuscript by Elizabeth Pearson-Griffith and Merrill Perlman. I appreciated the encouragement, insights, and good saves made by James C. Goodale, the valiant defender of a free press as the young lawyer on the Pentagon Papers case and a director of the *Paris Review;* Derek Holbrook, the English scholar in my time at Durham University; Gordon Crovitz; Tunku Varadarajan; Sidney Blumenthal, author of *A Self-Made Man: The Political Life of Abraham Lincoln, 1809–1849;* literary sleuth Donald E. Allen in Chicago; John Avlon, editor of the *Daily Beast;* and Isaac Lopez. I never expected that one day I would be edited by my own youngest daughter, but Izzy Evans went at drafts with zest and made many improvements.

"It goes without saying" is a phrase that speaks to its own redundancy, so by way of emphasis I take pleasure in indulging in the pleonasm to say it goes without saying that my wife, Tina, was brilliantly omnipresent. She sharpened her needle in the years editing *Vanity Fair* and the *New Yorker*, so I accepted her criticisms as a patient new to acupuncture accepts treatment: wincing, but much better for it in the end.

Do I Make Myself Clear? has a bit of a lineage. In 1966, after a time teaching journalism in Southeast Asia, I edited a little primer called *The Active Newsroom*. The board of the National Council for the Training of Journalists in Britain asked me to write an expanded version. The first of five books was *Newsman's English*, published more or less continuously from 1972 until the 1990s, when I accepted the suggestion of the editorial training committee of the Society of Editors, and the society's president Neil Fowler (editor of the *Western Mail*), that it should be republished and combined with my book *News Headlines*. I retrieved a few examples of my work from *Newsman's English* for this book. The new volume, edited with contributions by Crawford Gillan and published by Pimlico, includes contemporary work and avoids any suggestion of gender bias with the title *Essential English for Journalists*, in line with the society's *Essential Law for Journalists*.

ANSWERS TO "MAN OR MACHINE?"

The first two passages were by humans, the third and fourth by computers.

The second passage (the diffusion of innovations) was created from hundreds of papers by dietitians and catering companies responding with "rafts of measures" to a request from the British government for ideas on improving school food.

The *Daily Telegraph*'s Jemima Lewis, who provided the example, told me the nutritional and statistical details seemed just about comprehensible, but there was always something that didn't quite make sense. "And when we asked the sender to clarify, they'd admit they didn't really understand it themselves. We'd go back and back through the chain of command until we found someone who knew the answer, which mostly turned out to bear no relation to the original suggestion. It was a kind of telephone game, with bad writing and lazy thinking muddling the meaning at every stage."

Analysis: The Bomber

How 2,567 Words Became 1,030

This editing is based on the document released by the White House on January 7, 2010, which you can find in full in chapter 9. You can see how the fog that envelops the whole document is made up of particles: words that do not work, live images suffocated by abstractions, prefatory clauses too complex for any normal memory, dozy verbs in the passive voice. This is more than a question of style or grammar. Passive voice sentences may be grammatically pure, but they mask the identity of the doer. Not a security risk for the doer since a collective "we" does not name an individual or department. The report expresses regret for the lack of accountability in confronting the terrorist threat represented by Farouk 86, but its very language diffuses responsibility. "Steps were taken," it says, a sentence in the passive voice that epitomizes the whole report. The most telling phrase in it is "no single component assumed responsibility." It is a fair selection of the flatulence in much of the formal English we read; most corporation language is as bloated, and strong men and women lose their minds in marketing delirium. For bureaucracies and businesses, the deadening force is a defensive reflex. In the following analysis, I indicate a few passages where the context requires the passive voice, but throughout we find less clarity, vigor, and economy in the surfeit of passive-verb sentences. If treasuries would collect a dollar for every wasted word we'd overnight abolish the national debt.

WHITE HOUSE TEXT WITH
MY CRITICAL COMMENTS

Bold = questionable usage
( ) = number of words shorter

White House
First, it should be noted that the work by America's counterterrorism (CT) community has had many successes since 9/11 **that should be** applauded.

> *Comment:* "It should be noted" is passive, wordy, and distancing. Flesh-eater phrases like this abound in documents. Expunge them all. The direct statement below saves ten words and that's just a start in this long report.

> *Rewrite:* Since 9/11, America's counterterrorism (CT) community has had many successes we should applaud. (10)

White House

Our ability to protect the U.S. Homeland against terrorist attacks is only as good as the information and analysis **that drives and facilitates disruption efforts.**

> *Comment:* Wordy and inert, with a bloated subordinate clause.

> *Rewrite:* Our ability to disrupt attacks is only as good as the information we gather and analyze. (9)

White House

The thorough analysis of large volumes of information has enabled a variety of . and agencies **to take action to prevent attacks.** On a great number of occasions since 9/11, **many of which** the American people will never know about, the tremendous, hardworking corps of analysts across the CT community **did just that,** working day and night to track terrorist threats and run down possible leads **in order to** keep their fellow Americans safe.

> *Comment:* Who did the "thorough analysis"? Answer: "the tremendous, hardworking corps of analysts." Write the paragraph to focus on them and you make it shorter and clearer and actively suggestive of purposeful human activity. "Tremendous" is a rent-an-adjective, but we'll let them rent it for happiness all round.
>
> Tautology: "To take action to prevent attacks." How can you prevent attacks

without taking action? Consider the absurdity of the implied counterfactual: attacks have been prevented by the inertia of a variety of departments.

"Did just that." The writer has to backtrack with a participial phrase ("Working day and night to track terrorist threats and run down possible leads…") to say what the staff did on a great number of occasions.

Flesh-eater: "in order to."

Rewrite: Our tremendous, hardworking staff in many departments and agencies works day and night to analyze large volumes of information for terrorist threats. They have saved lives on many occasions the American people will never know about. (36)

White House

Yet, as the amount of information **continues to grow,** the challenge to bring disparate pieces of information—about individuals, groups, and vague plots—**together** to form a clear picture about the intentions of our adversaries **grows as well. These actions,** informed by the excellent analytic work of the very same individuals and **structure that is under review,** have saved lives.

Comment: The writers and, I suspect, multiple text editors failed the very same challenge—in this case, to bring together the elements of a simple sentence.

> *Rewrite:* As the amount of information grows, so does the challenge to bring together disparate information about vague plots by terrorist groups and individuals so that we can form a clear picture of their intentions. This is how the very same analysts in the same NCTC structure have saved lives. (11)

White House

Unfortunately, **despite several opportunities that might have allowed the CT community to put these pieces together in this case, and despite the tireless effort and best intentions of individuals at every level of the CT community,** that was not done. As a result, **the recent events** highlight our need to look for ways to **constantly improve** and assist our CT analysts, **who are at the forefront of providing warning of terrorist attacks and keeping Americans safe.**

> *Comment:* The predatory clause opening is a wordy way around delaying admission of error. The long-winded "several opportunities in this case..." phrase can be subsumed in a noun, *clues.* Note the deadly passive "that was not done." "Recent events" is redundant. And, yes, it's nice to acknowledge the good intentions, worthy efforts, etc., but we got the point first time around. "As a result" is a limp flesh-eater connector, avoiding the direct statement that they learned a lesson (or as they would say, "a lesson was learned").

> *Rewrite:* Unfortunately, the CT community missed
> clues scattered in different places. We have
> identified the human errors and a series of
> systemic breakdowns. We are fixing the
> blind spots and will keep the failings
> under regular review. (40)

White House

This report reflects preliminary **findings to facilitate immediate corrective action.** Neither the report nor its findings obviate the need for continued review **and analysis** to ensure that we have the fullest possible understanding of the systemic problems **that led to the attempted terrorist attack on December 25, 2009.**

> *Comment:* The appropriate place for this paragraph
> is at the beginning of the report. We don't
> need to be told again that this is all about
> "the attempted terrorist attack."

> *Rewrite:* This preliminary report identifies areas
> for immediate correction. We recognize
> that we need to investigate more to
> understand the systemic problems. (21)

White House

Note further that sensitive intelligence data **was removed** from this public report to protect sources and methods.

> *Comment:* Replace passive with active.

> *Rewrite:* We removed sensitive intelligence data
> from this report to protect sources and
> methods. (4)

White House

**The preliminary White House review of the events that led to
the attempted December 25 attack** highlights human errors and
a series of systematic breakdowns **failed to stop Umar Farouk
Abdulmutallab before he was able to detonate an explosive
device onboard flight 253.**

> *Comment:* Repetitious, unclear construction: We are
> insistently told this was an "attempted"
> attack because the bomb didn't detonate.
> Fine. But at the end of the sentence, we
> read that "he was able to detonate an
> explosive device" because a "series of sys-
> tematic breakdowns" failed to stop him.
> One can go quietly mad unraveling the
> meanings of passages like this.

> *Rewrite:* The preliminary White House review
> highlights human errors and systematic
> breakdowns that enabled Umar Farouk
> Abdulmutallab to board flight 253 with
> an explosive device. (16)

White House

The most significant failures and **shortcomings that led to the
attempted terror attack** fall into three broad categories:

- **A failure of intelligence analysis, whereby** the CT community **failed** before December 25 to identify, correlate, and fuse into a coherent story **all of** the **discrete** pieces of intelligence held by the U.S. Government related to an emerging terrorist plot against the U.S. Homeland organized by al-Qa'ida in the Arabian Peninsula (AQAP) and to Mr. Abdulmutallab, the individual terrorist;
- A failure within the CT community, starting with established rules and protocols, to assign **responsibility and accountability** for follow up of high priority threat streams, run down all leads, and track them through to completion; and
- Shortcomings of the watchlisting system, **whereby** the CT community **failed** to identify intelligence within U.S. government holdings **that would have allowed** Mr. Abdulmutallab to be watchlisted, and **potentially prevented** from boarding an aircraft bound for the United States.

The most significant findings of our preliminary review are:
- The U.S. Government had **sufficient** information **prior to** the attempted December 25 attack to **have potentially disrupted** the AQAP plot — i.e., by identifying Mr. Abdulmutallab as a likely operative of AQAP and **potentially preventing him** from boarding flight 253.
- The Intelligence Community leadership did not increase **analytic resources** working on the full AQAP threat.
- The watchlisting system is not broken but needs to be **strengthened and improved,** as evidenced **by the failure** to add Mr. Abdulmutallab to the No Fly watchlist.
- A reorganization of the intelligence or broader counterterrorism community is not required to address problems that

surfaced in the review, a fact made clear by countless other successful efforts to thwart ongoing plots.

Comment: Wearisome repetition. Being reminded of the subject so often is a form of Chinese water torture.

Overlong sentences. Passive voice.

Abstraction. "Analytic resources" is abstraction for people/staffers.

Tautology: "Strengthened and improved." Who would write "weakened and improved"? Or "improved and weakened"? This is the bloat that makes so many documents tiring to read.

I've had enough of "sufficient" as the genteelism (Fowler) for the shorter, bolder real noun: *enough.* Sufficient unto the day is the evil thereof.

Rewrite: The most significant findings fall into three broad categories:

- The U.S. had information about an emerging terrorist plot organized by al-Qa'ida in the Arabian Peninsula (AQAP);
- It had information to identify Mr. Abdulmutallab as a likely operative of AQAP;
- It had enough information to justify placing him on a watchlist to be

denied boarding for the U.S. at the discretion of screening officials.

But the CT community did not observe rules and protocols to assign responsibility for high-priority threat streams and track them through to completion.

Judgment: The watchlist system is not broken but needs to be strengthened.

The problems revealed do not require reorganization of the intelligence or broader counterterrorism community because the system had thwarted other plots. (159)

White House

It is important to note that the fundamental problems identified in this preliminary review are different from those identified in the wake of the 9/11 attacks. Previously, there were formidable barriers to information sharing among departments and agencies — **tied to firmly entrenched patterns of bureaucratic behavior as well as the absence of a single component that fuses expertise, information technology (IT) networks, and datasets — that have now, 8 years later, largely been overcome.** (74)

Comment: "It is important to note." Again, flesh-eaters are on the loose. Expunge the six opening words.

Second sentence: windy with additional reading burden of a long parenthetical set off by dashes; twenty-six words and "as well as" does not scan.

The reader has to carry the twenty-six words in his mind to the end of the sentence where he is invited to imagine tying something to nothing: "formidable barriers to information sharing tied to the absence of a single component."

Why "are different from"? *Differ* is a strong verb. It conveys the thought in one word, not the three where the verb is a form of *to be*, the most pallid of verbs.

"Firmly entrenched" is a candidate for the Adverb Annihilator promoted in chapter 4. Get rid of adverbs hitching a ride on adjectives and verbs. Pause a moment to think what *entrenched* means. If the pattern of behavior is entrenched, it is firm; if it is not firm — resistant to change, attack, assault — it is not entrenched.

Rewrite: The difference from 9/11 is that then entrenched barriers prevented departments and agencies sharing information: we had no single component to fuse expertise, IT networks, and data sets. Eight years later we have the NCTC. (38)

Comment: We now face a flaw in the basic organization of the report. The reader's next question is, Well, if those problems have been largely overcome, what went wrong? But the writer can't tell us without describing the reorganization since 9/11. He now proceeds to do that. It's an afterthought that should have been a forethought. It is also muddled writing. The afterthought breaks the thread of the argument and makes it harder to follow when the author resumes the thread. In my rewrite, I transpose an edited version of this section to a spot near the beginning.

White House

An understanding of the responsibilities of different analytic components of the CT community is critical to identifying what went wrong and **how best to fix it.**

> *Comment:* "How best to fix it" is good, but not the weak *be* verb in "is critical to identifying."

> *Rewrite:* To fix what went wrong requires an understanding of how the CT community works. (12)

White House

The National Counterterrorism Center (NCTC) was created by the Intelligence Reform and Terrorism Prevention Act of 2004 (IRTPA) to be "**the primary organization** in the U.S. government for analyzing and integrating all intelligence possessed or acquired by the U.S. government pertaining to terrorism and counterterrorism." Intelligence Community guidance in 2006 **further defined counterterrorism analytic responsibilities** and tasked NCTC **with the primary role** within the Intelligence Community for bringing together and assessing all-source intelligence **to**

enable a full understanding of and proper response to partic-ular terrorist threat streams. Additionally, the Director of NCTC is in charge of the DNI Homeland Threat Task Force, whose mission is to examine threats to the U.S. Homeland from al-Qa'ida, its allies, and homegrown violent extremists.

> *Comment:* We are told twice in this one paragraph that NCTC is the primary body—and we'll be told twice more. Then we have tedious fussiness: "full understanding," "proper response," "particular." The writer is as scared of a naked noun as the Victorians of naked piano legs.

> *Rewrite:* Intelligence Community guidance in 2006 more precisely defined responsibility for scrutinizing all sources of threat streams so the NCTC could respond. (100)

White House

Notwithstanding NCTC's central role in producing terrorism analysis, CIA maintains the responsibility **and resource capability** to "correlate and evaluate intelligence related to national security **and provide appropriate dissemination of such intelligence.**" CIA's responsibility for conducting all-source analysis in **the area of** counterterrorism is focused on supporting its operations overseas, **as well as informing** its leadership of terrorist threats and terrorist targets overseas.

> *Comment:* A monster. *Notwithstanding* is a refugee from a legal contract. The overlap or collision is best faced up front:

"Maintain...resource capability" is an ugly abstraction. Translates in English as "is able to."

"In the area" is a flesh-eater.

"Provide appropriate dissemination of such intelligence" is Mr. Micawber in full flow, pomposity on stilts. It means "inform leadership."

Rewrite: Both the NCTC and CIA are required to uncover specific plots like the attempted December 25 attack, but the CIA is more concerned with overseas terrorist threats. (36)

White House

Therefore, both agencies—NCTC and CIA—**have a role to play in conducting (and a responsibility to carry out)** all-source analysis to identify operatives and uncover specific plots like the **attempted** December 25 attack.

Comment: "Therefore" is a word we summon when we suspect we haven't proved what we set out to prove.

"A role to play" is a flesh-eater since the duties are made clear in the same sentence.

Rewrite: Both agencies have a responsibility to analyze all sources to identify hostile operatives and their plots. (19)

White House

The information available to the CT community over the last several months—**which included pieces of information about Mr. Abdulmutallab, information about AQAP and its plans, and information about an individual now believed to be Mr. Abdulmutallab and his association with AQAP and its attack planning**—was obtained by several agencies.

> *Comment:* Even when there is an opportunity for a positive statement, the writer skulks in the cloudy passive. Clarity demands abandoning the parenthetical and repetitious inclusion of this and that.

> *Rewrite:* Several agencies before December 25 reported fragments of intelligence about AQAP and its plans and association with an individual now believed to be Mr. Abdulmutallab. (26)

> *Comment:* Now a reader wants to know what the fragments of information were, but the writer doesn't keep hold of the thread. We have two more paragraphs of muddy prose.

White House

Though **all of** that information **was available** to all-source analysts at the CIA and the NCTC prior to the attempted attack, the dots **were never connected,** and **as a result,** the problem appears to be more about a component failure to "connect the dots," rather than a lack of information sharing. The information **that was** available to analysts, as is usually the case, was fragmentary and embedded in a large volume of other data.

> *Comment:* Epidemic of *be* verbs and the passive voice: "was available," "were never connected," "that was available."
> "All of" is bloat.
> "As a result" = flesh-eater, replace with *so*.
> "That was" is clutter.

> *Rewrite:* Analysts at both the CIA and NCTC had identified suspicious items in a large volume of information but failed to "connect the dots." (52)

White House

Though the consumer base and operational capabilities of CIA and NCTC are somewhat different, the intentional redundancy in the system should have added an additional layer of protection **in uncovering a plot like the failed attack on December 25.** However, in **both cases,** the mission to "connect the dots" **did not produce the result that, in hindsight,** it could have— connecting identifying information about Mr. Abdulmutallab with fragments of information about his association with AQAP and the group's intention of attacking the U.S.

> *Comment:* Repetitious—"in uncovering a plot like the failed attack on December 25."

> *Rewrite:* The intentional redundancy within the system failed as a backup layer of protection. (71)

White House

The majority of these discreet [*sic;* **discrete**] pieces of intelligence **were gathered** between mid-October and late December 2009. For example, on November 18, Mr. Abdulmutallab's father met with U.S. Embassy officers in Abuja, Nigeria, **to discuss his concerns** that his son may have come under the influence of unidentified extremists, and had planned to travel to Yemen. **Though this information alone** could not **predict Mr. Abdulmutallab's** eventual involvement in the **attempted** 25 December attack, it provided an opportunity **to link information on him with earlier intelligence reports that contained fragmentary information.** Analytic focus during December was on the imminent AQAP attacks on Americans and American interests in Yemen, and on supporting CT efforts in Yemen.

> *Comment:* Now at last the writer gives us a clue about what the famous fragments were, the dots that didn't get connected. But the passive voice persists ("were gathered").
>
> "Discuss his concerns" = tell.
>
> Two Mr. Abdulmutallabs jostle in the same paragraph. Make one "the son" and the other "the father" or Mr. Abdulmutallab Senior.

Rewrite: The dots that CT could have connected emerged between mid-October and late December 2009. On November 18, Mr. Abdulmutallab's father met with U.S. Embassy officers in Abuja, Nigeria, to tell them that his son may have come under the influence of unidentified extremists and planned to travel to Yemen. This information alone was not enough to predict the son's involvement in the December 25 attack but it might have connected other dots of fragmentary intelligence in December on imminent AQAP attacks on Americans and American interests. (28)

White House

Despite these opportunities and multiple intelligence products **that noted the threat** AQAP could pose to the Homeland, **the different pieces of the puzzle were never brought together in this case**[,] the dots were never connected, and, **as a result, steps to disrupt the plot involving Mr. Abdulmutallab were not taken prior to his boarding of the airplane with an explosive device and attempting to detonate it in-flight**.

Comment: Passive, repetitious.

This overlong sentence might be better with a full stop after *together.*

> *Rewrite:* CT staff never connected the dots, so no one attempted to prevent Mr. Abdulmutallab boarding the plane with an explosive device. (46)

White House

Intelligence is not an end to itself, nor are analytic products— **they** are designed to provide **senior** government leaders with the **necessary** information to make **key** decisions, but also to **trigger action, including further collection, operational steps, and investigative adjustments.**

> *Comment:* A dash conjunction is too frail a branch to sustain the succession of thoughts that follow. When in doubt start a new sentence ("They are designed").
>
> Extinguish the cavalcade of adjectives— "senior" government leaders, "necessary" information, "key" decisions. Again, it's not a bad idea to consider the sense of what we're writing. Are the "analytic products" (ugh) designed to provide leaders with the *unnecessary* information to make key decisions? Of course not, but the logic of the redundancy invites the parody: Analytic products are designed to provide really junior leaders with the unnecessary information to make dumb decisions.

> *Rewrite:* Intelligence helps senior leaders make decisions or exposes the need for more investigation. (27)

White House

As noted above, NCTC and CIA have the primary and overlapping responsibility to conduct all-source analysis on terrorism. **As with this intentional analytic redundancy,** the CT community also has multiple and **overlapping warning systems** to ensure that departments and agencies are kept fully aware of ongoing threat streams.

> *Comment:* Overlapping by agencies belongs in the place where the relationship between NCTC and CIA is explained.

White House

NCTC is the primary organization **that provides situational awareness** to the CT community of ongoing terrorist threats and events, **including through several daily written products that summarize current threat reporting for a broad audience,** as well as meetings and video teleconferences **that** provide the opportunity for the CT community to engage in a real-time manner **on this information.** While the threat warning system involves analysis, it also extends to other elements within the CT community **that** should be responsible for **following up and acting** on leads **as a particular threat situation develops.**

> *Comment:* The length of the opening sentence, fifty-eight words, is a giveaway of clumsy construction.

"That provides situational awareness" is robot-speak. It translates among humans as "to tell," "alert," "describe," a choice of verbs to provide situational awareness of the richness of the English language. "A particular threat situation" is another contortion.

Rewrite: NCTC is the primary organization for alerting the CT community of terrorist activities. Several daily reports summarize threats for a broad audience. Meetings and video enable the CT community to engage in real-time evaluation. Other elements within the CT community are responsible for following up and acting on leads. (43)

White House

In this context, the preliminary review suggests that the overlapping layers of protection within the CT community failed to track this threat **in a manner sufficient to ensure all leads** were followed and acted **upon to conclusion.** In addition, the White House and the National Security Staff failed to identify this gap ahead of time. No single **component** of the CT community assumed responsibility for the threat reporting and followed it through by ensuring that **all necessary steps were taken to disrupt the threat. This argues** that a process is needed to track terrorist threat reporting to ensure that departments and agencies are held accountable for running down all leads associated with high visibility and high priority plotting efforts, in particular against the U.S. Homeland.

> *Comment:* The paragraph amounts to "something must be done" but we don't know what.
>
> Verbiage substitutes for thought, lack of which is advertised by "a process is needed."
>
> Flesh-eaters gala: "In this context," "in a manner sufficient," "necessary steps were taken," "followed and acted upon to conclusion."
>
> Excisions of this wasteful wording affords the reader the glimmering of a more understandable paragraph.
>
> Is a "component" animal, vegetable, or mineral? If we probe deeply enough, maybe we will find a cognitive human being with a specific duty.

> *Rewrite:* No single part of the CT community took responsibility for disrupting the plot. The overlapping layers of protection failed and so did the White House and National Security staff. Government needs a system of checks to make sure every department and every agency knows what it is supposed to do and does it. (72)

White House

Although Umar Farouk Abdulmutallab was included in the Terrorist Identities Datamart Environment (TIDE), the failure to include Mr. Abdulmutallab **in a watchlist** is part of the overall systemic failure. **Pursuant to the IRTPA, NCTC serves** "as the central and shared knowledge bank on known and suspected terrorists and international terror groups." **As such,** NCTC consolidates all information on known and suspected international terrorists in the Terrorist Identities Datamart Environment. NCTC then makes this data available to the FBI-led Terrorist Screening Center (TSC), which reviews nominations for inclusion in the master watchlist called the Terrorist Screening Database (TSDB). The TSC provides relevant extracts to each organization with a screening mission.

> *Comment:* Such a head spinner, it invites a riposte in the same terms. The failure to be clear in these four sentences is part of the document's overall systemic failure. This time, the passive voice is not the issue. It's the construction.
>
> The information that Farouk was on a terrorist list is too important for the narrative to be mentioned as a throwaway in a prefatory subordinate clause. But what's "the" Terrorist Identities Datamart Environment (TIDE)? The reference to "the" organization implies we know, but we are not told until the next sentence, and then in a muddle of acronyms and prolixity ("Pursuant to the IRTPA [what?], NCTC serves").
>
> *Rewrite:* Umar Farouk was included in a knowledge bank of known and suspected terrorists

and international terror groups, consolidated by the NCTC. It's called TIDE (Terrorist Identities Datamark Environment). TIDE's data is available to a Terrorist Screening Center controlled by the FBI, which provides relevant extracts to organizations with a screening mission. The FBI also reviews nominations for inclusion in a master watchlist called the Terrorist Screening Database (TSDB). (41)

White House

Hindsight suggests that the evaluation by watchlisting personnel of the information contained **in the State cable nominating** Mr. Abdulmutallab did not meet the minimum derogatory standard to watchlist. Watchlisting would have required all of the available information to be fused so that **the derogatory information would have been sufficient to support nomination to be watchlisted** in the Terrorist Screening Database. Watchlist personnel had access to additional derogatory information in databases that **could have been connected** to Mr. Abdulmutallab, but **that access did not result in them uncovering the biographic information that** would have been necessary for placement on the watchlist. **Ultimately,** placement on the No Fly list would have been required to keep Mr. Abdulmutallab off the plane inbound for the U.S. Homeland.

> *Comment:* What "State [Department] cable"? What "derogatory information"? The writer keeps getting ahead of the reader.

> *Rewrite:* The State Department did nominate Mr.
> Abdulmutallab to the Terrorist Screening
> Center, but the center's personnel decided
> he did not meet the minimum derogatory
> standard to be placed in the TSDB and
> hence on the No Fly list. Watchlist personnel
> had access to databases other than TIDE
> but did not uncover his association with
> terrorism. (68)

White House

Mr. Abdulmutallab possessed a U.S. visa, but **this fact was not
correlated** with the concerns of Mr. Abdulmutallab's father about
Mr. Abdulmutallab's potential radicalization. **A misspelling** of
Mr. Abdulmutallab's name initially **resulted in** the State Department
believing he did not have a valid U.S. visa. **A determination**
to revoke his visa, however, would have only occurred **if there had
been** a successful integration of intelligence by the CT community, resulting in his being watchlisted.

> *Comment:* Again, need to distinguish between father
> and son.
>
> The impersonal passive prevails in the
> service of a reluctance to say what happened and when it happened after the
> alarm from the field that he might be a
> dangerous person.
>
> Everything is wrapped in cotton wool:
> "a misspelling"; "a determination" instead
> of "a decision"; "resulted in."

> *Rewrite:* Mr. Abdulmutallab had a visa to enter the United States. Initially, the State Department thought he did not because his name had been misspelled in the database, but even with that error corrected, the CT community did not integrate the information fully and so did not revoke his visa. (25)

White House

The U.S. government had **sufficient** information to have uncovered and potentially disrupted the December 25 attack—including by placing Mr. Abdulmutallab on the No Fly list—but analysts within the CT community failed to connect the dots that could **have identified and warned of the specific threat. The preponderance of the intelligence related to this plot was available broadly to the Intelligence Community.**

> *Comment:* The last sentence is redundant.

> *Rewrite:* The U.S. government had enough information to detect and disrupt the plot by placing Mr. Abdulmutallab on the No Fly list, but analysts failed to connect the dots. (35)

White House

NCTC and CIA are empowered to collate and assess all-source intelligence on the CT threat, but all-source analysts highlighted largely the evolving "strategic threat" AQAP posed to the West, and the U.S. Homeland specifically, **in finished intelligence**

products. In addition, some of the improvised explosive device tactics AQAP might use against U.S. interests **were highlighted in finished intelligence products.**

The CT community failed to **follow-up further** on this "strategic warning" by **moving aggressively to further identify** and correlate critical indicators of AQAP's threat to the U.S. Homeland with the full range of analytic tools and expertise that it uses in tracking other plots aimed at the U.S. Homeland.

NCTC and CIA personnel **who are** responsible for watch-listing did not search all available databases to uncover additional derogatory **information that could have been correlated** with Mr. Abdulmutallab.

A series of human errors occurred—delayed dissemination of a finished intelligence report and what appears to be incomplete/faulty database searches on Mr. Abdulmutallab's name and identifying information.

> *Comment:* First sentence repeats earlier description of duties of NCTC and CIA.
>
> "Tactics...were highlighted" and "that could have been correlated" are passive.
>
> "Follow-up further"—"Follow up" will do.
>
> The point being made about concentration on strategic threat can be crisper and shorter, and this is the place to say dissemination of one report was delayed.
>
> *Rewrite:* Analysts completed and submitted intelligence reports identifying the strategic

threats to the U.S. Homeland and the West; they also highlighted some of the improvised explosive devices AQAP might use. Then things went wrong. Dissemination of a complete intelligence report was delayed. The CT community failed to follow up the "strategic warning" by deploying the full range of analytic tools and expertise used in tracking other plots. NCTC and CIA personnel responsible for watchlisting made faulty and incomplete database searches on Mr. Abdulmutallab. (78)

White House

"Information sharing" does not appear to have contributed to this intelligence failure; relevant all-source analysts as well as watch-listing personnel who needed this information were **not prevented from accessing** it.

> *Comment:* Passive voice. "Not prevented from accessing it" means they were "not denied access." Better still, the positive: personnel who needed this information had access to it.

> *Rewrite:* The intelligence failure was not due to reluctance to share information. Analysts and watch-listing personnel had all the access they needed. (9)

White House

Information technology within the CT community **did not sufficiently enable** the correlation of data that would have **enabled** analysts to highlight the relevant threat information.

> *Rewrite:* Information technology did not correlate data well enough to help analysts highlight the threat. (11)

White House

There was not a comprehensive or functioning process for tracking terrorist threat reporting and actions **taken such** that departments and agencies are held accountable for running down all leads associated with high visibility and high priority plotting efforts undertaken by al-Qa'ida and its allies, in particular against the U.S. Homeland.

> *Comment:* Passive.
>> "Taken such"—only lawyers talk like this. A positive statement is hiding in here.

> *Rewrite:* The CT community needs a better process for tracking terrorist threats so that departments and agencies can be held accountable for running down all leads associated with plots by al-Qa'ida and its allies, in particular against the U.S. Homeland. (11)

White House

Finally, we must **review and determine the ongoing suitability** of legacy standards and protocols in effect across the CT community, including criteria for watch lists, protocols for secondary screening, visa suspension and revocation criteria, and business processes across the government.

> *Comment:* "Ongoing" is a flesh-eater.
> "Review and determine the ongoing suitability of legacy standards" says the same thing three times.

> *Rewrite:* We must review legacy standards and protocols across the CT community including criteria for watchlists, protocols for secondary screening, visa suspension and revocation criteria, and business processes across the government. (9)

HOW THE WHITE HOUSE STATEMENT SHOULD HAVE READ

(Revised to deal with all the faults identified in the analysis)

On December 25, 2009, a Nigerian national, Umar Farouk Abdulmutallab, attempted to detonate an explosive device while on board flight 253 from Amsterdam to Detroit. The device did not explode, but instead ignited, injuring Mr. Abdulmutallab and two other passengers. The flight crew restrained Mr. Abdulmutallab and the plane safely landed. Customs and Border Protection (CBP) took Mr. Abdulmutallab into custody, and the Federal Bureau of Investigation (FBI) later questioned him.

The President asked John Brennan, the Assistant to the President for Homeland Security and Counterterrorism, to review the terrorist watchlisting system. What follows is a summary of his preliminary report focused on identifying areas for immediate correction. To protect sources and methods, this report excludes sensitive intelligence data.

Background

America's counterterrorism (CT) community of departments and agencies works day and night to keep their fellow Americans safe. Since 9/11 they have saved lives on many occasions that the American people will never know about.

What Went Wrong in This Case?

Our ability to disrupt attacks is only as good as the information we gather and analyze. The volume has grown enormously, and with it the challenge to bring together disparate information—about individuals, groups, and vague plots—so that we can form a clear picture of hostile intent. The primary organization in the U.S. Government for analyzing and integrating all intelligence on terrorism is the National Counterterrorism Center (NCTC), created by the Intelligence Reform and Terrorism Prevention Act of 2004 (IRTPA). The Director of NCTC is in charge of the DNI Homeland Threat Task Force, whose mission is to examine threats to the U.S. Homeland from al-Qa'ida, its allies, and homegrown violent extremists. NCTC summarizes current threats in several daily reports to a broad audience. Meetings and video teleconferences enable the CT community to engage in real-time evaluation. Other elements within the CT community are responsible for following up on leads.

Both the NCTC and the CIA are required to uncover specific plots. Both have the resources to correlate and evaluate intelligence. The CIA focuses on supporting its operations overseas and informing leadership of terrorist threats and possible targets. Unfortunately, in this case the CT community failed to collate clues in different areas. We have identified the human errors and a series of systemic breakdowns. We are correcting them and will review the system regularly. The most significant shortcomings fall into three broad categories: intelligence analysis, follow-through, and watchlisting terrorists.

Intelligence analysis: Several agencies between mid-October and late December 2009 reported fragments of intelligence about AQAP and its plans and association with an individual now believed to be Mr. Abdulmutallab. The State Department was informed that on November 18, Mr. Abdulmutallab's father met with U.S. Embassy officers in Abuja, Nigeria, to say that his son may have come under the influence of unidentified extremists and had planned to travel to Yemen.

Follow-through: Though this information alone could not predict Mr. Abdulmutallab's eventual involvement in the December 25 attack, it provided an opportunity to link information on him with earlier intelligence reports about AQAP's evolving "strategic threat" to the West and the U.S. Homeland. Intelligence reports had highlighted some of the improvised explosive device tactics AQAP might use against U.S. interests. The CT community did not follow established rules and protocols to assign responsibility for tracking this high-priority threat stream, run down leads, and track them to completion. It did not move with the full range of analytic tools and expertise that it uses in tracking other plots aimed at the U.S. Homeland.

Watchlisting terrorists: The failure to name Mr. Abdulmutallab in a watchlist is part of the overall systemic failure. We had items of intelligence within the U.S. government to justify placing Mr. Abdulmutallab on a No Fly watchlist and likely preventing him from boarding flight 253. His name had been included in a knowledge bank, consolidated by the NCTC, of known and suspected terrorists and international terror groups. It's called TIDE (Terrorist Identities Datamart Environment). TIDE's data is available to a Terrorist Screening Center controlled by the FBI, which provides relevant extracts to organizations with a screening mission. The FBI also reviews nominations for inclusion in a master watchlist called the Terrorist Screening Database (TSDB).

Watchlist personnel considered that the State Department cable on Mr. Abdulmutallab did not meet the minimum derogatory standard for inclusion in TSDB. Watchlisting would have required all of the available information to be fused, but NCTC and CIA personnel did not search all available databases.

Mr. Abdulmutallab had a visa to enter the United States. Initially, it was thought he did not—due to a misspelling of his name—but the CT community would have revoked his visa only if it had integrated all the intelligence.

The watchlisting system is not broken, but it does need to be strengthened. We do not judge it necessary to reorganize the intelligence or broader counterterrorism community. It has thwarted countless plots.

Breakdown of Accountability

NCTC is the primary organization for alerting the CT community of terrorist activities, but the broader CT community failed to follow all leads. No single part of the CT community assumed responsibility for disrupting the plot. The overlapping layers of protection failed to detect the gap, and so did the White House and the National Security staff. Government needs a process for holding departments and agencies accountable for running down all leads associated with high-level plots.

A series of human errors occurred—delayed dissemination of a finished intelligence report and what appears to be incomplete/faulty database searches on Mr. Abdulmutallab's name. "Information sharing" does not appear to have contributed to this intelligence failure; relevant all-source analysts as well as watch-listing personnel who needed this information had access to it, but information technology did not correlate data well enough to help analysts highlight the threat.

The CT community needs a better process for tracking terrorist threats so that departments and agencies know they will be held accountable for running down all leads associated with high-level plots by al-Qa'ida and its allies, in particular against the U.S. Homeland. We must review legacy standards and protocol across the CT community, including criteria for watchlists, protocols for secondary screening, visa suspension and revocation criteria, and business processes across the government.

(End rewrite: 1,030 words; original: 2,567)

YOUR SCORECARD

2,000 words	Flabby
1,500 words	Good, provided no facts lost
1,000 words	The White House needs you.

BIBLIOGRAPHY

Abramoff, Jack. *Capitol Punishment: The Hard Truth about Washington Corruption from America's Most Notorious Lobbyist.* New York: WND Books, 2011.

Alley, Michael. *The Craft of Scientific Writing.* New York: Springer, 1998.

Amis, Kingsley. *The King's English: A Guide to Modern Usage.* New York: St. Martin's Griffin, 1999.

Angell, Roger. *This Old Man: All in Pieces.* New York: Doubleday, 2015.

Arendt, Hannah. *The Origins of Totalitarianism.* Boston: Houghton Mifflin, 1973. Digital.

Ashe, Geoffrey. *The Art of Writing Made Simple.* London: W. H. Allen, 1972.

Aslop, Joseph. *FDR 1882–1945: A Centenary Remembrance.* New York: Viking, 1982.

Barzun, Jacques. *Simple and Direct: A Rhetoric for Writers.* New York: Harper and Row, 1975.

Bates, Jefferson D. *Writing with Precision: How to Write So That You Cannot Possibly Be Misunderstood.* New York: Penguin, 2000.

Baxter, Jenny, and Malcolm Downing, eds. *The BBC Reports: On America, Its Allies and Enemies, and the Counterattack on Terrorism.* Woodstock, NY: Overlook Press, 2002.

Beard, Henry, and Christopher Cerf. *Spinglish: The Definitive Dictionary of Deliberately Deceptive Language.* New York: Blue Rider Press, 2015.

Beard, Mary. *Women and Power: A Manifesto.* New York: Liveright, 2017.

Bernstein, Theodore M. *The Careful Writer: A Modern Guide to English Usage.* New York: Atheneum, 1977.

————. *Miss Thistlebottom's Hobgoblins: The Careful Writer's Guide to Taboos, Bugbears, and Outmoded Rules of English Usage.* New York: Farrar, Straus and Giroux, 1971.

————. *More Language That Needs Watching: Second Aid for Writers and Editors, Emanating from the News Room of the New York Times.* Manhasset, NY: Channel Press, 1962.

————. *Watch Your Language: A Lively, Informal Guide to Better Writing, Emanating from the News Room of the New York Times.* Great Neck, NY: Channel Press, 1958.

Bernstein, Theodore M., Marylea Meyersohn, and Bertram Lippman. *Dos, Don'ts and Maybes of English Usage.* New York: Times Books, 1977.

Bernstein, Theodore M., and Jane Wagner. *Bernstein's Reverse Dictionary.* New York: Quadrangle/New York Times Book Company, 1975.

Block, Mervin, and Joe Durso Jr. *Writing News for TV and Radio.* Chicago: Bonus Books, 1988.

Bragg, Melvyn. *The Adventure of English: The Biography of a Language.* New York: Arcade, 2011.

Brewster, William. *Writing English Prose.* New York: Henry Holt, 1913.

Buckley, William F., Jr., and Samuel S. Vaughan. *Buckley: The Right Word.* New York: Random House, 1996.

Burns, James MacGregor. *Roosevelt: The Soldier of Freedom.* New York: Harcourt Brace Jovanovich, 1970.

Calkins, Lucy McCormick. *The Art of Teaching Writing.* Portsmouth, NH: Heinemann, 1994.

Cappon, Rene J. *The Associated Press Guide to News Writing.* Lawrenceville, NJ: Thomson/Peterson's, 2000.

Carey, John, ed. *Eyewitness to History.* New York: William Morrow, 1987.

Christian, Darrell, Sally Jacobsen, and David Minthorn, ed. *The Associated Press Stylebook and Briefing on Media Law 2013*. New York: Basic Books, 2013.

Churchill, Winston S. "The Scaffolding of Rhetoric." November 1897, Winstonchurchill.org. https://www.winstonchurchill.org/images/pdfs/for_educators/THE_SCAFFOLDING_OF_RHETORIC.pdf

———. *The Speeches of Winston Churchill*. Edited by David Cannadine. London: Penguin, 1989.

Claiborne, Robert. *Our Marvelous Native Tongue: The Life and Times of the English Language*. New York: Times Books, 1983.

Clark, Roy Peter. *The Glamour of Grammar: A Guide to the Magic and Mystery of Practical English*. Boston: Little, Brown, 2010.

———. "The Shakespeare Sentence That Changed My Writing—and Can Change Yours." Poynter.org. April 23, 2014. http://www.poynter.org/2014/the-shakespeare-sentence-that-changed-my-writing-and-can-change-yours-draft/248954/

Cobbett, William. *A Grammar of the English Language*. New York: Oxford University Press, 2002.

Crystal, David. *The Fight for English*. Oxford: Oxford University Press, 2007, plus many scores of other books by this prolific author.

Crystal, David, and Ben Crystal. *Shakespeare's Words: A Glossary and Language Companion*. London: Penguin, 2002.

d'Ancona, Matthew. *Post Truth: The New War on Truth and How to Fight Back*. London: Ebury, 2017.

Davis, Evan. *Post-Truth: Why We Have Reached Peak Bullshit and What We Can Do about It*. London: Little, Brown, 2017.

Davis, Kenneth S. *FDR: The New York Years, 1928–1933*. New York: Random House, 1994.

Demick, Barbara. *Nothing to Envy: Real Lives in North Korea*. London: Granta, 2014.

Doty, Mark. *The Art of Description: World into Word*. Minneapolis, MN: Graywolf Press, 2010.

Edelhart, Mike, and James Tinen. *America the Quotable*. New York: Facts on File Publications, 1983.

Edwards, Ruth Dudley. *Newspapermen: Hugh Cudlipp, Cecil Harmsworth King and the Glory Days of Fleet Street*. London: Pimlico, 2004.

Enright, D. J., ed. *Fair of Speech: The Uses of Euphemism*. London: Oxford University Press, 1985.

Epstein, Edward Jay. *Extra: The Inventions of Journalism*. Create-Space, 2014.

Evans, Harold, ed. *The Active Newsroom: IPI Manual on Techniques of News Editing, Sub-Editing and Photo-Editing*. Zurich: International Press Institute, 1961.

———. *The American Century*. New York: Knopf, 1998.

———. *Essential English for Journalists, Editors and Writers*. London: Pimlico, 2000.

———. *Newsman's English*. New York: Holt, Rinehart and Winston, 1972.

———. *They Made America: From the Steam Engine to the Search Engine; Two Centuries of Innovators*. Boston: Little, Brown, 2004.

———. *War Stories: Reporting in the Time of Conflict from the Crimea to Iraq*. Boston: Bunker Hill, 2003.

Fahnestock, Jeanne. *Rhetorical Style: The Uses of Language in Persuasion*. New York: Oxford University Press, 2011.

Felsenfeld, Carl, and Alan Siegel. *Writing Contracts in Plain English*. St. Paul, MN: West Publishing, 1981.

Fiske, Robert Hartwell. *The Dictionary of Disagreeable English: A Curmudgeon's Compendium of Excruciatingly Correct Grammar*. Cincinnati, OH: Writer's Digest Books, 2005.

———. *The Dimwit's Dictionary: 5,000 Overused Words and Phrases and Alternatives to Them*. Oak Park, IL: Marion Street Press, 2002.

———. *Robert Hartwell Fiske's Dictionary of Unendurable English: A Compendium of Mistakes in Grammar, Usage, and Spelling with Commentary on Lexicographers and Linguists*. New York: Scribner, 2011.

———. *To the Point: A Dictionary of Concise Writing*. New York: W. W. Norton, 2014.

Flesch, Rudolf. *The Art of Readable Writing*. New York: Harper and Brothers, 1949.

Forsyth, Mark. *The Elements of Eloquence: How to Turn the Perfect English Phrase*. London: Icon Books, 2014.

Fowler, H. W. *A Dictionary of Modern English Usage*. London: Oxford University Press, 1968.

Fry, Katherine, and Rowena Kirton. *Grammar for Grown-ups: A Straightforward Guide to Good English*. London: Square Peg, 2012.

Gallo, Carmine. *Talk Like Ted: The Nine Public-Speaking Secrets of the World's Top Minds*. New York: St. Martin's Griffin, 2015.

Garner, Bryan A. *Legal Writing in Plain English: A Text with Exercises*. Chicago: University of Chicago Press, 2013.

Garst, Robert E., ed. *Style Book of the New York Times*. New York: New York Times Company, 1956.

Garst, Robert E., and Theodore M. Bernstein. *Headlines and Deadlines: A Manual for Copy Editors*. New York: Columbia University Press, 1964.

Gellhorn, Martha. *The View from the Ground*. New York: Atlantic Monthly Press, 1988.

Gibbs, Wolcott. "Time…Fortune…Life…Luce." *New Yorker*. November 28, 1936.

Goodwin, Doris Kearns. *No Ordinary Time: Franklin and Eleanor Roosevelt: The Home Front in World War II*. New York: Simon and Schuster, 1994.

Gowers, Ernest, and Rebecca Gowers. *Plain Words: A Guide to the Use of English*. London: Particular Books, 2014.

Grant, A. M., and T. G. Pollock. "Publishing in AMJ—Part 3: Setting the Hook." *Academy of Management Journal* 52 (2011): 873–79.

Graves, Robert, and Alan Hodge. *The Reader over Your Shoulder: A Handbook for Writers of English Prose*. New York: Random House, 1979.

Gunning, Robert. *The Technique of Clear Writing*. New York: McGraw-Hill, 1968.

Gunning, Robert, and Richard A. Kallan. *How to Take the Fog Out of Business Writing*. Chicago: Dartnell, 1994.

Gwynne, N. M. *Gwynne's Grammar: The Ultimate Introduction to Grammar and the Writing of Good English*. New York: Knopf, 2014.

Hampson, Roger. "A Study of D.H.S.S. Leaflets: The Language of Bureaucracy." Thesis, University of Bristol, 1978.

Heffer, Simon. *Strictly English: The Correct Way to Write…and Why It Matters*. London: Windmill Books, 2011.

Holmes, Charles S. *The Clocks of Columbus: The Literary Career of James Thurber*. London: Alison Press/Secker and Warburg, 1973.

Huddleston, Rodney, and Geoffrey K. Pullum. *The Cambridge Grammar of the English Language*. Cambridge: Cambridge University Press, 2002.

Humphrys, John. *Lost for Words: The Mangling and Manipulating of the English Language*. London: Hodder and Stoughton, 2004.

Johnson, Boris. *The Churchill Factor: How One Man Made History*. London: Hodder and Stoughton, 2014.

Johnson, Edward D. *The Handbook of Good English*. New York: Facts on File Publications, 1983.

Johnston, David Cay. *The Fine Print: How Big Companies Use "Plain English" to Rob You Blind*. New York: Portfolio, 2012.

Kaufman-Osborn, Timothy V. *Politics/Sense/Experience: A Pragmatic Inquiry into the Promise of Democracy*. Ithaca, NY: Cornell University Press, 1991.

Kempton, Murray. *Rebellions, Perversities, and Main Events*. New York: Times Books, 1994.

Kenneally, Christine. *The First Word: The Search for the Origins of Language*. New York: Penguin, 2007.

Kermode, Frank. *The Art of Telling: Essays on Fiction*. Cambridge, MA: Harvard University Press, 1983.

Kilpatrick, James J. *The Writer's Art*. Fairway, KS: Andrews, McMeel, 1984. Kindle edition.

King, Stephen. *On Writing: A Memoir of the Craft*. New York: Scribner, 2000.

Kotlikoff, Laurence. "12 Secrets to Maximizing Your Social Security Benefits Under the New Rules." PBS.org. November 12, 2015. http://www.pbs.org/newshour/making-sense/12-secrets-maximizing-social-security-benefits-new-rules/

Levin, Bernard. *Speaking Up*. London: Jonathan Cape, 1982.

Lewis, C. S. *On Stories: And Other Essays on Literature*. New York: Harcourt Brace Jovanovich, 1982.

Limburg, Peter R. *Stories Behind Words: The Origins and Histories of 285 English Words.* New York: H. W. Wilson, 1986.

Marsh, David. *For Who the Bell Tolls: The Essential and Entertaining Guide to Grammar.* London: Guardian Books, 2014.

Marsh, David, and Amelia Hodsdon, eds. *Guardian Style.* London: Guardian Books, 2010.

McDonell, Terry. *The Accidental Life: An Editor's Notes on Writing and Writers.* New York: Knopf, 2016.

Mencken, H. L. *The American Language: An Inquiry into the Development of English in the United States.* New York: Knopf, 1945.

Metzler, Jack, ed. *The Solicitor General's Style Guide.* Washington, DC: Inter Alias, 2013.

Mills, William Haslam. *The Manchester Guardian: A Century of History.* London: Chatto and Windus, 1921.

Mira, Thomas K. *Speak Now or Forever Fall to Pieces.* New York: Random House, 1995.

Mitchell, Richard. *Less Than Words Can Say.* Boston: Little, Brown, 1979.

Montague, C. E. *A Writer's Notes on His Trade.* London: Penguin, 1952.

Munnell, Alicia H., Steven A. Sass, Alex Golub-Sass, and Nadia Karamcheva. "Unusual Social Security Claiming Strategies: Cost and Distributional Effects." Working paper. Center for Retirement Research at Boston College, 2009. http://crr.bc.edu/wp-content/uploads/2009/08/wp_2009-17-508.pdf

Olson, Lynne. *Troublesome Young Men: The Rebels Who Brought Churchill to Power and Helped Save England.* New York: Farrar, Straus and Giroux, 2007.

Orwell, George. *Nineteen Eighty-Four: A Novel.* New York: Harcourt, Brace, 1949.

———. "Politics and the English Language." *Horizon.* April 1946. Mountholyoke.edu

———. *Why I Write.* London: Penguin, 2004.

Osen, Diane, ed. *The Writing Life: National Book Award Authors.* New York: Random House, 1995.

Parr, D. Kermode, and Ernest Weekley. *Collins' Senior Etymological Dictionary.* London: Collins Clear-Type Press, 1952.

Partridge, Eric, and Janet Whitcut. *Usage and Abusage: A Guide to Good English*. New York: W. W. Norton, 1995.

Perlstein, Rick. *Nixonland: The Rise of a President and the Fracturing of America*. New York: Scribner, 2008.

Phillips, Tim. *Talk Normal: Stop the Business Speak, Jargon and Waffle*. London: Kogan Page, 2011.

Phythian, B. A., ed. *A Concise Dictionary of Correct English*. London: Hodder and Stoughton, 1979.

Plain English Campaign. *Utter Drivel!: A Decade of Jargon and Gobbledygook*. London: Robson, 1994.

Plimpton, George, ed. *The Writer's Chapbook: A Compendium of Fact, Opinion, Wit and Advice from the Twentieth Century's Preeminent Writers*. New York: Modern Library, 1999.

Plotnik, Arthur. *Spunk and Bite: A Writer's Guide to Bold, Contemporary Style*. New York: Random House, 2007.

Poole, Steven. *Who Touched Base in My Thought Shower? A Treasury of Unbearable Office Jargon*. London: Hodder and Stoughton, 2013.

Potter, Simeon. *Our Language*. Baltimore: Penguin, 1967.

Potter, Stephen. *Sense of Humour*. London: Max Reinhardt, 1954.

Provost, Gary. *100 Ways to Improve Your Writing*. New York: New American Library, 1985.

Ragins, Belle Rose. "Editor's Comments: Reflections on the Craft of Clear Writing." *Academy of Management Review* 37, no. 4 (2012): 493–501.

Roosevelt, Franklin D., and Winston Churchill. *Roosevelt and Churchill: Their Secret Wartime Correspondence*. Edited by Francis L. Loewenheim, Harold D. Langley, and Manfred Jonas. New York: Saturday Review Press, 1975.

Rose, Jonathan. *The Literary Churchill: Author, Reader, Actor*. New Haven, CT: Yale University Press, 2014.

Rosenbaum, Sara, David M. Frankford, Sylvia A. Law, and Rand E. Rosenblatt. *Law and the American Health Care System*. St. Paul, MN: Foundation Press, 2012.

Ross, Lillian. *Reporting Back: Notes on Journalism*. New York: Counterpoint, 2002.

Safire, William. *How Not to Write: The Essential Misrules of Grammar.* New York: W. W. Norton, 2005.

———. *Let a Simile Be Your Umbrella.* New York: Crown Publishers, 2001.

———. *No Uncertain Terms: More Writing from the Popular "On Language" Column in the New York Times Magazine.* New York: Simon and Schuster, 2003.

———. *On Language.* New York: Times Books, 1980.

———. *The Right Word in the Right Place at the Right Time: Wit and Wisdom from the Popular "On Language" Column in the New York Times Magazine.* New York: Simon and Schuster, 2004.

———. *Take My Word for It.* New York: Times Books, 1986.

Schlesinger, Robert. *White House Ghosts: Presidents and Their Speechwriters.* New York: Simon and Schuster, 2008.

Seely, John. *The Oxford Guide to Effective Writing and Speaking: How to Communicate Clearly.* Oxford: Oxford University Press, 2013.

Sellers, Leslie. *The Simple Subs Book.* Oxford: Pergamon, 1985.

Shea, Michael. *Personal Impact: The Art of Good Communication.* London: Sinclair-Stevenson, 1993.

Siegel, Alan, and Irene Etzkorn. *Simple: Conquering the Crisis of Complexity.* New York: Twelve, 2013.

Sieveking, Paul, ed. *World's Weirdest News Stories: From the Pages of Fortean Times.* London: Magbook, 2010.

Social Security Advisors Group, LLC. http://www.social securityadvisors.com/

Stephens, Cheryl. *Plain Language Legal Writing.* Vancouver, BC: Plain Language Wizardry Books, 2008.

Stewart, James B. *Follow the Story: How to Write Successful Nonfiction.* New York: Simon and Schuster, 1998.

Strunk, William, and E. B. White. *The Elements of Style.* Boston: Pearson, 1999.

Swaim, Barton. *The Speechwriter: A Brief Education in Politics.* New York: Simon and Schuster, 2015.

Sword, Helen. *Stylish Academic Writing.* Cambridge, MA: Harvard University Press, 2012.

———. *The Writer's Diet*. Auckland, New Zealand: Auckland University Press, 2015.

———. "Zombie Nouns." *New York Times*. July 23, 2012.

Tabor, Nick. "No Slouch." *Paris Review*. April 7, 2015.

Thompson, Mark. *Enough Said: What's Gone Wrong with the Language of Politics?* New York: St. Martin's, 2016.

Thurber, James. *My Life and Hard Times*. New York: Harper Perennial Modern Classics, 1999.

Tomalin, Nicholas. *Nicholas Tomalin Reporting*. London: Deutsch, 1975.

Truss, Lynne. *Eats, Shoots & Leaves*. New York: Gotham Books, 2004.

Van Noorden, Richard. "Publishers Withdraw More Than 120 Gibberish Papers." *Nature*. February 25, 2014. http://www.nature.com/news/publishers-withdraw-more-than-120-gibberish-papers-1.14763

Wallace, David Foster. "The Weasel, Twelve Monkeys and the Shrub." In *The Best American Magazine Writing 2001*, edited by Harold Evans, 107–12. New York: Public Affairs, 2001.

Waugh, Evelyn. *Scoop: A Novel About Journalists*. London: Chapman and Hall, 1933.

Wills, Garry. *The Kennedy Imprisonment: A Meditation on Power*. Boston: Little, Brown, 1982.

Winkler, Matthew. *The Bloomberg Way: A Guide for Reporters and Editors*. Hoboken, NJ: Bloomberg Press, 2012.

Wise, Jessie. *First Language Lessons for the Well-Trained Mind*. Level 1. Charles City, VA: Peace Hill Press, 2010.

Yglesias, J.R.C., and I. M. Newnham. *Mastery of English*. London: Longmans, Green, 1965.

Zinsser, William. *On Writing Well: The Classic Guide to Writing Nonfiction*. New York: HarperCollins, 2006.

———. *The Writer Who Stayed*. Philadelphia: Paul Dry Books, 2012.

Readability Bibliography

www.checktext.org

www.countwordsworth.com

www.editcentral.com

www.hemingwayapp.com

www.online-utility.org

www.readabilityformulas.com

www.readability-score.com

www.writersdiet.com

"Car Seat Instructions Too Hard, Study Says." *St. Petersburg Times.* March 3, 2003.

"Comparative Ages, Grades and Exams—US vs UK." *The Good Schools Guide International.*

DuBay, William H., ed. *Unlocking Language: The Classic Readability Studies.* Costa Mesa, CA: Impact Information, 2007.

Jewell, Andrew. "Experimenting with the Future of American Literary Study." Library Conference Presentations and Speeches. Paper 16. University of Nebraska–Lincoln, 2006. http://digitalcommons.unl.edu/library_talks/16

Liberman, Mark. "Willa Cather Was Skeptical of Analytics Before You Were." *Slate.* April 9, 2014. http://www.slate.com/blogs/lexicon_valley/2014/04/09/analytics_novelist_willa_cather_squabbled_with_the_university_of_nebraska.html

"Limitations of the Readability Formulas: Two Chapters of *Know Your Reader* by George R. Klare and Byron Buck, New York: Hermitage Books, 1954, pgs. 136–151," http://www.impact-information.com/impactinfo/Limitations.pdf

"Reading Aloud." The Writing Center, University of North Carolina at Chapel Hill. http://writingcenter.unc.edu/handouts/reading-aloud/

Schrock, Kathy. "Fry's Readability." *Kathy Schrock's Guide to Everything.* September 30, 2015. http://www.schrockguide.net/frys-readability-info.html

"The SMOG Readability Formula." University of Utah, Spencer S. Eccles Health Science Library, Patient Education, Patient Education Workshop, Handouts, Module 4. http://library.med.utah.edu/Patient_Ed/workshop/handouts/smog_formula.pdf

"Test Your Document's Readability." Microsoft Office Support. https://support.office.com/en-gb/article/test-your-document-s-readability-0adc0e9a-b3fb-4bde-85f4-c9e88926c6aa

Wegner, Mark V., and Deborah C. Girasek. "Do Child Safety Seat Installation Instructions Need to Be Simplified?" *Children, Youth and Environments* 13, no. 1 (Spring 2003).

Wikipedia Contributors. "Flesch-Kincaid Readability Tests." *Wikipedia*. June 21, 2015.

———. "Rudolf Flesch." *Wikipedia*. June 19, 2015.

———. "SMOG." *Wikipedia*. July 17, 2015.

Williams, C. B. "A Note on the Statistical Analysis of Sentence-Length as a Criterion of Literary Style." *Biometrika* 31, no. 3/4 (March 1940): 356–61. http://www.jstor.org/stable/2332615

Blogs

An American Editor
  https://americaneditor.wordpress.com/
Angry Sub Editor
  http://angrysubeditor.blogspot.com/
Apostrophe Abuse
  http://www.apostropheabuse.com/
Arnold Zwicky
  https://arnoldzwicky.org/
Arrant Pedantry
  http://www.arrantpedantry.com/
Ask Copy Curmudgeon
  https://askcopycurmudgeon.com/
The "Blog" of "Unnecessary" Quotation Marks
  http://www.unnecessaryquotes.com/
Blogslot
  http://theslot.blogspot.com/
Caxton
  https://caxton1485.wordpress.com/
Chicago Style Q&A
  http://www.chicagomanualofstyle.org/qanda/latest.html
Copyediting
  http://www.copyediting.com/
DCblog

http://david-crystal.blogspot.com/

Draft
http://opinionator.blogs.nytimes.com/category/draft/?_r=0

Editor Mark
https://markallenediting.com/

Explorations of Style
https://explorationsofstyle.com/

Fritinancy
http://nancyfriedman.typepad.com/

Good Copy, Bad Copy
http://www.daccreative.co.uk/goodcopybadcopy/

Grammar Girl
http://www.quickanddirtytips.com/grammar-girl

Grammar Guide
http://grammarguide.copydesk.org/

Harmless Drudgery
https://korystamper.wordpress.com/

Iva Cheung
http://www.ivacheung.com/blog/

Johnson
http://www.economist.com/blogs/johnson

Language: A Feminist Guide
https://debuk.wordpress.com/

Language Corner
http://www.cjr.org/language_corner/

Language Log
http://languagelog.ldc.upenn.edu/nll/

LawProse
http://www.lawprose.org/lawprose-blog/

Lexicon Valley
http://www.slate.com/blogs/lexicon_valley.html

Lingua Franca
http://chronicle.com/blogs/linguafranca/

Linguischtick
https://linguischtick.wordpress.com/

Logophilius

http://logophilius.blogspot.com/
Macmillan Dictionary Blog
   http://www.macmillandictionaryblog.com/
Madam Grammar
   https://madamgrammar.com/
Mededitor's Paragraph Factory
   http://mededitor.tumblr.com/
Mighty Red Pen
   https://mightyredpen.wordpress.com/
Mind Your Language
   http://www.theguardian.com/media/mind-your-language
Motivated Grammar
   https://motivatedgrammar.wordpress.com/
Random Idea English
   http://random-idea-english.blogspot.co.uk/
Sentence First
   https://stancarey.wordpress.com/
Separated by a Common Language
   http://separatedbyacommonlanguage.blogspot.co.uk/
Sesquiotica
   https://sesquiotic.wordpress.com/
Sin and Syntax
   http://sinandsyntax.com/category/blog/
Strong Language
   https://stronglang.wordpress.com/
Stroppy Editor
   https://stroppyeditor.wordpress.com/
Style and Substance
   http://blogs.wsj.com/styleandsubstance/
Subversive Copy Editor
   http://www.subversivecopyeditor.com/blog/
Ten Minutes Past Deadline
   https://tenminutespastdeadline.wordpress.com/
Throw Grammar from the Train
   http://throwgrammarfromthetrain.blogspot.com/
We All Need Words

http://weallneedwords.com/blog/
The Writing Resource
http://thewritingresource.net/
You Don't Say
http://www.baltimoresun.com/news/language-blog/

INDEX

ABOUT THE AUTHOR

~~~

Sir Harold Evans is celebrated for his editorship of two of the most renowned newspapers, *The Sunday Times* and *The Times* of London, and his seven years as president and publisher of Random House in New York. He was already a number one bestselling author in his own right in Britain with his *Good Times, Bad Times,* the story of political intrigue in a dispute with Mr. Rupert Murdoch over the integrity of the political coverage by *The Times.*

He has since written two epic histories. *The American Century,* illustrated with nine hundred photographs, dramatizes a people's struggle to achieve the American Dream, and in thirteen essays analyzes the causes and significance of the great movements in the one hundred years from the end of the frontier to the Reagan presidency. It spent ten weeks on the *New York Times* bestseller list.

The sequel was *They Made America: From the Steam*

Engine to the Search Engine — Two Centuries of Innovators. It was selected by *Fortune* magazine as one of the best books of the past seventy-five years. WGBH produced a four-part television series for the PBS network. Of his memoir *My Paper Chase* (2009), *The Economist* wrote: "Gripping and timely.... Sir Harold 'Harry' Evans remains one of the great figures of modern journalism."

As editor of *The Sunday Times,* Evans led his famous Insight team in unmasking the cover-up of the treacheries of the greatest Soviet spy, Kim Philby; took up the lost cause of the thalidomide children, winning them long-denied compensation; and liberated the British press with a victory in the European Court of Human Rights. The twenty-four international judges ruled 13–11 that the British practice of imposing indeterminate gag orders in civil cases was a violation of the free speech clause of Article 10 of the European Convention for the Protection of Human Rights. The achievement was recognized with the award of the European Gold Medal from the Institute of Journalists. Netflix recently released the prizewinning documentary of the dramas, by Jacqui and David Morris, *Attacking the Devil.*

Evans has been a leader in the training of journalists. His five-volume study of newswriting, editing, and design was adopted by the British Society of Newspaper Editors. His *Active Newsroom* was published by the International Press Institute. In 2001, British journalists voted him the all-time greatest newspaper editor. (On being told, he remarked, "Anecdotage has most effective editors running the gamut from certifiable lunacy to homicidal mania.") He was knighted in 2004 for services to journalism.

As editor at large for Thomson Reuters, he is a commentator and interviewer; the opinions in this book are his.

Evans is married to Tina Brown, the former editor of *Tatler, Vanity Fair,* and *The New Yorker.*

CREDITS

The author is grateful for permission to reprint the following: